Publishing Information

Disclaimer and Legal Notice

The Layman's Seduction Guide:

How To Meet & Seduce The Most Beautiful

Women Into Bed

(Regardless Who You Are)

Table of Contents

Introduction

It would not be true to say that, men have wondered for hundreds of years how to meet, impress and date women—actually, they have been wondering, learning, and debating for *thousands of years*. Perhaps, this could be millions, if our distant ancestors were smarter than we give them credit for. Yes, building up the courage to talk to women does not always seem like the key issue. The real challenge is more in finding the conversational and flirting skills necessary to make a woman feel something; the capacity to stir a woman's emotions and to elicit a response beyond politeness.

That is the secret and that is what a man wants, because as anecdotal evidence shows, the man who can do this will instantly be perceived as an alpha male, a stronger and more potent member of the species, who has his pick of women and who is never left alone or made to feel undesirable.

What I intend to do in this book, is to show the readers, the "Tao" of attraction and of seducing the female mind, although the complexity of attraction is far deeper than just seduction. The aim is to learn how to create chemical and what they sometimes call "gut-level" attraction, whenever you please, at will, and regardless of the obstacles that appear.

In the next eight chapters, I am going to discuss some of the fundamentals of becoming an alpha male, and what exactly it is that a man is doing when he "seduces", "plays", or "womanizes." These are all colloquialisms referring to a far greater act, which is the ability to alter a woman's perspective, change her attitude, and to make her feel an emotion that is entirely of your creation.

This Tao of attraction is something beyond dating clichés, pick up lines, and seduction strategies. It is more like a mental place or a new understanding in your mind, and one that once you learn it, you will never go back to being the poor "friend" who finishes last.

In the first chapter, I am going to discuss a little bit more about what being an "alpha" means with respect to conversation, relationships, and even on an instinctual level.

Chapter 1

What Is An Alpha Male?

The term "alpha male" may not be universally known to all men except for some vague references. For example, canine behavior, or perhaps the urban expression "alpha dog", which refers to the leader of a gang or group of friends. Informally speaking, an alpha dog is a man who is regarded as a leader and someone who is the social center of a group.

However, the idea of a leader is more biological than simply the "most popular guy in the room." An alpha has such a strong personality that he often intimidates other men. They may feel inferior or introverted in the alpha's presence, either because of an alpha's willful action, or even inadvertently because the alpha male is far more entertaining or interesting to talk to in a group.

The dating community has latched onto the phrase "alpha male", because that is presumably, what all men want to be. They want to be the "best show" at the party, the most entertaining fellow in a group of friends. They want to be an "alpha" that constantly attracts women, without having to try to "sell" themselves.

It is a perfectly natural desire, and yet one that is often misconstrued. For example, men often believe that in order to create instant attraction, they have to be:

- Good looking

- Rich

- Funny

- Or do some special "shtick" that forces women to take notice of them.

(For example, the proverbial pick up line)

However, this is a misconception, and it is often not the peripheral qualities that ultimately create attraction between two people. Looks and first impressions can certainly grab a woman's interest, but an attraction is something that develops as the result of physical, mental, and emotional interaction.

Engagement is what causes attraction. Whatever seduction means, or constitutes, is surely something based on interaction, since all of what we know about psychology is primarily focused on behavior. The definition of behavior is "the way in which one acts or conducts oneself, esp. toward others."

When we discuss a man attracting a woman, we are discussing the chemistry that a man actively creates, activates and maintains, in a rather systematic approach. This may well be in contrast to what many people "feel" about love, sex and attraction. For instance, ideas of:

- Someone having an unexplainable "it" quality.

- A woman who prefers one "loser" over another, who seems right for her.

- A special emotion or passion for someone that is not based on rationale but on sexual "spark".

This is the chemistry that takes place in dating. If one feels chemistry, he knows it. If the feeling is mutual, the couple usually goes to bed in a short period of time. If the feeling is one-sided, it is heartache. However, if the feeling is coming from the woman and directed towards a man this is chemistry . This chemistry creates powerful, instinctual attraction.

Maybe He's Born With It

Another common misconception is that some men are simply born with sexual charisma, or that some men just have a natural inclination towards being sociable, attractive, and flirtatious, while other men are forced to "pick up the scraps."

There is one mistake in this perspective. The mistake in this perspective is that you either have it or you don't, which is inconsistent with what we know about man's ability to adapt and improve his lifestyle. As intelligent beings, we all have the ability to make changes, to adopt new personality traits, and to build positive qualities, To say that we are either born with it or not, would mean that we are preordained to live a certain way and be enslaved to a predetermined persona. That is almost as absurd as believing in fate or destiny.

The truth is we make our own destiny. While it might be true that some people are born with an innate sense of leadership, confidence, or extroverted personality, this does not mean that these qualities cannot be learned. Just as a man is capable of learning a skill, like playing a piano, so is a man capable of learning seduction techniques.

Yes, it helps to be a naturally suave and confident man by good genes, of course. Is it the only way? Consider this: self-taught pianists are just as talented and wonderful to listen to, as natural, play-by ear geniuses are. Once a person commits himself to learning an art, he can learn it, whether it takes the person a few months or a few years to perfect the skill. What matters is the art, not where our skills come from.

When it comes to dating, it could be argued that the "pick up artist" or the "player" imitates and borrows ideas from the naturally gifted men, who communicate deep confidence and have a natural way of talking to women. The player "plays" a role, assuming the actions and personality of someone who can be observed to have success.

Once again, it is the genius vs. the craftsman analogy. In the end, they both get what they want. If the craftsman or "artist" is able to get over resentment of the natural performer, he may find a new perspective or set of tools that can help deliver success.

What really matters is how determined the man is, who does not have natural charisma, to learn this skill and apply these suggestions. It could be said that men on the outside looking in, the ones who were not born with natural conversational skills, took an overly scientific view of dating and introduced concepts brand new to the dating scene. For example, techniques like neuro-linguistic programming, and other psychological approaches.

Macro-Evolution: The Rise Of The Educated Pick Up Artist

2

In many ways, the educated pick up artist has the capacity to *surpass* the naturally inclined seducer and sort of macro-evolve into an even more powerful and attractive presence. The learned pick up artist actually prepares for a variety of scenarios and obstacles, including rejection, and uses the chance to improvise. A man who is naturally charismatic relies on impulse and may not have the intellectual versatility that a pick up artist learns.

The point is, a man seeing his lack of genetic success as an excuse for failure or an abandoned attempt, is a self-sabotaging behavior. For all that we have seen in psychology and in the more informal pick up artist community, chemistry between people can be controlled, manipulated, and altered, according to the wishes of one person. Simply knowing and accepting this will put a man higher above the rank of defeatists, who believe that attraction is beyond their control.

When a man is defeatist he becomes the subordinate male, the one who follows the alpha; ultimately hoping the alpha's association will provide some benefit, or he will seek exile from the rest of the pack and give up the challenge.

Therefore, what we have here is the classic situation of a pack of males, and one striving to be dominant, while the others remain passive. This is a much more realistic way to look at attraction and dating, rather than retreating to the same cliché of "either attraction exists or it does not". It is comparable to saying that some males are just born leaders and if they are not, that is just their destiny and it won't change.

The overwhelming message in the attraction community and all of psychology really, is that the individual, who has knowledge of what thinking patterns exist, has full potential to change them and move towards more productive behavior. The result of giving up the content, the struggle, is a dangerous exercise in self-effacement. They will either wait for something magical to happen to them and jump into a relationship prematurely (since they figure they are lucky enough to attract just one woman), or they become embittered towards the opposite sex and the "rules" of dating.

Ironically, there are no real rules about attraction, outside of marketing gimmicks that suggest you only need "one remedy" to change your luck. However, there are perceptions that women form based on a man's behavior, and that is the reality of dating. It is not really about following the rules ,so much as, it is about influencing these perceptions with deliberate actions.

Now Here's When You Come In

It is imperative that you let go of these antiquated notions about deserving someone, or having a disadvantage when it comes to dating. You do have the potential to create strong levels of attraction in women, regardless of whether you are a natural group leader, a ladies' man, or the best-looking guy in the room. Part of your mission will be simply accepting this objective perspective, and to stop identifying yourself as a man at a disadvantage or a man who feels intimidated by a woman outside his own level of attractiveness.

One strange phenomenon in the dating world is that many men will oftentimes date women, who are more on "their own level" of attractiveness, rather than pursuing the most attractive women, or at least the one they see as the most perfectly shaped and flawless specimen. The belief is that these men are more comfortable around women they can see themselves with, and yet are more nervous around women who look to be a class above them. He

3

never relaxes to the point that he can comfortably date "10s", and usually ends up with "6s" or "7s."

This attitude has to change, if you are to outgrow the limitations, of being second best. Much of the battle is in overcoming subconscious attitudes that you are worthless or that you must defer to an alpha male, or in some cases, the "alpha female" that intimidates you.

Much of dating involves, how we as men, react to what is happening around us. A capable man does not just wait passively as life passes by. He will start a conversation with a woman he likes and then slowly create sexual tension, using his best qualities to exhibit a confident attitude and presence.

Is Being Alpha Truly Being "Yourself"?

This brings us to a legitimate issue many men (and women) might have with the idea of "seduction." If one uses seduction techniques, is that person compromising his ethics and trying to be someone else? We grow up hearing life lessons that we ought to be ourselves and to hold true to our values, or perhaps our honesty.

Moreover, in discussing complex concepts like neuro-linguistic programming, you may even provoke some people who believe that amateur forms of hypnosis are an unfair advantage. Unfortunately, "hypnosis" is just a part of everyday life, whether we realize it or not.

Consider for example, when you try to sell a product at work; persuading clients to buy something, you are using hypnosis techniques. When you watch television or read magazines and see a barrage of ads urging you to buy something, you are subjecting yourself to commercial forms of seduction.

Ironically, many women have no problem consulting love-relationship articles in *Cosmopolitan,* and that sort of ilk, because it is presented as harmless "suggestion". When, in fact, it is a form of manipulation—using someone else's ideas, or using a psychological advantage, to manipulate a man.

It is the same thing that men do when they seek out seduction classes or learn what are sometimes called "quick lay" strategies. All of these things are forms of seduction—the only difference is in the presentation, and of course, the complexity of the source. Women consulting *Cosmo,* want simple strategies; men paying lots of money for a seduction "seminar weekend" want layers of complexity that culminate in what's ultimately on their minds—sex.

The "presentation" of seduction technique is yet another aspect in understanding seduction in general. People who try to "sell us" something must meet us at our level of comprehension and ultimately give us a product that we already want.

What has happened is that the pickup artist has simply found a way to manipulate emotion and thought processes that are male-centric, as opposed to unisexual. The biggest lie in dating and relationships is that we never use seduction in getting what we want. Seduction is all around us and used in every aspect of life, particularly dating.

- Women are manipulative in attracting attention, persuading a man to do what she asks, and in ensuring that a man stays faithful.

4

- Men are manipulative, even at the earliest stages of dating, oftentimes resorting to buying women gifts, or displaying kind and gentlemen's behavior, or persistently nagging a woman until they get a date.

All of this is a form of manipulation and seduction, even though one can argue that to be kind, it is not necessarily hiding your true self—it is simply presenting your best foot forward. Likewise, being seductive and persuasive in dating is not a lie. It is simply a man presenting himself in an aggressive and attractive way that is more in line with psychological theory, not to mention the base instincts of alpha male behavior that we observe in all of nature.

Guaranteed or Your Money Back?

What is truly ironic is that most women are not offended by the idea of subliminal seduction, but at the idea that this behavior can be *learned,* rather than simply the gift of a natural born charmer. Men, who they ordinarily would filter out because of a lack of social grace, can learn how to bypass a woman's filtering system and proceed to a point beyond the notorious "friend zone", where men without that special chemistry or "spark" are condemned. They may in fact fear the lack of control they suddenly have in the dating process, as if any man can learn hypnotic "tricks" to bed women, lie, and exit the relationship. This, of course, is all myth.

First, there is no guarantee that any man can seduce any woman at any time. We can certainly build ourselves to a level of self-confidence that makes us capable of such actions, but there is no guarantee we can actually force a woman to follow through with "imbedded" commands. That is the stuff of science fiction. Even clinical and intensive hypnosis cannot work if there is resistance in the patient. Anybody claiming otherwise, that you can alter a person's mind and implant new thoughts in there, is obviously exaggerating this up to a fault.

Second, seduction strategy uses thoughts and feelings that a woman is already experiencing, and allows a man to use these states of mind to bond with her. It is similar to, what we do with our gender, when we meet a new friend, try to impress a new boss, or give advice to our little brother. It is a form of bonding to maintain a deeper level of conversation that just happens to be female-centric.

Third, seduction strategy does not necessarily mean that it is a misogynistic war on women and that the newly empowered man is going to seduce and "dump" every woman he meets. Most men who use this strategy simply want more success in dating, and want the same experiences as naturally gifted men. These men have their pick of partners, similar to attractive women, who sometimes go through multiple trial relationships before deciding that one lover really completes them.

Some men may only desire one special woman, and will use all these techniques as leverage to get this woman to commit. Ultimately, a man's actions—and how a woman responds to this "new personality" exhibited—is a matter of free choice. Nobody does anything that they do not already want to do. What the seduction community does is eliminate many of the obstacles that prevent these relationships from starting in the first place.

Confidence + Intelligence = Seduction

Usually, confidence is recommended as the solution to unsuccessful dating, but it is actually the combination of confidence and intelligence. A man who is cocky and overly antagonistic towards a woman may be confident, and perhaps successful to an extent. However, he will not enjoy the same success as the learned pick up artist, who knows when it is time to strategize and bond with a female prospect, rather than simply adhering to a "shtick" or stereotypical character.

You will find that learning more about dating, female psychology, and seduction—not to mention increasing your experiences in the "field"—will help you to become more internally confident to the point where you do not have to fake an image of success or macho posturing. You will simply be confident because of your *new outlook on life*.

Indeed, many men who learn how to be better "seducers" actually learn how to become more capable and successful men in general. They learn how to be leaders, how to be alphas, which means they can demonstrate skills in a variety of fields even beyond dating. They are better friends, better parents, and better workers. They are no longer followers, but step up to assume a more responsible role in life. They are in control of their own destiny, and no longer content to be "on the outside looking in" when it comes to finding the good things in life.

This brings us to our first principle in the Tao of seduction.

Control Over Yourself

Controlling yourself is the first step, because in order to wield any "power" or skill, you must be firm control of your thoughts, feelings, and actions. The very idea that you can be a man, who has the capacity to seduce anyone at any time, requires that you must use your body and mind as a weapon; you have perfect restraint and the ability to strategize and "strike" whenever it is advantageous. Your total control of the situation prevents outside obstacles from becoming a factor. You have power over your:

- State of mind

- Body language

- Self-image

- Conversational abilities

The fact that you have control over yourself also means you have control over your interactions. You are no longer an observer to what happens, nor do you allow "chance" or some outside element to determine compatibility.

Control might well be a deceptive word because control and seduction are almost opposites. Control means you manage the situation, oftentimes by force, whereas seduction means persuading someone to follow through with your suggestion.

All we really can control is our own bodies and our own minds. The more you learn about dating, the more you realize that you *controlling your natural urges,* is the key to impressing women and persuading them to look at you differently.

For example, even if you were to present a confident and sexy persona on your first date and convince a woman that you were truly a compatible alpha male, with a lack of control you could still easily ruin the experience.

A lack of control might entice a man to:

- Exhibiting jealousy

- Becoming overly rude or antagonistic

- Become too insulting in his humor

- Flirt with other women

- Get drunk

- Become sexually aggressive before she's comfortable

Once you let go of this control, all the rapport you have successfully created up until now, dies. Her perceptions of you have not only altered but have also been spoiled.

Sometimes, control is not about stopping yourself from making an error; sometimes, it is about simply projecting the feeling of control, that you are in control of the situation, and are ensuring the comfort of both, you and your date prospect.

For example, a man who appears to "know people"; might be perceived as an attractive man, in the same way as he will be expected to have control over the entertainment, the venue, and the romantic scene unfolding. So much of dating behavior is hindered because of awkward tension. A man in control always makes his date or future date feel at ease in the situation.

He controls the scene. What about the man who shrewdly requests the band play his date's favorite song? He demonstrates his control in a proactive way, by taking direct action and creating a moment of heartfelt connection. Only a man who is in full control—of not only the setting and venue, but also of the dynamic energy between two people—can manage this.

How about the man who gets a kiss because he takes action? He feels the moment building and so he controls the scene by reading his partner's cues and knowing when to reach out and make a move. This is entirely a game plan of control. Men who lack control, or who do not own the moment, will be left second-guessing if "now" is the right time, and will sabotage their chance at success.

The time to act is when you feel it, and you know your date feels it, because of the control that you maintain throughout the experience. Indeed, guiding someone through a process is the sign of confidence, and this is true outside the world of dating as well.

When we have someone who can show us the way through unknown territory, we follow that person; relieved that we do not have to come up with solutions to unknown problems. It is the same reason a younger woman might feel attracted to an older man; he has dating experience and can make her feel like the star of the show, guiding her on what to do, and how to enjoy the experience.

It might even be preferable to a better-looking man who shares the same awkward, nervous energy as the girl. If neither person has any control—not over each other but over the experience—then the date will probably feel forced. The woman will feel there is a lack of chemistry, because the man really has no idea how to preside over the experience and show the woman something special.

And yes, a woman wants to feel something special, she wants something to click. Otherwise, there is no sense in pretending as if this is going to be a successful dating experience.

This probably does fly in the face of many of the life lessons we were taught about having "love at first sight" or having natural chemistry. The truth is we are compatible with a high number of partners - maybe not everybody on the face of the earth, but a good number. We are all human and we all have the ability to bond with each other emotionally, to learn about each other, and to experience a shared intimacy.

So the question is, can you master control over yourself and the moment, by reading and applying the lessons that we learn? If so, you will soon be capable of maximizing your chances with more women, even "opposite personalities" and women that you instinctively feel are "10s" and out of your range.

You could say that control is a form of social intelligence. It is a process of eliminating self-doubt (the feeling of having no control) and ridding yourself of anxiety. Lastly, it is about having the ability to influence positive circumstances, by simply understanding concepts of psychology, and being able to study your "target audience" to produce the reaction you want.

The art of seduction; believe it or not, is a logistics game. Logistics is the "things that must be done to plan and organize a complicated activity or event." While you probably have been taught that the female mind is irrational, unpredictable and impossible to learn, we are here to tell you, no! - and that it IS a logical process. The logical process is you understanding the emotional female mind and then you using scientifically proven techniques and strategies that have worked historically.

There, are you not relieved? Dating is a logical process and you do not have to be a natural, abstract genius to have your pick of attractive partners. All you need is control and a little bit of time in your hand, as we discuss further insights into what becoming the alpha male really means.

Chapter 2

Understanding The Biology Of The Courtship Process

So much of the problem coming from most dating gurus is that they lack specifics. Much like your mom and dad, who also gave you "good advice" about dating. They told you it was merely a lack of confidence and of course, not being or believing in yourself. Just be yourself and be confident and everything will fall into place.

Surprise! It is not always just about confidence, perhaps, you have already noticed that personally or through the behaviors of your (unsuccessful) friends. Sure, they are confident. They are trying. But they're not really succeeding. More importantly, they do not seem to be landing the dream girl they are always hoping for—they are usually dating 5s or 6s; average looking women who are available, but nothing really to write home about. However, isn't the whole point of dating to find someone beautiful, someone as close to perfect as possible? Settling on what is available does not seem to make much sense.

This clearly indicates that something more than just vague assurances of confidence is necessary if you want to change the way other people feel you. When we discussed confidence in the previous chapter, we discussed how to create attraction - merely by reinforcing your presence as a territorial and dominant male. However, more is involved if you want to proceed beyond attraction.

The next step involves assuming the qualities that a woman expects from an alpha male. The confidence you project *advertises* to women that you are an alpha male, someone who understands attraction and how to give them exactly what they want in a man. You might even say that having confidence is being passed the ball in court. To "drop the ball" means to disappoint this woman after promising all this beaming confidence. This would indicate that either you are ignorant of how the dating process works from point A to point B and so on, or that you are a celebrity rock star who deserves sex for free, solely because of your fame.

Assuming of course you do not have this type of celebrity buzz, you can't slack off or do a halfway job of displaying confidence with no technique. Learning the technique is paramount to success. Doing the routines halfway or trying to coast on your instincts is just going to get you occasionally laid, which is not the image makeover that you need.

What Is Chemistry Beyond Attraction?

The scientific understanding of chemistry is that it is the biological reaction of substances interacting, combining and changing. In dating and courtship, chemistry is the complexity of emotion and interaction that happens between two individuals. You feel chemistry with all sorts of people on an unconscious level.

Your instinctive behavior will produce a basic effect, and will draw some sorts of people to you while repelling others. The "secret" to dating, if you want to call it so, is that this chemistry can be manipulated. It is not just a matter of physical biology because our minds and subsequent conversations are still a form of biological communication. Talking is how we send signals in nature, showing what we want and why we deserve it.

The Slow Build—Why?

9

One of the first things you will learn in seduction is that a woman requires a slow buildup of strong emotional attraction (even if that process is "sped up" as we will discuss in a later chapter) before she deems you a man worthy of her sexual attention. The slow build up process is in contrast to the male "visual" attraction system, which usually only requires a beautiful woman desiring sex as the igniting factor.

It is arguable whether this is a social construct; that women have been taught to be sexually inhibited by society, whereas men are encouraged to be the aggressors. What seems more apparent is that women have differently wired brains, not to mention unique female hormones that—statistically speaking—do give them greater emotional capacities than men. At least, in the sense that they can more often respond to non-verbal cues, using an estimated 20,000 words daily compared to that of men, which is approximately 7,000. Men's brains are slightly larger but women's brain's have more neural connections. Men also primarily use one hemisphere to process information while women use both. This indicates that whether due to social constructs, genetics or biology, women will more often respond to emotional stimulation, which takes time to build. It is not instantaneous like a male visual system, and cannot be based solely on such peripheral factors, which of course, would be the lazy man's wish.

So what is chemistry and why does it work? At the heart of the matter, the slow build up results because we make a consistent pattern of eliciting positive reactions from other people. Soon enough, they will start to associate positive feelings with our presence. As the bond grows, they may even start to overlook our faults and see primarily those positive points.

Now determining what those positive reactions are, is part of the game. Not all women are alike, nor do they think alike. However, by our words, we can draw them out and see how they react, and what kind of attention they like to see. You could say that the "chemistry" we feel with a suitable partner is the direct result of the attraction, plus the cultivation of shared emotional experiences.

Naturally, all you ever hear are vague answers when asking this person how he did it, and what makes the chemistry so remarkable. Either because the one confessing has no clue, as to why it happened, or maybe even because the guy does not want to reveal his secrets. However, analyzing the courtship process is relatively easy.

First, consider the importance of positive associations.

Even before you begin to think about chemistry, you must ensure that your target woman is in a positive frame of mind. If she is not, and you are already walking uphill, it will be an exhausting process; bending over backwards to please someone who is not looking forward to being pleased.

However, it goes beyond just first impressions. Logically, by sheer nature, we seek out people who reinforce these positive feelings. Therefore, your aim should be to avoid being negatively associated, whether that is because of the frame of mind of the woman, or because of the image you're projecting—that could easily be one of negativity.

Frame of mind is a major part of what builds chemistry, along with conversation. A lot of men out there tend to hold bad attitudes or negative and nervous attitudes when approaching women, which immediately creates a bad state of mind. That is instant association of negativity.

This is precisely why average or below average looking guys are capable of creating attraction and chemistry. This is because, they understand that consistent positive association is just as important or more than mere appearance or the first impression. In theory, you could give a bad introduction, or a non-introduction, (as in falling below the woman's radar, not making any impression) but still reverse that momentum by reinforcing positive associations from this moment on.

Re-Familiarizing Yourself With The Courtship Process

Much like a writer sometimes needs to review the rules of the story, structure and language, so too will a confused man find it beneficial to re-learn the dating and courtship process; clearing his mind of all the bad advice other people have given him about dating.

What helps is to remember that much of life involves adapting to a fast-changing environment. We cannot assume that a constantly changing environment is natural or that everything is just going to fall into place. Sometimes the only way to survive is to adapt to the things happening around you. Therefore, try to understand that your instincts on what to say and when to say it might be slightly off, even if it is your natural reaction; learning to adapt to the way women think is a part of evolving into a smarter and more attractive alpha male.

Now, merely familiarizing yourself to the course of being an alpha male is not the entire courtship process. It is a great way to get attention but the next progressive step is to become a knowledgeable man, who knows precisely what behavior a woman expects.

Now this is the part where most guys give up. They figure, who can possibly understand the female mind? Is it not complex? Well yes, but then again men are complex and still remarkably easy to figure out. The difference is that women are wired differently and in the courtship process you have to treat them accordingly, in contrast to how you might behave with a fellow male friend, a parent, or even someone you are just casually nice to in a day's time.

The Importance Of Targeting

Now some dating coaches are going to tell you that you can sleep with anyone at any given time using these techniques. Others will tell you that it is exaggeration, you really cannot tell. What is the truth of it? Honestly, speaking on a purely scientific level, no one is absolutely sure, since you're talking about a situation with an infinite number of variables. As we said earlier, if a woman maintains a negative frame of mind then it does not matter if you are Casanova or Johnny Depp—you are not going to force her to like you.

However, by using these techniques you can learn to summon her instinctive responses and definitely increase your probability of finding romance. You will have the capacity to seduce anyone you want, because any sentient being can facilitate a friendship with another sentient being—especially if that relationship is short-term. When our relationships are tentative, it is much easier to forge them. That is why we are devoting an entire chapter later on to discussing how to make a relationship last beyond all the suave moves and seduction techniques.

In fact, the secret to female seduction is surprisingly specific, and human-bound and not gender-specific. You can seduce a woman the same way a salesperson "seduces" a buyer.

By targeting this person, deciphering what she wants, and then giving it to her in just the right way.

The principle of the matter is that you, as the salesperson, should become familiar with your "target woman" before trying your routine, as much as your resources allow. This is impossible, you might say. After all, women are complicated and it can take years to figure them out, right?

Not necessarily. This is why companies invest in what is called "market research." They do not have the resources to learn every single customer out there, but they can invest in statistical information and use these trends to develop their campaign. The same thing is true in dating. No, all women are not alike, of course not.

However, you can work according to established types and categories of women, who will likely demonstrate a somewhat standard set of values, even among diverse personalities.

Is it not true that when you date certain categories of women, you do get a reasonably predictable reaction?

For example, in dating when you meet the following types:

- Religious women

- Political or activist-minded women

- Younger college girls

- Older mature women

- Single moms

- Married women

- Bisexual women

- Educated women

- Rich women

- Working class women

- Celebrities

Stereotypes aside, it is highly probable that you are going to confront recurring social patterns based on lifestyle choices that each of these women have made. Rather than working against those lifestyle behaviors by trying to develop a method that "works on all women, exactly the same way", you would be wise to *adapt* your behavior to fit in with the lifestyle of the woman you want to develop a relationship with. This is a perfect example of adapting to the environment rather than just blindly trying whatever works (which is usually nothing, if you don't have it planned)

Spending a few moments of your time learning about different lifestyles, and researching how women in a certain category statistically feel and think, will be valuable in helping you "learn and understand" each person you encounter later on.

Familiarity Breeds...Comfort?

When we say familiarity brings contempt, what we actually mean is complacency brings contempt. Familiarity is something that we typically find comforting; it allows us to relax, to sleep, and to enjoy peace and serenity. If we were constantly in a state of agitation, life would be miserable. If there is ever a doubt, become an ER doctor or move to the Middle East and then determine if you really hate all this familiarity!

No familiarity is good. When we become accustomed to something, we gain confidence in doing it. We lose our fear. We grow and alter our perspective. It is this way for women and perhaps even amplified in the female mind. Some men can perform sexually under stress. However, for a woman, the more common case is the comfort that you make her feel; it allows her to feel sexual and to engage you in the courtship process.

Most women do not respond sexually or socially to stressful situations. If you are nervous or give off an "Attitude" that suggests you're not enjoying yourself, you are adding to her stress level and in essence, pushing her farther away. The natural player or suave fellow understands that making a woman feel comfortable in his presence is key to building rapport.

Confidence creates familiarity. Right? That is certainly a great deal of it. When a woman sees you performing well, being comfortable in her presence and your own skin, she determines you are a fun guy to be around—someone that can make the courtship process enjoyable and not a chore.

However, familiarity is also based on understanding motivation. This is exactly why many women do seem to go after the same "types" rather than constantly changing up her selection for one bizarre match right after another. (And yes, I'm aware there are exceptions to the rule...congratulations to those women for developing their romantic palette).

Women respond best to men who seem familiar (as in men she has already learned how to deal with) or men whom they are capable of learning quickly. So yes, believe it or not, women are already one step ahead of you—they think they know what you are, what you want, and how to manipulate you! By reading this book, you are merely increasing your own social intelligence.

One common suggestion on how to increase your "familiarity" with women is to spend more time studying what they like; women's lifestyle magazines, chick-lit books and movies, TV shows, and the places where they like to go frequently.

Naturally, reading all of this statistical information is no match for actually dating a large number of women. Experience is the best teacher. After allowing yourself to join the dating pool and date different women, you will be able to learn and predict how a woman responds to the things you say.

13

Let me guess, the very idea terrifies you! Understood, but rest assured, we will get to that soon enough. For now, accept the fact that familiarity means comfort. Only by appealing to a woman's longing for familiarity, something she can understand and not fear, will endear her to you, even at the most infinitesimal level like talking.

What Are A Woman's Needs

Women want alphas as we established in the previous chapter, but discovering "what kind of alpha are you?" is the primary task at hand. Not all alpha males behave in the same way. Some are very different...why, some men are naturally introverted and yet speak with such great weight that they retain all of that clout even when conversing with more extroverted personalities. Your job is to discover what type of alpha male *you have to be* to impress the woman you want in particular.

No, not just any woman will do. And no, being a guy and "available" is not enough (Since most women will not actually try the "I'm going to sleep with the next guy I meet!" That is a bet!).

The alpha male is merely a man who stands out; who controls himself and gets what he wants, regardless of fear or judgment from others. Women do want an alpha male, but different alpha males have different qualities. The setting and the environment becomes a major player in this context.

Personally speaking let me say this; the alphas focus on their strengths, not their weaknesses. They do not bluff, and they don't feel intimidated. For example, if you're an alpha-hopeful and desiring to bed a woman who plays basketball, but you don't watch basketball or enjoy it, then it does not make much sense to compete with other men to become her basketball alpha, does it? You are out of your league and the only option is to lie and to scam your way into a position of respect. This is desperation.

A true alpha male would simply choose a discussion he is more suited for, perhaps using basketball as an analogy, to better communicate with the woman he likes. Nevertheless, "posing" in this way and trying to compete in an area where you're just going to lose is never the way to go.

Think about men like Bill Gates or Mark Zuckerberg, who were certainly not alpha males in physique, in power, or in movie-star like sex appeal. Still, they demonstrated their alpha abilities in an area they could control and excel. They are both happily married and their respective spouses would not trade them for all the money in the world...probably because they have all the money in the world! Just a joke there, no need to take notes on that.

You know they recently did a study in which women were surveyed and asked to describe their ideal man. At first, many of the women disagreed with what they wanted. However, when they were told to narrow down all of their most important qualities, they all seemed to say the same thing: strength was the most important. In contrast, most men say loyalty is the most important factor in a woman.

Can you begin to see a biological pattern here? This is why they often say that a woman must respect a man before she finds him attractive. What earns respect? Strength; whether that strength is conveyed in the peripheral or the internal.

Primal Needs And Biological Urges

Now here comes a heady discussion. There are some scientists and biologists, who speculate that ALL women want strong men because it is a primal need ingrained in them. The theory is that women biologically look to men to keep them alive, since they are the proverbial home keeper to the man hunter. The stronger a man is, the better he is able to take care of her in building a family. And obviously, men who have high status in a community (which could be anyone from a DJ in a concert, to the manager of the plant, or even a pastor in church) are perceived as having exceptional strength in some aspect of character.

On the other hand, the theory for men suggests that they admire loyalty in women because for millenniums, men were unable to know if women were cheating on them with other mates. Hence, there was no way to know if the woman's baby was actually the husband's child or a mysterious guest. Loyalty became a quality associated with love and attraction because this was the pre-scientific age.

Now I am not necessarily saying that this is 100% true. In fact, many scientists and philosophers argue that all we know about male and female biology is the result of social construct. Namely, that we act male or female because of the attitudes of society thrust upon us. This too is possible, and with rapidly changing roles in society, including working women and househusbands, nothing is as predictable as we would hope.

Still, at the very least we must assume that strength in character is closely related to standing out from the crowd, producing better genes for your future children, and speaking in terms of pure personality matching. It is easy to assume that "strong" individuals are able to showcase their personality and positive qualities in ways that "weaker" men cannot.

It is like the old adage says; men want sex with anyone, but women want sex with men who are special. So, we have another important principle in attraction: always maintain your strength. Without it, you defer to other males. You surrender the alpha position. And that really does you no favors, unless of course, you want sloppy seconds—taking whatever the alphas are generous enough to leave you.

It is not about machismo or being a man's man. It is about standing your ground to other men and to women, letting them know that you are content in who you are. You understand your needs above all else. The very idea of you knowing what you want, and knowing what the woman wants, is the "spark" you need to ignite this coupling.

In fact, you can safely say that this primal urge that a woman feels to be with a strong alpha male, is probably more important than any other individual qualities, she holds dear.

And yes, you can probably attest to this from bitter past experience. The right woman "should" fall for a nice guy like you. But what works is a stronger nature, and a more confident attitude in a man—even if he is completely wrong for her. This should speak volumes as to the power of attraction.

Once a woman senses that you are an alpha and know the importance of maintaining this strength *throughout the courtship*, she will already feel attracted to you, associating you with all sorts of good things like familiarity, comfort and safety.

15

You might liken this dynamic to a VIP pass in a club. Once you show that you understand the chemistry of attracting and dating, even when put in her presence, you will get the VIP pass and get her full attention. All the other guys in the waiting line are trying too hard to learn and fit her superficial list of qualities. They cannot connect with her on the level she wants because it is something special, something beyond average. Average does not make for sexy. Display of strength is what draws a woman's attention.

An Evolving Primal Urge

At the same time, understand that women do go through several changes in their life, starting as young as their transition from teen into 20-year-old. Young girls may feel attracted to cute movie stars, only to switch to bad boys in their late teens. Their 20s are a time of experimentation, while their 30s are typically a period of more stability; creating a family. During these transitional times, she may decide that one man is "stronger" in a particular aspect than another man. A man with a job and a confident and loving demeanor may impress a woman looking for a husband and father to her children, even if he is not as "strong" in personality as a hard-nosed biker who wants to ride around all day and drink.

Her perceptions and values change but her attraction to strong-minded men will not. No woman ever "decides" to marry a weak man, she "settles" occasionally on a weak man. But that is not what she is looking for. She is looking for passion, for chemistry, all of which is activated by this volatile quality, this manly fortitude that we must never take for granted, less we become the very women we desire!

Creating the New You

So it is not enough to say that you just need confidence, the first step would be to understand what you have to feel confident about. This includes the qualities and characteristics you possess that are going to make you attractive in the eyes of women.

In general, people are not very adept in remembering high volumes of information...maybe that is why we just love our tablets and Smartphones. On the contrary, we remember simple things, and the more repetition used the better. In like manner, it is not really a great idea to describe the hundreds of reasons why women should like you. It is better to find just a few of your "sticking points" or "prime assets" that you want to sell to the loveliest girl in the room.

In addition, you may find it helpful to list the qualities of yourself that you are not satisfied with, or that you feel incompetent about. Being aware of your strengths and limitations is the first necessity to "competing" against other men. You want to maximize your strengths, use your assets, and minimize or improve those weaknesses.

We discussed avoiding vagueness in general and it is essential here because these are the aspects you must know explicitly, before you can improve your presentation.

So rather than say, "I lack confidence" or "I'm not good with women," think of something specific to say, something that you can identify for strategic purposes.

For example:

- I am not good with introductions.

- I do not know how to make conversation.
- I get too nervous when I start talking.
- I do not know how to make conversations that last more than a minute.
- I talk too fast or have trouble breathing in the presence of beauty.
- I cannot seem to keep eye contact without shivering.
- I sound sleazy and weird when I am just trying to flirt.
- I feel out of the league of most women.
- I am self-conscious about my appearance or one physical aspect of myself.
- I hate my job and dread she will ask me about it.
- I have had so many bad relationships and do not want to be hurt again.
- Sex ruins friendships and so I do not look forward to it.
- I do not have a lot of sexual experience and I fear not being able to please a woman.
- I become afraid and feel myself making nervous gestures.
- I am afraid of rejection and how it will make me feel.
- I am afraid of being embarrassed publicly.
- I need drugs or alcohol to feel comfortable.
- I hate the "qualifying" part of dating and it ends up frustrating her and me.
- I am funny but too funny. I do not know how to switch from funny to sexy.
- My funny comments are always mistaken as rude or insulting, when I am just trying to be friendly.
- I am out of practice with dating.
- I am still in love with someone else and my heart is not into it.
- I do not want to come across as desperate, clingy or scary.
- I talk too much.
- I have so much respect for women; I feel guilty trying to be sexual in conversation.

- I have guilty feelings about dating and sex.

- I feel unattractive because of a recent physical change.

- I think women are prejudging me and it makes me agitated.

- I am too quiet.

- I am too intense when I speak.

Now that you have an idea of what you do not like about your dating style, you can more accurately determine what criteria you have to change to become "naturally" charismatic and attractive. After all, what is the difference between you and all the popular guys out there?

At this point, it is only about specific negative traits that you do not like about yourself. If you were to change these behaviors, or at least minimize them to a manageable extent, you could become that ideal man and speak comfortably. Focusing on specific issues will also help you increase your aura of confidence and stop thinking in terms of "I can't do it!" or "I'm not charming like those other guys." This is because you are no longer focused on not being good enough. Rather you are focusing on what aspects are not good enough and that you have power to change.

Highlighting Your Best

In like manner, it is helpful to create a list for yourself and determine what qualities you do possess that are competitive with other men—perhaps even the characteristics that allow you to outshine others.

For example:

- What are your favorite things about yourself?

- What do other people tell you that they like about yourself?

- What TV characters or movie stars do you like and try to emulate? What are their qualities that you enjoy and also have?

- What are some of the best memories you can remember, and what qualities did you display to have those memories?

- What do you enjoy doing the most?

- How do you express love?

- How do you give to others?

Answering these questions will begin to provide insight on your "best" qualities, the sticking points you want your date to remember, so that she will feel attracted to you and continue to associate positive qualities with your presence.

After serious introspection, you might determine:

- I have a great sense of humor.

- I take good care of myself physically and mentally.

- I am intelligent and a good teacher.

- I am active and ambitious.

- I am artistic and have goals I want to fulfill.

- I am a giving person.

- I am a good lover.

- I am a good listener and empathetic.

- I am a good counselor and give good advice.

- I uphold my core values and morality code no matter what.

- I am open-minded about all things.

- I am adventurous.

- I am a great performer at my hobby or interest.

- I feel comfortable speaking my mind when I get to know a woman.

- I am not afraid of debate.

- I am a romantic soul.

- I am fearless.

You see, all of these things are traits that "sell" to women looking for a compatible partner. However, if all you are focused on is your shortcomings, she will never even know why you are such a good catch in the first place. You have to show her why you are special, qualifying yourself for her attention.

Very often, you may be unaware of some of the good qualities you do have. Therefore, it is a smart idea to speak to others, male and female, about what they consider to be your greatest assets, the things they would find attractive about you. Or in the case of other guys, the admirable qualities that would qualify you for a date with a close friend or sister. Take these compliments seriously and do not brush off honest statements.

Now that you have become aware of these positive qualities, it is time to showcase them— indeed, to *live them* and highlight them in everything you do. This includes, the show stopping moments of the night (as in, let me play guitar for you!), all the way down to the little things ("I remember what you told me about..."; showing you are a good listener). You do not have to be a braggart because that would certainly be interpreted as a negative quality. However, you should try to alter your behavior slightly, so that you resist old patterns of "trying too hard" and instead try social patterns that emphasize selling points.

What Is Supposed To Happen On A Date

One more tidbit to help you stay focused, as opposed to blindly moving in for romance and getting the big hand in front of the face, is to remember that dating is a goal-oriented process, and not just an intuitive "let's hope it all falls into place" experiment. There is a definite formula and a beginning, middle and end. It goes like this:

Part I: Creating Attraction

Creating attraction - through first impressions, confidence, strength and interest in the other person. Think of this as the animal phase, something we share with our lesser sentient furry friends, since we give off some strong body language showing our mating availability. Usually this involves:

- A straight, firm posture

- Smiling and sweet facial expressions

- Strong eye contact

- Excellent grooming

This is the mating dance we all subconsciously take part in and more often, than not, a woman can tell if you like her in that way—but rest assured if you approach her in an attitude of weakness, she will deny ever seeing these signals. That is her prerogative. If you are going to do it, do it right!

Part II: Reading Your Date

Read your date, sense her attraction and if she is responding favorably to the energy in the room. Establishing rapport and comfort is key here, as a rushed, nervous, or uncomfortable energy will drain the attraction.

Part III: Verbal Communication

The theme of conversation is somewhat irrelevant. Rest assured, plenty of dumb guys out there have made it to first base with thick-headed conversation. The difference between them and you is that these guys know conversation is not really about debating or persuading but about *connecting*. It is about communicating on a subconscious level and imparting your desires to her in an intellectual and comfortable way. The conversation is to establish rapport, friendship and a reasonable degree of trust. It is the perfect time to show your strengths in subtle and self-confident (but not bragging) ways. Then, after demonstrating your positives, it moves into the reactionary phase where you respond to the favorable cues or "signals" you are receiving. This helps you determine if you have permission to progress further—if you have successfully developed and maintained attraction.

Now yes, I realize that you may take your conversation very seriously and that you want to be known as a smart guy who is interesting to talk to. We will get to that later. For now, rest assured that while intellectual conversation is important, the emotions behind all this data is what is actually getting your future primed for courtship.

Part IV: Physical Touch

The physical touching stage precedes sex and romance because it is a preliminary step to establishing a much deeper connection after the initial chemistry is discovered. If a woman allows you to touch her; inviting you directly or responding favorably to your test touch, this is a good sign and you can progress from innocent bumping to sitting close to one another, to eventually expressing affection in a safe and yet comfortable way. This phase is important as it will ultimately determine whether you are chemically compatible and if you can go ahead and move on with the courtship phase.

If your date does not respond well, something is not working right and you are losing the positive associations and attraction you had maintained up until this point. It is time to regroup.

Part V: Intimacy

Intimacy becomes more assertive the more trust you build. Polite or light touches eventually turn into cuddling, hand holding, gazing and stroking, and then ending with that 'all-important' kiss. You will even notice that as you progress forward and start to feel the sexual chemistry igniting, her skin color may change; her eyes may become starry; and your voices may go up or down an octave as you begin speaking with a "sexual voice."

Some guys go for the physical touch or sexual voice early and it's definitely a hit or miss strategy. In traditional courtship, you do try to move forward in a logical and step-by-step manner. There is a quick lay strategy, which we will discuss later, however; if romance and courtship is your goal this is the proper way to build the relationship's foundation.

As we move into Chapter 3, we are going to discuss some of the specifics of what keeps good men down, and unable to relax around beautiful women.

Let us start with introductions. For many men out there, one of the most confusing and intimidating parts of the dating experience!

21

Dynamic Introductions That Last a Lifetime

For a lot of men out there, even the ones who do feel reasonably confident and flirty, the introduction is very difficult. This is understandable, as our society has rightfully been trained to avoid talking to "strangers", since we never really can tell who is friendly and a nice person, and who might be a ticking time bomb of a crazy person! It is natural to take introductions slowly and to be a little suspicious when one meets new people. For example, how comfortable do you feel when a salesperson approaches you in the mall, running circles around you and acting overly friendly, or when a religious person comes to your door offering good news?

You might even feel apprehensive about a *woman who approaches you and starts flirting with you.* It is such a strange behavior that you might think something is up and not quite right. For example, you are on a busy street in a big city like Las Vegas or London and a gorgeous woman approaches you, makes small talk and seems attracted to you without any explanation. Your first guess? "Hmmm is she a hooker?" Of course, there is no way to ask that politely. That is the suspicion though; people suddenly interjecting themselves into your life are a bit conspicuous. The first thing you want to know is, "What do they want from me?"

Furthermore, we usually do not believe whatever that person is saying. We want to know what the catch is, what their real motivation is, after "hooking you in" with what sounds like a great idea.

So here is a thought; Instead of feeling sorry for yourself and lamenting on why women don't seem to like you, try to think of this game from their perspective. If they are the "commodity" and you are pursuing them, why should they trust you? What is your "catch"? Why do they owe you their attention?

Now you are beginning to see the reality of what introductions are and why seduction is so important in framing the introduction. An alpha male does not merely approach a woman but has an agenda, and has a strategy. Sometimes the worst mistake you can make is approaching a woman in clueless wonder, hoping the scene will just play out naturally. Unfortunately, in most cases, it will not. Figuratively speaking, you do not speak the same "language" until you are able to establish common ground. No wonder when some guys nervously approach a woman jabbering on about some nonsense, a woman becomes defensive and quickly puts up a shield of cynicism. You might as well be speaking ancient Hebrew and flailing your arms, because without that all-important common ground, she has nothing to say to you.

The Pre-Approach

So let us talk strategy. You are absolutely correct in assuming that successful men don't just walk up to a woman and improvise—unless of course, they have naturally extroverted tendencies. More specifically, they have the innate ability to strategize and think of ideas and scenarios quickly. They involuntarily do what the usual introvert has to go through the process of planning to do. Still, the result is the same. All men carry out the pre-approach process before actually approaching a woman.

So we come to step 1 in the pre-approaching process.

Analyzing the Situation: The first step is to access the scene and take in the environment. This will naturally play an important part in determining your success for the night. Perhaps, it is the *one* thing that you have in common with this strange new woman; a shared environment and a shared experience. When you do enter a room, what is the first thing you do? It might serve you well to:

- Notice the facility, the background scene, and the ten different things that are happening all at once.

- Notice the faces of the people; what their behavior and body language indicate about their mood.

Taking note of these small details can help you gain confidence and also come up with conversations later on.

Playing the "I See You Game": Now we are going to let you in on a little secret. Women are not as oblivious as you might think, nor are they as gullible as they sometimes pretend to be. For instance, the majority of women will probably notice if you stare (if you make eye contact), and they will definitely notice when you hover around them, trying to work up the courage to say something. Women are highly sensitive to changes in environment, and it is not too narcissistic of them to think that you are probably smitten and gawking, because you usually are...aren't you? So, just as you are assessing the situation, believe that women are doing the same thing. They might just be hiding it much better than you are. The corner of a woman's eye is like a fully functional infrared radar!

The point being...

You Should Be Strategizing to Make a Move...Now!: There's no sense in strategizing if you're just going to sit there for 20 minutes thinking about what you could do. This is not what is meant by strategizing, because the strategy is simple at this early point: go up and talk to her. That is it. And maybe show her that you're not a stalker, a lunatic, a criminal, or a man-boy who is too afraid to talk to a lovely face.

The problem is that so many men psyche themselves out of the experience by worrying about the woman's reaction that they either avoid the woman after minutes of nervous pacing, or they take too long and lose all of their positive momentum. In fact, by the time a man "works up the courage" to talk to a woman, he has probably already lost points with her. This is because:

- She has sensed his weakness.

- He has exhibited strange behavior, usually reminiscent of stalkers or anti-social individuals (which is often associated with psychotics in the female mind)

- He has not done anything to attract her, but has already suggested he is lacking in good qualities. After all, why else would he hesitate unless something was seriously wrong?

This is precisely why some men travel in "packs", so that they do not seem awkwardly placed, as if waiting for a moment or waiting for the courage. They play it cool and make

23

themselves look busy, talking to someone they know. This is why, virtually, every player's guide and gifted extrovert will tell you:

Approach her right away and show her that you are a friendly, rational and fairly confident human being. This immediately tells her you are worth talking to, worth getting to know, and not somebody who is asking to be avoided. It is the three-second rule that a lot of guys talk about. If you are too afraid to approach a woman within three seconds, you probably will not approach her at all, or she will not be as receptive to you; since you have already second-guessed yourself. If you must pause and strategize for moments on end, then you better start talking to another gent. Once you make eye contact with the woman you like, you are on a timer. And every second you waste, is another point being lost. Think of dating in terms of basketball...now you are getting the picture!

Knowing What You Want

The second biggest problem with introductions besides the whole "kind of, sort of, want to try my luck, and summon up courage!" is that men tiptoe about why they are there, why they like the girl they like, and what exactly it is that they want to happen. Some men will even summon up some great confidence early on but then quickly burn out as they realize they are too shy or perhaps too confused about how they want things to proceed.

This is why natural born players are more successful in dating than shy and inexperienced men. Players know what they want, whether that is a bonking in bed, or a dance, or a dinner date, or even just a specific conversation with a beginning, middle and end. On the other hand, inexperienced men simply know they want to speak to the girl but have no clue about what or why. And that is usually the woman's first reaction: why? Why are you talking to me? Why am I listening? Why should I care? Why are you so special to think you deserve me? (Yeah, that's a ball-buster for you but it is true)

So you could say that part of the secret of a great introduction is showing the woman you are approaching something specific; a goal you are interested in, or a direction to the conversation. This shows intelligence, confidence and your researching abilities, if nothing else. The good news is that when you know what you want to talk about and what way to steer the conversation, it puts a woman at ease. It is the basic "path of least resistance" life lesson. People do not always want to think. Sometimes they just want to feel or to react to what is being said. In that respect, a man who guides the conversation will always have an easier time evoking emotion and conversation from a woman than a shy guy who's still scratching his head, trying to think of what "move" to do next.

So coming to terms with, what you want in the pre-pick up stage, is essential to actually getting what you want and setting an achievable goal. Do not think that you have to go for a quick lay if you really just want to take it gradually. It is okay to take small steps, and honestly, most women are probably more comfortable with slow-moving romance rather than ultra-liberated sexual escapades. (Unless you both hang out at Mardi Gras)

You can always make a phone number, a date, a name, even a simple conversation that you start and finish – your goal. Knowing that and working towards it will give you the momentum you need to get started.

Being a Positive-Minded Pick Up Artist

Ever noticed that there aren't a lot of negative-minded pick up artists walking around? Sure, negative minded guys might occasionally get laid, but it is really nothing compared to the guy who is positive, magnetic, always happy and flirty, and generally just an optimistic guy. Well, this optimism easily converts into an assertive, "I can do anything" attitude that is hard for a woman to resist.

For example, what do most men do when an obstacle is placed between them and their potential date? Well of course, the natural reaction is to be pessimistic and think, "I have to bow out." When a woman says that she has a boyfriend, or if she looks especially hostile, or even if she is with a large group of other women, these are warning signals that are meant to deter men. An ordinary guy takes that suggestion quickly.

A pick up artist views these obstacles as positives; not only the proverbial "challenge" but also simply looking past the obvious disadvantage and seeing the potential for a good time.

For example:

- The hostile or angry woman. (Positive thought: She is going to scare everyone else away, meaning I will have less competition!)

- The woman in a group (Great, so I can hit on a lot of girls at once!)

- The woman with a boyfriend (She is probably missing something in her relationship; if I find out what that is, the rest of it is easy!)

It is not really a matter of memorizing these positives; it is learning to look at a situation with a positive attitude and not simply accepting an obstacle as the final impediment to your happiness. A successful ladies' man does not think pessimistically because, by nature, doing so does not bring about change, or lead to new opportunities, but stubbornly remains the status quo.

Outcome-Dependent Behavior

One common problem among single men is the huge value we put on rejection or acceptance. Many are so afraid at the very idea of rejection that either they talk themselves out of opportunity, or they judge their own behavior harshly when they do get a friendly or not so friendly "No, thanks."

On one hand, rejection is difficult and it is difficult in all walks of life. It is hard to hear someone reject you, and sometimes the only way we can live with rejection is to remind ourselves that it is not personal—well, in dating, it is personal and that is the worst kind of rejection!

One of the biggest leaps you can make is to lose your fear of rejection. That tidbit alone will make you super-confident in the eyes of a woman because that is pretty much the only defense a woman has, except of course, to get a restraining order. Most men are so terrified or devastated at rejection that they cower when a woman tells them she is not interested. This is one of many filtering processes, a woman will put you through, just to see if you are serious dating material.

So guess what? The men who cower away at the first sign of disagreement do not really have much to offer in her eyes. Yes, it is kind of a sick game, but that is what people do.

So you can take one of two approaches to a woman attempting to restrict you in this way.

A.   You can be determined to laugh it off and joke about the rejection, even mocking her for so quickly dismissing you, and then continue with your current dating goal.

B.   Or you can alter your perspective slightly, and start "elevating" your standards a bit when looking through the dating pool.

Think about the typical nice guy's point of view. He is so lonely and horny he would probably date just about anyone, since he wants sex, and wants to prove himself worthy of a girlfriend. In doing so, in taking this attitude, he has decided to lower his standards. He accepts that he wants to sleep with a woman he finds attractive and nothing can deter him. However, he never stops to think, "What if I don't like her? What if something about her turns me off?" This attitude is so strong in a man that women can sense it—and their radar immediately goes up, suggesting that you are not that special. And what did we learn about female attraction? You have to be the alpha male if you are going to attract her on a subconscious level.

So one simple solution that might change your dating luck is to give yourself the option of rejecting a woman. It seems shocking to you, especially if the woman is beautiful, especially if you hardly have any female attention. However, this small dynamic shift is a cataclysm to the typical female mind and will often provoke women who insist on putting up a witchy exterior shell. More to the point though, elevating your standards gives you the self-confidence you need to be true to yourself and to not fear rejection that stops men dead in their tracks.

The 10 Game

One way to get over your fear of rejection is to stop idolizing women so much, and instead to start treating them like the flawed human beings that they all are—that we all are. For instance, there is such a thing called the 10 Game, where you rate women according to the perfect 10 standard.

You start by rating women that you believe are a perfect 10. There is no sense in denying they exist, maybe some of your favorite Hollywood bombshells, past and present. Now move on downward and start rating some 9s and 8s. Then 7s and downward until you reach 0 and the ugliest woman in a dress.

Now, the next time you go out and see an attractive woman, rather than instantly saying she is a 10 or the most beautiful you have ever seen, start being a little bit more critical and rating her realistically. A 6, a 7 maybe an 8 if she really tries. You might even start subtracting points based on her behavior and personality (i.e. she is good looking but she smokes; but she is a few years older than myself; but she has an annoying laugh).

Now that you have taken a critical look at her, she is far from the 10 that you have built her up to be. She is just another single person, like you, with selling points and with negative points that could make her incompatible with your lifestyle. You might even make a list of the woman's assets, bad points, and fatal flaws that could potentially ruin the entire relationship.

As you mold your mind to think differently from your old perspective, and actually be secure enough to decide what you do and do not want, your interactions with others will start to change. You will stop thinking silly things like, "She's out of my league" or "I'm not good enough for her" and will instead start to wonder:

"Well, she is cute…but what else does she have to offer? Is there any substance behind that pretty face?"

You may actually be surprised to learn that there isn't. A lot of men have such low self-confidence that they actually chase after women who don't match them intellectually, or socially, never realizing that they could do better—they could find that perfect 10 if only their standards were a bit higher.

So in the interest of getting this right, the pickup stage coming up, adjust your perspective and ready yourself to approach a woman in confidence. Now you have mastered the internal pre-pick up process, and it is now time to work on converting your internal enthusiasm into something externally smooth and articulate.

A Woman's Prerogative

It is a woman's prerogative to decide who she wants to sleep with and it is often said that women know within the first few minutes of meeting you if she's going to sleep with you. This revelation certainly makes introductions and first impressions seem so much more important, doesn't it?

You will find the more often you date that projecting mystery is an attractive quality. Men do seem to ruin their chances with women by revealing too much early on. This includes their strange thoughts, their neediness, their controversial opinions or attitudes, when in fact they should be more concerned with learning who the woman is, and how to adapt his personality to fit hers.

So let us consider some of our most and least favorite openers.

The Lame Kitten

For lack of a better word, the lame kitten is what happens when a guy loses all his nerve, and instead of roaring like a lion, meows like a kitten! He says something terribly obvious and unsatisfying like, "Come here often?" or "So…you like this place?" or whatever other filler conversation he can come up with at a moment's notice. All of these statements are wishy-washy and only seem to disguise the fact that he can't think of anything to say, and certainly cannot admit what he wants. You force her to think of something negative, like your lacking social kiss, instead of keeping her positive mood going. At this point, you might as well tell her you are a millionaire or reveal yourself to actually be Brad Pitt, because that is all that can save you at this point.

The Pick Up Line

Men are so obsessed with introductions that they have invented the pickup line over a number of years—you know the secret "key" required to grab a woman's attention, one that will unlock that daunting door of attraction every single time. Ironically, pickup lines all end the same way. The guy delivers the cheesy line and the woman either rolls her eyes or laughs. (Once in a while, she gets offended which is actually quite the spectacle)

So right away, what does this tell you? The fact that women pretty much all have the same reaction to a pickup line? Right, it is irrelevant. It does not really matter if you say something cheesy, something romantic, something goofy and absurd, or even something shocking.

The opening line serves only one purpose to get her attention. It is almost the same thing as saying "Hi!" sadly enough, since your "Hi!" can be just as friendly, joyous and good-humored. Now this is not necessarily to discourage pickup lines. They are fun to use and sometimes they are good icebreakers when the environment is not entirely comfortable.

However, you cannot over think this one because the truth is there is no secret word or sentence that earns her respect. A line is just a hello, and what she actually responds to is your physical approach, as well as the inflection of your voice. As soon as she senses your happiness (indicated by a sincere smile), your confidence, and your newly found standards of excellence that you're holding out for, she will respond favorably. She has no reason not to, unless of course she is putting on an ice queen façade to scare you away.

So all you are really doing with an opening line is *starting communication*. You are letting her know that it is okay to feel comfortable in your presence and that you are not going to be a "stressful" guy to deal with. Some of the best reactions guys get is the laughter that *follows* the pickup line. Sometimes the guy laughs at the cheesiness of the pickup line and the woman joins him. It is really about the experience you share rather than anything brilliant you are saying in just one sentence.

An open-ended question (meaning one where she must express an opinion or offer a perspective) immediately grabs a woman's attention and forces her to think about what the man is saying.

Of course, since all of this is positive association, it is imperative that the conversations be kept light. Simple questions about tattoos, favorite costumes, or dating etiquette go a long way in opening up a dialog without getting into anything too heavy. Another alternation is to disguise the open-ended question as a survey of some sort, though it is a fairly transparent ploy. A woman might even become wise to your seduction techniques if she senses that you're using "lines" or obvious "questions" in an attempt to make her feel something.

Therefore, some guys absolutely prefer the direct approach, which is casual conversation, perhaps even boldly romantic, rather than playing too many tongue-in-cheek games. This suggests an honest approach, which is right in line with the personality a man might be trying to portray.

The Conversation Starter

Pickup lines are out of date, even if they are retro-terrific sometimes. This is why many guys have progressed beyond the standard pickup line and are more into starting conversations with a simple "hi" or "hello." This immediately lets the woman know this is friend material, which is not necessarily a bad thing. A new friend is good (a lifelong friend zoned friend, not so good). This is a good strategy if you want to escape the stigma of dating. The simple introduction and straight transition into conversation is not as intimidating for you or for her because there isn't necessarily a need to impress right away. In fact, your approach could even be suggesting something completely innocent—like that of a platonic friend or neighbor. Not where you want to end up long-term, but being ambiguous in the beginning is an effective way to alleviate her suspicions. This gives you the opportunity to build rapport as a fellow intelligent being.

Asking about a woman's day and simply relating to her as one human being to another, as a friend first, is an option to consider, especially if she seems standoffish about being pressured into a date.

The Instant Casanova

This is a bit of an unorthodox strategy, but it can work in many cases, especially if you have mastered self-confident body language and what is called "the sexual state", which we will discuss a bit later. Instead of coming up with creative ways to engage her, the instant Casanova move emphasizes the romance, and will fixate on a woman's beauty rendering her into giggles, or at least a cynical goose face if it doesn't work. It is a somewhat hit or miss strategy, and does seem to be a move straight out of the 1970s. (Just witness Gene Wilder's amazing magnetism whenever he saw a "beautiful woman" that moved him to fawning, charismatic disbelief). He looked as if he was ready to hop into bed with her, and hey, with that movie star presence and soft voice, most of his fans would have accepted the invitation.

The good news is if you do work up enough courage to use this strategy, you will immediately activate and spread that sexual tension and will make a dramatic introduction—even if she rejects you at first. The potential negative is that you will scare her away and be forever labeled as a man chasing her for sex, and probably not a friend she will feel comfortable with. So it's a 50/50 in most cases. It is also far less effective with higher numbered women (10s and 9s) than it is for 6s and 7s who really don't get that much attention and crave it.

Another twist to add into the Casanova approach is to up the drama and actually create a minor "scene" or happening, directing not just her but also everyone else's attention to you both, making a romantic and embarrassing memory to last a lifetime. This adds a little more dramatic flair, and certainly gives you the impression of being someone special.

The Instant Casanova approach also works if you work some innocent touching into it, such as gazing into her eyes while touching her hand. The key to this is to be *low key* however and to exude a natural and calm state. Using this approach but being too excitable is surely going to scare her away and paint you as an unstable suitor.

The Shocker

No, not that type of shocker! However, the "shock" effect sometimes works in dating, especially if you are beaming with confidence and are feeling like spreading some of that madcap humor. Shocking statements, inappropriate observations, absurd antics and satirizing dating culture (for example, guys who pretend as if all women are stalking them, or guys who brag incessantly about their sexual prowess) are desperate moves that do have a way of getting you noticed, (by women and maybe talent scouts wherever they're hiding). However, it is definitely a huge risk. If you fail to do this correctly, you could scare a woman away for good. Or perhaps she'll sense that something about you is "fake" and so she will reject you anyway.

One example of the shocker gimmick is called "grandmaster"; lingo in the dating world referring to an alpha male who is blatantly propositioning women but with a funny and cocky approach, essentially entertaining women (and other men who watch) with a show. It is enjoyable to an extent, but again, it comes with a huge risk; one of the ways to offend the woman you like. Much like the other shock jock moves you can try, it may get an honest laugh. It may lead to a quick lay…sometimes. But usually, you will have to leave the grandmaster façade behind and get serious if you want to progress into real conversation. This is a strategy to try when you have a major caffeine-sugar high. Otherwise, leave it to late night talk show hosts of the world.

Good Humor And Gimmicks

Good humor is not necessarily shocking, nor is it smarmy or condescending like satirizing dating culture. It is simply going for laughs. You can do this by literally orchestrating a skit (for example, using your cell phone as a prop and describing a woman who's sitting next to you, pretending to talk to someone else) or using a prop like a pez dispenser, or a puppet, or whatever is strange and quirky that you can work into a joke. Just be very clear about why this is funny, and that you are just trying to get her attention, or else you may simply come across as a mental patient with a pez dispenser.

Actually, take some of these gimmicks seriously, as in "I'm a magician!", "I am a scientist!", or "I am a psychic!" They are gimmicks in and of themselves and make for a great introduction. Even something as obvious as "I am a musician" or "I am a writer" are interesting gimmicks you can play up, instantly conveying to her that you have special value beyond the average.

Familiarizing Yourself

Familiarizing yourself is a clever technique, and particularly goal-oriented, since your intention is to become familiar with her, in her presence, so that her comfort level with you increases. The level of familiarity you feign is a progressive sequence. When you have established that you are a non-threatening presence (usually leading with a smile and friendly persistence) then you can proceed into casual touching which activates her kinesthetic awareness of you. It is always subtle at first, such as a jocular "high five", or touching someone's elbow or hand in a gesture of friendliness.

It can become more overt as you increase intimacy, such as "platonic" hugging, handshaking or even what is called; the 'boyfriending' technique. You politely go into her space and perform boyfriend-esque tasks, subconsciously showing her what it would be like. For example, you could move her hair with your hand, and tell her it would be better if she combed it that way. Or you could touch her cheek, pretending to remove an eyelash (even if there is no eyelash). Or you could touch her lips with your fingers, pretending to remove a tiny amount of saliva or food from her lips (even if none exist).

Some men will actually use the concept of familiarizing themselves in the opening line, and pretend to know the woman they are interested in, or try to make it seem like the woman should know him from somewhere. This is a great manipulative technique because the woman feels compelled to know him, at his request, but cannot seem to place the face. Within seconds, an impostor form of intimacy is achieved…and then let go, when she realizes he is playing her. Still, it is an effective way to introduce yourself, if a bit obvious.

Using comparative illustrations might well be considered another form of the familiarity technique, as you will compare the woman you are interested in to a well-known celebrity or international figure. Some men have found even greater success by simply refraining from the actual comparison, instead simply observing, "You look like...", and then leaving her hanging. This is a great way to manipulate her curiosity, and the "hook" as we will soon call it is always a powerful motivator. You have her attention, you engage her and then cease. She wants to know the answer to the question you just posed.

The Hypnotic Intro

The hypnotic intro can be very well said to be the most effective strategy, but also the most difficult technique to pull off. In this instance, you are actually suggesting to the woman of interest what you want her to feel by very subtly, and practically subconsciously, imbedding commands into your conversation. Logically speaking, she will be held captive. She will feel what you tell her to feel. At any point, she has the option to turn off her empathetic "switch" and stop listening to you, but if there is an attraction already there, this is the best way to explore it.

It starts simply enough by acknowledging what she is already thinking. This is one of the principles of hypnosis in the first place - the establishing of common ground. You don't want resistance but agreement. Therefore, the introduction consists of describing (or even joking about) what she is feeling, and the experience you are both taking part in. This is a type of "pacing reality" as some pickup artists call it.

Keeping your comments measured (not necessarily vague, but non-committal) will continue to hold her curiosity. She will suspect you like her but will not know for sure, and hence will be a captive audience. From then on, the "learning stage" of hypnosis continues, with you, playing therapist, asking her open-ended questions that actually *reveal who she is*; her likes and dislikes, her dreams and memories, and future ambitions. Once you have established a common ground, all that is left to do is guide the conversation into discussion you can manage.

One of the most effective techniques after delivering a hypnotic intro is to leave her with a question, rather than simply allowing her to shut down with a close-ended yes or no statement. The "yes or no" question is one of the worst things you can do in the conversation, because ideally, you don't want the woman saying "no" for any reason, since this is bringing negative associations of you into her mind.

You can also continue to guide her attention, holding her as your audience, by further imbedding commands into her head, all the while pretending to freely converse. Conversations like these are best served with an emphasis on sincerity and engagement.

As in:

- I was just thinking about childhood experiences...

- I was just thinking about how life is unpredictable...

- I was thinking about the time when...

- Today I was feeling down but then something cheered me up...

31

And so forth.

With these sentences, we can clearly see that the pickup artist is prepping her for a hypnotic pull. He is hiding behind "I feel" or "I think"; when in actuality he is going to tell her what she should be thinking. He might use carefully placed words such as "amazing", "delightful", "powerful", and so on when describing a seemingly commonplace or sentimental experience. However, what he is actually doing is appealing to her emotion.

The only way a woman (or anyone for that matter) can understand what you are saying is to feel or know what you tell them. So if you spend a couple of minutes describing something with strong emotional content (and have a good backup story or "excuse" on why you're saying this to her) you will awaken something inside of her.

You can either describe the short-term past (what she was doing or thinking before you started a conversation) or even the present tense, offering a bit of a humorous observation. When you do talk about this shared experience, she cannot disagree with you, and so this only goes to improve positive associations. She will agree with you and continue to nod, to find common ground, until you give her a reason to reject where you are going. This is when you create the connection.

The conclusion, specifically the future tense is how you end this introduction. Now you go to the stage of saying what you would like to be true, instead of what is true and what is shared. This is a little bit of a risk, since this is where you open the box of sexual tension and let her know why you are doing this; that you believe she thinks you are handsome, and is happy you approached her, or even that the two of you should go and continue this conversation on a date.

Because up until now she has mostly been agreeing with you, she might feel more inclined to say yes and agree that there is a connection, perhaps "unexplainable" that she feels toward you. When, in fact, all you have really done is taken a brutally honest approach to this game, which brings us to a very important point: honesty is respected. Dishonesty, avoidance and flattery tends to wear away at her attraction-level.

It is important at this stage that you do not push too hard with the embedded commands and that you keep things positive and a bit on the conservative side. After all, you are not Freud doing a 30-second hypnosis experiment. You are just a guy trying to relate to an attractive girl sharing an experience.

Neg-Hitting

Neg-hitting is a bit of an ego buster, something men use to get the attention of a high-ranking woman (usually a 9 or a 10), who assumes that every guy wants her and is waiting for that "special one" to come along. What better way to let her know she's not the grand prizewinner in the game of dating than to very subtly imply that you could do better? A neg-hit is the introduction she needs, to actually notice you, because you are subconsciously telling her "I don't want sex. That's not what I am looking for, and you are not what I thought you were."

This instantly activates the "push and pull" dynamic, daring her to chase you just a little bit, after you've clearly signaled you're not interested, or she's done something to offend you. This works well on women with big egos, who are not used to guys standing up to them and holding their own ground. Women who are 10s are usually desensitized to compliments and perhaps even a little bored with most of the other introductions they get, assuming they get plenty from across the board.

The neg-hit slaps her back down to earth, because it plays on her vanity by giving a backhanded compliment. In other words, a nice insult. You don't insult her, you don't behave aggressively. What you do is appeal to her immaturity by giving a cloaked criticism of her persona (but usually her personality, not her figure), by indicating she is lower than your usual standards. This instantly provokes your woman of interest, since she suddenly feels compelled to prove herself to you—even though you have completely avoided the part where she turns you down. You turn her down first and the war is on.

As you continue to play the game, she will attempt to gain an upper hand trying to *turn you into the nice guy*, using ploys to get you to surrender control back to her, showing you this is all an act. Little does she know she likes this game, because it is fun and flirty, and because, sometimes the guys like to play hard to get too.

When you engage in negging she will usually, neg you back, until she sees that you are not going to back down. This causes her to re-think the situation and try to "win you over", eventually dropping her defensive façade.

You really cannot push too hard on this, because constantly insulting her will most likely drive her away, perhaps eventually breaking through her shields and hitting her where it hurts. This is precisely what self-loathing girls with daddy issues usually like, but rest assured most women have a threshing point and eventually the neg-hitting has to relent a little bit. It is a great way to open a conversation with a 10.

However, at some point, you want to proceed away from the witty and memorable introductions—important though they are—and then proceed into more artistic and scientific techniques, namely the date conversation.

The "hook" is another principle in introductions, but it is a somewhat complicated discussion since the nuances of conversation start at the introduction and then proceed to thread through the entire conversation, and even for the final goodbye. In our next chapter, we are going to consider what makes a conversation flow.

33

Chapter 4

The Art, The Science Of Good Conversation

The painful truth is that it is easy to make a good introduction, at least when compared to engaging in a full conversation with a member of the opposite sex—and with a complete stranger for that matter. First impressions count, but men have an even greater struggle ahead of them. How can they maintain common ground over time, eventually building more intimacy until an emotional connection is felt?

For that matter, if finding common ground is the key, why is it that women can tell right away if they are going to sleep with this guy? It seems confusing at first, that is, until you realize that maintaining common ground in dialog is basically an extension of the same attitude you introduce. You are not necessarily exploring new territory but trying to keep sending the same message, without saying anything incongruous to your presentation so far. In other words, don't blow this opportunity that you have created for yourself. Don't betray the projection you've given her thus far.

Ongoing dialog is similar to the dynamics of an introduction; your mission is to capture a woman's curiosity and then keep her engaged until she begins to feel something for you—or more to the point, continues to amplify what she already suspected in the first few seconds of meeting you.

The Transition

The transition from smooth introduction to long and meaningful chat is a tricky trap because it is easy to infuse personality and enthusiasm into an introduction you memorize. It is more difficult to be entertaining for minutes, even hours, on end without losing any of your charm. Don't most guys run out of things to say? When do you know when it is right to ask a woman out? And then, what in the world do you say when you do have her undivided attention?

One of the first things you realize in dating is that you have a natural gift of gab around people that you are not sexually attracted to. You probably don't have much trouble making small talk with a relative, a neighbor of the same sex, your childhood guy friends, and your work colleagues. Conversation comes easy. Sure, maybe you are not exactly close with these people but consider how you feel when you speak to them, versus when you speak to an attractive woman. It is a major difference, isn't it?

And the reason you have such palpable tension on a date is because you have almost zero comfort established. Comfort that you take for granted with family and friends because your conversations have become routine. Once you have this comfort, you do have the entitlement and the ability to create conversations at will, and to be as funny and interesting as you want.

What is conversation but basic communication between two separate beings? You are not really conveying anything deep. Instead, you are imparting information, or in most cases in the dating scenario, providing free entertainment. You are not performing a stage show; you are customizing the night's entertainment for the woman you are trying to attract. So whatever follows the introduction has to match the same feeling as the introduction; something new, something interesting and a little bold.

The more you both engage in conversation, the more familiar you become to her and the greater a connection she can feel. What begins as attraction can amplify and become a desire for more intimacy, as long as you maintain that same feeling.

Obviously, the conversation cannot be one-sided with you doing all the talking, or with her telling you the story of her life. Chemistry is created when two people talk to each other, equally engage, and respond to what is being said.

Good conversation never seems forceful. It seems natural, relaxed, fun and comfortable. It is more entertaining, more exaggerated than the typical 'getting to know you - chitchat' because of the sexual dynamic. As we learned a long time ago, an alpha male does not fear sexual tension, but invites it, toys with it, but without ever seeming too desperate to "score", "succeed", and "win" at this game. He is content in himself and this game; this push and pull dynamic sets the stage for an emotional tug of war.

Transitions are as easy as learning the English language. You finish one thought and then use a connective word or phrase to lead into another or a similar discussion that can be tied in to the original thought. For example, "Speaking of enjoyable memories", or "Actually that brings me to my next question." You guide her along the train of thought not interrupting abruptly since this implies awkwardness and maybe even fear.

The next step that comes is the *discovery process*. You communicate instinctively, following the signals of courtship. However, the primary objective here is the discovery process, learning what you can about your potential date so that you can begin assuming the qualities of the man she wants. When it is time to get serious and start learning about each other, it is best to continue the emotional pull by evoking her curiosity. One of the best ways to do this is through "hooks."

Hooks are what she gives you, and what you run with in the conversation. A good hook is a full dialog, an opinion or a story she feels like sharing with you. A bad hook we can all sense right away; it is when a woman answers your questions or statements with one-word responses, and sends strong signals of disinterest. Your goal in conversation is fairly minimal. Continue building attraction by reemphasizing your higher caliber hooks, while deflecting those low caliber hooks, which might as well be low caliber bullets!

There is no great way to answer a "yes" or "no" response and she is not necessarily putting up a shield by answering this way. This could be the reaction to an awkward introduction. In this case, it is best to remember your hook-defenses, ten different ways you can *react to the hooks she is giving you.*

Let's start the countdown.

1. The Open-Ended Question

An open question cannot be answered with one word. Therefore, if you want to draw your love interest out, use questions that demand a sentence or several sentences worth of response. This not only gives you more to work on, but also encourages her to speak. The rule is the more a woman talks the more comfortable she is becoming in your presence.

35

At some point, she is bound to stop talking and to shift the pressure back to you. If you cannot think of anything else to ask, or if you sense that she is doing all the talking, then it is time for you to move on to hook #2.

2. The Factoid

You can say something fact-based and it does not all have to be about her. In fact, if you mostly let her talk without interjecting—indeed, showing that you're paying attention—then you run the risk of exposing yourself as either a pickup artist or just a somewhat dull guy. Either way - not where you want to be.

Stating a factoid about her hook (meaning directly tying into what she just said) is a great way to relieve the pressure off her, and she will tire quickly of discussing herself, especially if she has limited expertise in the hook subject. For example using a hook of what city she is from could easily convert into a lead for you. You could give less than common knowledge facts about the city, and what you know of it, creating more of a relaxed atmosphere.

3. The Opinion

By the time you are ready to discuss opinions, you have established some trust and are ready to start evoking more emotion from her. The best way to do this is to give your opinion on something related to the previous hook. Be confident and downright aggressive when it comes to expressing yourself, because she needs to see your passions at work. It is safe however to avoid discussing any controversial topics, or really anything close to her heart. You can be negative in that you dislike something, but it should be an object or entity, with which she has no attachment. The worst thing you can say is something deferring like, "That's nice," or anything comparably safe and non-expressive. It is too 'gentlemanly' and it is not really alpha male behavior.

It is important to note that the objective here is not to disagree with everything, just to get a rise out of her, but to let her see your power, your strength in character. Rather than intentionally disagreeing with her and wearing her out arguing, occasionally flex your muscle by expressing something contrary to what she says. It is conflict, which is good for flirtatious behavior, but it is also balanced with honest communication. Don't force it. You are sure to disagree on something!

4. Defusing An Argument

At some point, you are probably going to land yourself in an argument and if this happens, you do have to defuse the tension, lest your potential date marks you off the list for having too much attitude. If you get to the boiling point, you must drain the air of all heated debate. After all, it is push and pull not constantly push! The best way to do this is to state that you do not agree but that you admire her tenacity, and that you are both passionate people. You essentially give her a medium-level compliment, congratulating her for the mental effort she put forth.

5. Challenging Her

Challenging her is another emotional trigger you always have the option of pulling and it works well, particularly if you do not clash on any issues. Challenging her means teasing her, and is a funny form of artificial conflict. Of course, there is no real conflict and you should avoid needlessly offending her. You are playing with her, exaggerating assumptions to the point of comedy. By the time she "defends" herself against this silly attack (but not an actual character criticism) she will probably laugh the discussion off. It is what we tend to do with everybody *except* the gorgeous woman in the room. We do it to our younger siblings all the time and with hardly a thought. A lot of men resist becoming antagonistic just for fun because they feel it is disrespectful. However, all it really does is entertain your date, stimulating her emotions and tickling her funny bone. Remember you can always "defuse" the situation if she takes any of the fake argument too seriously. The inability to challenge a beautiful woman will work against establishing yourself as an alpha male. It will suggest weakness, or at the very least inexperience. You care too much about winning, not enough about having fun and "connecting" on a deeper level than just peripheral beauty and politeness.

6. Turning Regular Subjects Into Comedy Gold

Unfortunately, many men resist saying anything funny and seem to downplay their sense of humor entirely, figuring it to be some sort of risk. Perhaps that his date won't laugh or will find his sense of humor strange or offensive. Well, all right, if your idea of humor is making Fatty Arbuckle references from the early 1900s, you might be pitching jokes a little over her head. However, as long as this is humor that makes other people you know laugh, there is hardly a reason to resist sharing a laugh with her.

Believe it or not, the nervousness of the encounter (hopefully coming from her end and not yours) will probably elicit laughter anyway; she laughs when she's not sure of what to say, or because she thinks that's what you want to see. So rest assured, whatever your sense of humor might be, she will probably laugh anyway. And doubly so if you are a naturally funny guy. In fact, you should aim to make this woman laugh at least a few times a night, saying something outrageous just to test her reaction. You have to experiment because you have to gauge what kind of person she is, what she reacts to, and what she admires in you. You have to learn this information so you can assume these attributes for future encounters with her.

What happens though if she throws you a curve ball? What if she stares at you cold, either intentionally not laughing or just not getting the joke in general? If this happens, your first reaction might be to cower or nervously try to regain your dignity during a long, awkward, painful pause. However, the best reaction is an overreaction. *Maintain eye contact.* Don't cower. Make fun of the fact that the joke bombed and move on.

That is precisely what David Letterman always did on *The Late Show*. Sometimes the funniest moments on the show were watching the host tell a joke that bombed and then getting a funny reaction. It was a satirical commentary - it was irony. It made him look like quite the alpha male, as if he was always above the material. The same is true of a date—in fact, it is far more important that you retain your alpha male positioning. Don't apologize, don't allow her the gift of making the scene awkward.

In fact, you could even neg-hit her slightly and make it seem as if her lack of enthusiasm is a character flaw on her part. Start challenging her, indicating that you are unhappy with her reaction and exaggerate it to comedic proportions.

One important point to realize is that when you crack jokes and offer hilarious commentary you're not actually trying to be funny. You are not trying to be the funniest guy in the room or get a huge ha-ha reaction. It is all power play.

In fact, you may even be creating a future problem for yourself if all you ever do is make people laugh without actually standing up for yourself when it counts. Court jester type guys, funny guys that constantly entertain—and who are self-deprecating—don't earn respect. They are laughed at…oh yeah laughed with too, but also laughed at. The whole point of making relationship talk, the fodder for comedy, is all about *your amusement*. You are sending a strong alpha male signal when you are confident enough to laugh at yourself, and not really care about the reactions of other people. It is a strong signal that will provoke proud women who are used to guys catering to their every whim. It will probably reduce your date to giggles because your *attitude* is contagious.

7. Tell A Story

Telling a story that relates to the hook is always a great lead because it involves the woman's emotions. It actually has the potential to be even more emotionally volatile than challenging or debating, but with the added effect of hypnotic suggestion. As we reviewed earlier, when you tell a story you are actually telling her how to feel. Everyone loves a good story because we all want to vicariously experience the lives of others, particularly if it is a suspenseful or funny episode.

Now what you do have to guard against is the urge to tell stories that are extra long, boring, pointless and of no particular consequence. Raconteurs make it a point to make sure that stories feature excellent timing (meaning the build up and release of suspense, vivid description (allowing them to picture what is happening in their mind's eye) and strong emotional reactions from the subjects of the story. You might directly relate the hook to your own life experience or may choose to tell the story of a friend. You could even make the story up out of thin air, if you prefer.

What matters is how you include the listener into the story. Not only is it imperative to make the scene vivid and emotional, but you must also give them plenty of discussion to ponder on. The worst thing that can happen , besides the woman becoming bored and wandering off, is for her to say nothing. The story might be awesome but if all she can do is just stare at you in acceptance then you have not stirred her emotions. Telling the story was useless.

So make sure that when you do tell a story, you create what are called "follow up threads"; that is dialogs that can naturally and smoothly flow after the story is told. This gives *her something to say*. She isn't put on the spot to react to your storytelling ability, but on the contrary, feels compelled to add her own two cents. That is what gets her involved, that is what makes her remember the experience.

Essentially, you allow her to be a good guest to your "interview." You set her up. You let her say funny things, you let her contribute something from her own life to match your point, or debate your point. This is a story that is inclusive and gets her involved with the scene, and most importantly, with the emotions of the moment.

8. Favors

Now we are talking! What better way can there be to prove you are an alpha male than by immediately putting the woman, you want, to work for you? Now of course, she has no reason to do this and merely suggesting a task for her to perform is not going to work. Unless of course you can do it surreptitiously. When you learn how to make small, almost mindless requests and she follows through, you are creating instant familiarity, facilitating a connection based on suggestion.

You can use it based on a hook (for example, after she tells you that she speaks a foreign language, you could ask her to say something in that language) or you could simply use it without a hook, because it's just that effective. The main point here is that you are encouraging interaction. Simply saying something hardly noticeable as "Show me" or "Tell me" is one way of enticing her to do you a favor. Some men will actually give her a task to complete, using their jovial voice and a friendly face, and make it part of a gag. For example, telling her to turn around, to hold something, or to give an opinion on a survey. All of these are examples of assigning a task. The men who use this tactic usually do not ask and that is part of the dynamic. Asking a woman, begs permission. Instead, they just tell her to do a simple thing, and of course, since she does not want to think to over-think the situation, she simply does what he says.

The point here is that you are establishing a pattern that you can continue. She is agreeing to do these favors for you, without even realizing it subconsciously. Guiding her behavior in the future will be easier once you establish this power early on. Remember also that if there is a lull in conversation you can use the favor lead to generate more hooks, by actually telling her to name you specific things of her life—having her give you the hooks, you need to continue the conversation.

9. Assumptions

Assumptions are bad in business, and yet seem to go naturally with dating. We are dealing with an area of life that is so closed up and so reluctant to speak about that sometimes talking for the other person, who seems tight-lipped, is the best way to draw conversation out of them. Similar to challenging, assuming too much is an intentional way of provoking the other person—not in a malicious way but merely in exaggerating an assumption about them, so that they feel compelled to clarify.

Assumptions mean you try to figure the other person out, taking a hook and then stating your theory on what they do, why, and how. You use the information you previously learned to build an assumption, multiply it with a little bit of humor, and then wait for the clarification (Or in some cases maybe a complete agreement; you guessed correctly!). She may object your summary of her life and actually give you more information to work with.

This tactic usually works when you are specific, since vague assumptions only get vague answers. If you happen to be wrong, you can laugh it off, downplay the error by continuing the hook conversation, or you can admit you were wrong and express surprise—as if the woman has been elevated up to your level. In any case, you win. You are talking and you're discussing her life. In case you do not want to be wrong and want to look like a perceptive individual, you can always offer one of two options. Give her two polar opposite scenarios and then after she answers expound on how she seems to be an "extreme" person. Even if she corrects you, or argues you, she is playing right into your game.

The point is, make the assumptions detailed because vague does not take much risk. This is a high-risk move and when it pays off it works well. Women enjoy the details we come up with and want to be wowed; whether due to perception or just a wrong guess.

10. Validation

Validation is one of the most important lessons for pickup artists who want to shift the dynamic and stop begging for a woman's attention. Instead, they reverse the process and through clever wit and strategy, actually end up making the woman they like seek approval from them. In theory, we all seek validation, but only from figures that we consider "above us."

Hence, self-conscious men always seek approval from women, a validation that they matter, they are attractive. This actually puts the female in the "alpha" position, which is not really a turn on for most women. Hence, we have the relationship dynamic of "what we chase runs from us." The more we try to please women, the more they run away, the more difficult they become to manage. When we start to lose interest, to "flee" in the sense that we do not want to keep trying, then they chase us.

What explains this strange gut-level attraction, seemingly based on opposite natures of men and women? Is it low self-esteem? Is it a biological need that women have to "nurture"?

The theory of some psychologists, admittedly a bit of a dated concept, but one still stereotypically true for some, is that women feel the need to make men happy and to make them feel proud. In other words, to reach his superior level, his higher standard. Once she believes he is out of her league, (mainly because he is imbedding that into her subconscious) she tries harder to please him and to qualify.

Is this a sexist or antiquated reasoning? Possibly, given the constantly evolving roles in society, the prevalence of strong-minded women, and the questionable science behind the whole "women need to nurture men and take care of their home" cliché. What we can say is that many women do feel this way, and it could be because of "daddy issues", immaturity, or whatever you want to call it.

So it might not work on all women, but then again, that's why we have 10 hook leads instead of just one or two. You play it by ear and you use the technique that you feel is the most evocative, that has the most potential for producing strong emotion and positive associations. In general, making women feel as if they must validate themselves to you works on vain women in much the same way neg-hitting does. They might not literally try to validate themselves, but at the very least, they will appreciate the satire of what you are doing. Some women will actually take the challenge seriously and will seek your approval, trying to prove a variety of "positives" about themselves.

That she is:

- Really, really out of your league

- Really smart behind all that beauty

- That she needs and wants a strong man's approval

This dynamic mirrors the lesson we taught in the beginning. Women respect a man with higher standards more so than a man with low and "accept anything always" standards. If a man will sleep with anyone for any reason, that does not really make him special, nor does it make the woman feel particularly special. Again, the emotional lure of a relationship is powerful motivation.

Now a mistake some men might make, which actually ruins the whole game and gives them away as a pickup artist, is that they focus on the negatives, treating validation as a form of neg-hitting. As if, no woman is good enough for me...I am special. It is funny for a while but you cannot really create a lasting conversation out of that. It is a far better idea to use *positive validation*, and like a respectful interviewer, give her clear signals that she's impressing you. However, she does not impress you as a man who's easily pleased with the female body and a female talking to him. Rather, you as a high value man, an alpha, are pleasantly surprised that she is rising above the "average girl."

This validation might come through career choice, intelligence, or some form of uniqueness—usually something opposite her looks, body, and most peripheral features. It also helps to compare her to lesser examples of her gender, and indicate why you are pleased and how she trumps other women who fail to make the grade. This will immediately appeal to her jealousies; the competitive nature she feels against other women.

Remember that a woman will generally accept whatever it is you say. So if you are embedding commands telling her to see you as high value, she will either (A) see you as someone on her same level, or (B) someone in a superior position. She may even become addicted to the subtle approval you continue to give her.

Now, 'negative validation' is the exact opposite, and should actually come after positive validation. What you actually do is lower her value slightly, indicating something is wrong with her but in a very flirty, humorous way. You might say something along the lines of, "You're too nice for me," or "Another woman was wearing the same dress," and other snide but non-aggressive comments that appeal to her vanity.

Much like neg-hitting, negative validation requires a large ego to begin with. Women who already have self-image problems might not get the joke so well and will take your cheeky comments as criticism, ruining the dynamic.

Remember that negative validation does not always mean criticism. Simply "sighing" or making a subtle facial expression indicative of disappointment gets the point across powerfully—especially if you have been validating her positive qualities for a while. This "puts her back into place" and makes her eager to please you just to get back the positive validation once again. You can even tease her curiosity by pretending as if you do not want to tell her until she interrogates the truth out of you. You may be surprised by how quickly she changes her tune, *just to meet your approval*. What you have done is basically create a job interview where she just barely qualifies, and she wants the position. (Not that position...not yet!) You have successfully shifted the power role and put it in reverse. Your alpha confidence now has the woman trying to impress you.

Hey, good validation is an addiction. And what better way to remind women that they need it, than by denying it to them right off the bat?

The positive and negative validation is essentially the "push – pull technique" that so many men "naturally" pull off. Unfortunately, a lot of the naturals also have the tendency to push way too hard and wind up being cruel or insensitive. However, that is not what women are attracted to, (or at least the normal, well-adjusted women that you want). What they crave is the positive validation, the "pull in", and they work harder to get that after experiencing "pushes" through negative validation.

Push and pull goes one-step further. In this case, you are not qualifying the woman for your own standards. You are actually toying with her curiosity, making her wonder if you are genuinely interested in her, or if it is all in her mind. Even if she figures out that you are toying with her, it's still a positive attraction. You are unpredictable. You go from hot to cold and keep her guessing. She learns to crave your attention and will go nuts over the curve balls that you throw at her.

Just remember the key to the trick. Unapologetic but without the need to offend. Do not give yourself away but keep it very subtle. If you master the push and pull technique, you will always have the attention of a woman, wherever you go, because she will anticipate an emotional roller coaster whenever she speaks with you.

Thus far, we have reviewed some great ideas on how to introduce yourself and how to keep the conversation flowing. However, maybe that is not what you need, especially if you have been living life as an introverted nice guy for far too long. If that's the case, it might well be time to work on yourself—improving your physical and emotional self—before trying out all these techniques. Persona and image are an important part of the process and that is what we're going to discuss in the next chapter. How can you conquer your fears and backward instincts?

Chapter 5

Conquering Your Fears And Backward Instincts

So much of seduction theory is the *natural state of being a man. By nature, we are aggressive. We are funny. We are horny. We like women and want to impress them, tease, them, and strut our alpha male stuff. By our own intuition, we should be naturally charming and have our own pick of the highest caliber women wherever we go.

What seems to have happened though is that respectable society seems to have figuratively "castrated" men, shrinking their machismo, correcting their behavior, and convincing them to be nice boys, nice guys, and perfect gentlemen incapable of offending anyone.

Perhaps this social shift was inevitable. Years ago, there was no such thing as feminism, at least in the mainstream. There was no such thing as women's rights. For thousands of years, women have been viewed as property, with limited mental capacities. This erroneous attitude had to be corrected, and when that happened, men took a step back. They stopped making jokes. They stopped attacking ambitious women or trying to sabotage their careers. They stopped making sexist or violence-promoting jokes. And it was necessary for the time.

Now we are telling you, as a self-confident man, it's time to step forward just a little bit. We are telling you that it's okay to be strongly opinionated. It is okay to be defensive; it's okay to feel that you are above a woman's standards. It is okay for you to tease them and to argue with them just for a little harmless fun.

Women never desired men to lose their strength, only to stop the bullying behavior. Displays of power, whether creative, physical or emotional, are always attractive. Maybe it did not help matters when mom and dad gave you advice, but to be completely honest not a lot was known about seduction theory in the 20th century. Only towards the 1980s and onward was any scientific and psychological research done on the subject.

So a lot of the old techniques that we learned as teens, as younger boys, might well be outdated in this age of what we call the "post-seduction" era, where women are wiser to the tactics, but still respect alpha males who know how to play the scene, and who know the behavior a woman expects to see.

So I know what you might be thinking. "How do I do all of this when I have no self-confidence?" Or, "What if I get tongue tied and nervous? It won't matter what I say if I look like a train wreck." You are right; half of the battle is in controlling your physical behavior and managing your dating signals. So what we'd like to do in this chapter is introduce you to ways that will help you conquer your fears, and realign your dating instincts towards what women actually want as opposed to what we've been taught is proper courtship behavior.

Before you decide to change your personality and routine, it is important to reflect on why you feel the way you feel. How your present attitudes and dating patterns developed. A little introspect might help you. In fact, I recommend creating a list of your attitudes, past experiences and feelings that may be contributing to holding you back. For example, how many of you feel any one of these statements applies?

- I usually don't ask girls out because I just can't work up the nerve.

- The scene was awkward…it was too noisy. I couldn't think of what to say.

- I just feel shy around women.

- I feel guilty wanting sex. I keep thinking women want marriage. I want marriage.

- All I want is sex. I don't know how to talk to women.

- She is too good. I can't approach her without feeling like I'm out of her league.

- I respect her too much to flirt with her.

- I feel awkward when I flirt.

- I want to say something funny…but can never think of anything to say.

- I was in love with a woman. But she said she just wanted to be friends.

What all of these statements have in common is the men are battling internal issues. They are revolting against the "rules" in their own mind.

Part of being a successful man in dating is understanding yourself. This is why, oftentimes, men who are older, wiser, and introspective about their past mistakes, *are* more attractive than younger men who are still making the same mistakes. A little introspection does you well. It will help you to see *why* you are nervous around women. (Is it because you have trained yourself to avoid them?) Why you are afraid of sex. (Was it because you received conflicting messages about sex growing up?) Why you fixate on one woman and why that ends up leaving you in the friend zone.

Getting To Know Women As People First

Sometimes a great deal of dating anxiety can be avoided simply by taking the time to know women—to understand their perspective as fellow human beings, and not the "goddesses" that we always tend to see them as.

First of all, a lot of guys seem to think that they only have a chance with a certain type of woman; that she has to instantly feel attracted to him, that she has to be "into him" before she'll even consider going out with him. This is a major misconception. Most women do not put that much stock into appearances and even the ones that do are willing to give you their attention. They want to see your alpha male behavior. They want to see what you have to offer.

Women get lonely just like you do. And just like you, they find a new and interesting person to talk to. The problem is that so many men are intimidated by these beautiful women (eh, beautiful is not the word…let's say 7s and 8s) that they never really take a chance. They might not ask her out at all. They might create conversation and share weird tension. Some guys might manage to ask a girl out without actually offering anything in the way of interesting topics, funny conversation, or anything memorable.

So what we have here is an entire population of men who are lonely because they can't attract women, and a population of lonely women who can't attract any men who are fearless, who are not intimidated by their beauty. How tragic the whole scene is!

You may be relieved to learn that so much of successful dating is based on the concept of passing through a woman's dating filters. If you can show yourself worthy of her undivided attention, you have probably surpassed the hundreds of other guys she's bound to meet. Let us think of it with a simple analogy.

Your object of affection has three filters, which gets rid of most guys for her. Using these filters allows her to the gift of not thinking. And thinking gets her a little flustered, which is good news for you.

Filter 1: Remove all the creepy guys, stalkers, psychopaths and weirdos from her life. Practically all girls are afraid of the mentally ill and anti-social population. They do not actually want to be attacked, threatened or injured; they just like the aura of danger that any nice guy is perfectly capable of showing. Men who forget to smile, who work up some convoluted introduction that is too confusing to follow, and men that simply stare instead of making conversation fail this filter and get locked out quickly.

Filter 2: Men who are too afraid to actually converse with a woman and who seem socially lacking are easily screened out. She is actually doing you a favor in her mind, since she thinks you can't "handle" her. You do not know how attraction works, you are going to make this "relationship" awkward and boring, not any fun for either of you, and she wants to spare herself heartache, guilt, and all the other negative emotions that come from dating a guy who just doesn't get it.

So what she's actually doing is locking you out with her filter by either being nice and instantly rejecting you (yes, it burns, we all know), or she actually puts up a mean and intimidating face so that you will actually be spared the sting of rejection, and will just flee in terror. Either way, she doesn't have to deal with you, so all is well.

Filter 3: Men who can only summon enough power to ask for friendship. They don't have the guts, the power, to break out the sexual tension—the very reason anyone wants to date ever. So they just wait and wait, and become friendly, without actually committing anything or alluding to anything sexual or romantic. They carry an ambiguous vibe, which the woman really has no idea how to react to and so she files them in the friend zone. And of course men hate being friend-zoned even though she gave them precisely what they asked for...go figure.

So once a man proceeds beyond these filters, he becomes a sexual threat, a man she takes seriously, and who has real dating potential. He feels like a man to her. He creates a spark. He has "it", that chemistry that makes romance feel intense and not just like an obligation to settle down and marry. Make no mistake, every woman wants to feel something intense. Whether she calls it love or lust, she responds to the emotional involvement, not just the idea of sex.

Seduction Starts With Hello

We devoted an entire chapter to the quick lay strategy because, for the most part, seduction is a gradual process and each woman has a different time frame of when she opens up and learns to trust you. The good news is that seduction does literally start at "hello." Once you make a statement and get through all those wimpy guy filters that instantly turn her off, you enter the seduction phase. So much of the "seduction" happens in the first few minutes. You might even say that if you can survive the brutal introduction stage, the rest of the conversation flows easier than you think. Assuming you get the dynamic of the conversation, which we discussed in the last chapter, you can probably at least bluff your way through a date or pre-date discussion. We gave you ten different ideas on how to use a woman's "hook" to keep her interested.

The seduction stage involves both ends, the intellectual connection, but also a much more profound physical connection and compatibility. That is a little bit of what we're going to teach you now, or more specifically, give you some ideas on how to manifest this strong physical presence in social situations, even if you have been doing it all wrong for decades.

The Sexual State is perhaps the most important physical element of seduction, and it is possibly the only thing keeping you from enjoying a satisfying sex life. It is the same mesmeric quality that movie stars have, that irresistible French guys have, and that even your creepy friend from college once had. (You know the ugly guy that somehow still got the girls and you could never figure out why) It is called the sexual state, and it is brilliantly simple. It is when a man is open and proud about his sex desires. That is it.

When you can admit to yourself what you want from a beautiful woman, that you do not respect her so much that you are completely oblivious to how hot she is, you have officially crossed the line from wimpy friend to reasonably self-confident man. You know what you want and you are not afraid to start and experience sexual tension. You do not want women to feel "safe" around you. You want them to be aware of your libido, your "shame" (so to speak), your "weakness" (so to speak) for a pretty face. Because without this simple activation phase, the part where you *communicate that you want to have sex with her*, she will never know what to do with you, and will probably send you to the friend zone where such man-boys belong.

This doesn't mean that you're instantly going to get laid, because as stated, this only puts you on the same level as Creepy Calvin from College, the sexist pig at the strip club, and the average porno actor walking the streets of LA. A lot of guys have figured this much out.

The next step is to figure out how you, as an alpha male on a far superior plane than "those other guys" can express your sexuality *without directly telling her and sounding like a sailor who stubbed his foot*. Save the dirty talking for Chapter 10! A lot of guys figure out that the sexual state is important but never take the time to learn how to approach it with intelligence, and how to sneak past a woman's pervert filter without getting caught.

The irony is that most women do not care if you're a pervert or not. They are usually not afraid of raw sexuality. They are not afraid of what men want, because ultimately they do want to give it to them, just as you're so anxious to please a woman, right? What really scares a woman is a lack of comfort, the awkward tension that a horny man brings to the room because he is *all out of ideas on how to impress a woman*. So yeah, he is going around catcalling, making sex jokes, and sneering at every double entendre and it is not extremely attractive because he is lazy. He is not willing to invest in real conversation.

What are the ways you can approach the sexual state?

What works the most for a natural charmer includes:

- Admitting that you think a woman is attractive and saying it in your own unique way.

- Asking her out on a date, or simply desiring to be in her company alone and with a purpose. This tells at least that you want to be boyfriend material.

- Talking about sex naturally, without gloating or sneering, and making flirty comments about what could happen between the two of you. A sense of humor is important in this instance because simply talking about sex all the time (or being vulgar without invitation) sends a woman a warning signal. Women want to be seduced, romanced, or at least entertained before you start running your worst gutter mouth. If you are trying to get cookies without being invited into the jar, well expect some hostility.

- Physical suggestion.

How To Project Your Sexual State

The best way to be sexual and to communicate to a woman of your interest, beyond friendship, is to tell her how you feel with your body language, gestures and voice, so that she absolutely senses how you feel—even if she can't quite figure out your mysterious presence. Mystery is a good thing, it is very Phantom of the Opera-esque. Wouldn't you agree women love that show?

Let's not worry too much about "telling her" that you like her. Because you should always have the option to withhold compliments, or any admission of attraction if you feel it is necessary. Instead, focus on communicating attraction with your body. Before we discuss body language and review the rather obvious gestures that communicate emotion, let's first discuss the simple difference between a weak state and a strong sexual state.

Rather than identifying a weak state as by a cluster of gestures, let's simply paint how it feels. It is the same walking on eggshells feeling you get when you:

- Speak in public

- Go to a job interview

- Meet your favorite celebrity

- Meet with the boss

- Interview a serial killer

And so on. That palpable tension says, "I really got to watch what I say and how I say it because I don't want to embarrass myself." This is the state of mind that you have to escape because sex is all about intimacy. You crave intimacy, we move in confidence during the act. And most people seem so terrified of sexual tension that they immediately reach for a drink when they start talking. It is not exactly honest or brave, but hey, alcohol works better than simply being a nervous guy and gulping your way through an uncomfortable interview.

The key is to be able to enter the strong sexual state at will, without the need to deaden your anxiety with an artificial substance. First, let us examine the weak state. What are the characteristics of the weak state?

- Shaky nerves

- Fidgeting hands or feet

- Tapping fingers, twiddling thumbs

- Scattered, distant eye contact

- A weak voice

- You shift your weight back and forth

- Your arms seem to bounce around having nowhere to go

Just imagine if you were making all these gestures on purpose. What kind of message would you be conveying? Here is the kicker: you may not be aware of these things but you are constantly sending signals to the women you talk to, and if you approach them in the weak state, you probably are making these gestures and being noticed.

You are far better off approaching in the strong state, a state of mind that is self-confident and *controlled*, so that you are comfortable in your own skin and in her presence. Oddly enough, when you are around people you are not sexually attracted to, or better yet people whom you feel superior to, you tend to naturally project a stronger state. You feel like an alpha because of their obvious shortcomings. You feel total control over your body and can easily dominate the conversation if you choose.

Ah, if only you could convince your mind that the hot girl you're approaching is actually a weak-state person! In the first chapter, we discussed some of the concepts of visualizing yourself as a more confident person. In this chapter, we are going to focus more on maintaining control of yourself. You might not be able to convince your mind that this perfect 10 of a woman is no big deal, but you can always maintain control over your actions.

Instead of thinking vaguely about your nervous body language, be aware constantly of your most important "teller" parts that is:

- Your legs

- Your arms

- Your hands

- Your face

- Your eyes

- Your voice

Rather than attempt to keep all of your parts "still", which will make an awkward stance anyway, your goal should be to consciously give each of your body parts something to do.

Let's start with the legs and end with your voice.

Legs: Nervous shifting can be controlled by simply not giving your legs enough flexibility to split. Keep your legs about a shoulder's width apart, at all times, so that your weight is evenly distributed. Make sure your feet remain grounded and visualize that they are practically immobile. When you sit down, keep your legs slightly farther apart. Your unwavering stance sends a message that you are unafraid and comfortable in the setting.

Arms: Rather than let both arms go wild make it a point to put one arm to your side (you can grab a loop or put part of it in a pocket if you must) and keep the other hand free. With the free hand, gesture naturally with a view towards emphatic (emotional gestures), and descriptive gestures only. Do not gesture just because you feel like talking with your hands. Too much hand action indicates hyper-enthusiasm, which can be misconstrued. With one hand busy and the other hand in limbo, you can avoid nervous hand in hand gestures.

Hands: In general, hands are troublemakers! You're going to use them later (wink, wink) but for the time being understand that hands have a bad habit of revealing way too much about you. For instance, hands can often indicate nervousness when you touch your face or cover your mouth with a few fingers. Hands can also be invasive, especially if you invade a woman's space and finger-gesture too close to her face or breasts, which can communicate too much aggression. Control your hand and try as hard as you can to keep your palms down or pointing towards the woman's stomach (a safe and non-invasive place to point). Palms up (as in the come on, please!) gesture usually indicates desperation of some sort. You want your hands to be one of the best physical qualities about you: strong, deliberately moving...and of course super clean fingernails!

Eyes: You probably know by now that intense and unwavering eye contact is a sign of dominance, and you certainly want to show your alpha stature when you do make eye contact; that's at the beginning of the pre-date period, the conversation, and all the way to the end. Strong eye contact suggests, not aggression, but that you want this encounter to continue. You are interested in her. Your eyes do all the talking that your nervous demeanor cannot possibly explain.

However, you do not have to stare, stare, glare, and keep glaring until the woman feels violated! Strong eye contact is not defined by longevity, or even the "unflinching" variety. It is simply looking into her eyes at the right time, namely, when there is something important to say or when there is going to be a shift in mood. These pivotal moments require strong and unwavering eye contact because this is going to become a memory that she remembers for years on end. When it counts, look into her eyes and look hard.

But don't feel the need to keep staring when the point has already been made. You can cut away and it is actually normal to do so, because most men do not just stare at one another in a casual conversation but also observe the environment around them, taking turns looking around, at others, and then back to their dates.

Here is the key to success. Instead of breaking eye contact when you feel threatened which suggests weakness, stay strong. Stare and glare, but with a friendly or cocky smile. If a woman throws you a curve and perhaps even makes a snide remark, indicating rejection, keep your eyes on her and do not relent. When a challenge has been made you must answer the call or lose all respect—even the points you have earned up until now. It is Double Jeopardy time!

49

Another interesting note: when you break eye contact make sure you are leaving her face in the right "direction." Breaking away by looking up is a bit coy, perhaps shy, while looking down suggests total humiliation. As in, you have been defeated and are retreating, having been beaten by a superior opponent. For a much hotter emotional conflagration, try breaking eye contact and going to the side, as this indicates you are simply done with this point of conversation and are leaving of your own choosing. You are not intimidated, you are just calm and centered.

Face: Your face is usually a dead giveaway as to how you are feeling, so the whole idea of reading a person's mind is largely gratuitous. You know what a woman is feeling inside just from the look on her face. Likewise, she knows what you are feeling and is busy reading your mind. It is not easy to control the faces you both make; you make these expressions involuntarily. Obviously, people can see your "tells" of nervousness, embarrassment, or doubt, and these are negative traits that can affect your date's evaluation of you. In poker, they call it a bad poker face, since you give away your weaknesses in just a few stretches of your face. Celebrities are sometimes interviewed on camera and will often give themselves away through nervous ticks.

It's something you can really only learn through experience, which is why students who major in broadcast journalism are given public speaking and reporting experience so they can get accustomed to performing in front of others. If you do gain more experience in social situations you will learn to control yourself and feel your expressions coming on before they happen. You will feel them coming on and you will refrain from making that face that suggests weakness, surprise or discomfort.

When it comes to dating it is a similar experience to appearing on television, or in a movie, or dare we say even playing poker. You are literally being yourself; you are exposing your nerves and jitters to the world. You are controlling your emotions in order to deliver the performance that people are expecting—in this case the performance that your lady friend wants.

When people play poker, the players make a special effort to be straight-faced, to not let themselves show any emotion, whether positive or negative, so that they can retain an aura of mystery and objectivity. In dating, of course, you do not want to appear straight-faced and risk creeping your date out. A smile is what they want to see. However, are you smiling "for the camera" or are you smiling because you are losing yourself in boyish excitement?

Guess what a movie director would say if he caught you smiling too much or with a little bit too much emotion? "Umm, good, but let's take it down a notch." That is what you would hear, and do not assume that women are any different. They are highly sensitive to over-excitement because once again, they are looking for reasons to disqualify you, to filter you out.

You may wonder, if you do manage to wear a poker face in dating, how will you respond? What does your body do involuntarily if you train it to not react naturally? What happens is that you listen more. You maintain stronger eye contact. And when you smile, you smile to yourself, as opposed to a people-pleasing court jester smile that most people associate with nice guys. You know the smile with plenty of teeth, huge dimples and slanted eyes that suggests your happiness knows no restraint. For many women, (granted not every woman) such unreserved happiness can be a turn off. Because if you give her the impression that you're ecstatically happy now, you really have nowhere to go but down. You leave no room for improvement, no "reward", nor any "validation" that she can get from you by continuing this banter. You are too eager too soon and you compromise your alpha male stature.

The nervous laugh is another problem in the same vein. It is natural to laugh nervously because dating does make people nervous. However, if you could manage to control your nervousness and laugh only when something is funny, or better yet use the funny moment as a "hook" to further stir up the interesting conversation, you can show yourself to be a man in control of his emotions. Perhaps, you may appear as a more mature and confident person than the woman, who is probably cackling and giggling by now.

This does not only show control—it also shows a superior state of mind. Your calm and collected nature is overpowering her. Soon, she will surrender to your stronger mind because your "sexual state" (your strong eye contact, gentle and calm smile, and controlled body language) is palpable. She cannot deny there is a huge attraction there and it is all resulting from you simply being the dominant figure in the conversation. At this point, she has to adapt to your style to please you.

Lady Gaga sang the song "Poker Face", which was a song about sex and hiding real emotions from sex; i.e. the pickup artist-dating scene. This is a fitting metaphor to remember as you go about communicating with women who are into these head games and who "negotiate" through a relationship, rather than simply wearing their hearts on their sleeves. Remember you are expected to play the game. Being too much of a nice guy and overzealous with your emotions is moving away from the script, away from what she wants. Dance the way she wants to dance and enjoy the spoils that come from a good game of poker.

Voice and Tone: Voice is an element of physical communication that is even more important than facial expression and body positioning. If you have "the voice", the voice that screams sex, you can get away with making a few mistakes here and there. Just look at the power of the late Barry White's voice and how he made his sexual state voice his entire Hollywood gimmick. The power of a man's voice may well tell the story as to whether he is a man or a boy.

A boy speaks lowly, anxiously, eager to impress a new friend or even his parent. A man speaks confidently...but what does confidence really mean? It is not merely the volume or the pitch of a voice, even though lower tones and firmer syllables always help to heighten the sexual tension.

However, there is a greater component to a sexual voice than just deep and sexy dulcet grunts and whispers. It is the power of your words—your ability to make profound shifts in conversation, and actually alter the mood of a person or group of people with the power of your words and the strength of your voice. This is in stark contrast to the man who talks with doubt; not merely using a higher pitched voice but even using words that immediately put doubt in a woman's mind. How about the guy who asks questions but trails off before the end of the sentence? He might say something like, "So when you listen to music...you do like music, don't you? Or do you like..." You see, he does not even have the confidence to finish the sentence. He lets the woman fill in the blanks for him. He is feeling uneasy and at this point, she might even be thinking he is losing interest in her, or worse yet; he is just not emotionally ready for a relationship.

One recommended solution is to phrase your questions as statements. This gives your questions a stronger tone and can actually make them sound like assumptions, which we discussed is a great way to provoke a woman to speak and set the record straight.

51

In other words, do not invite the woman to "lead" in the conversation. Know where you're going with each discussion and eliminate gratuitous words at the end of your sentences, like "or?" or "and?"

You do not have to literally phrase every question as a sentence, and yes, telling a woman, "You DO go to the Laundromat," in a definitive statement sounds strange. However, just as an experiment, try to ask a few practice questions with the ending word spoken in a monotone. Our natural inclination is to raise our pitch towards the end of the sentence, since this asks permission or makes a request of a person. While grammatically correct, this is actually not preferable during dating. Alpha males do not ask permission to be themselves. They simply state what they think or feel and deal with the reaction of the woman in the most entertaining way possible.

Asking questions "naturally" may cause you to raise your voice slightly, particularly during the questions, and make it seem as if you are trying to impress her. For this reason, it is safer to speak questions as statements, and have the emphasis on the end of the sentence in a definitive matter. As if you are telling the woman the "question", you are asking.

This highlights another important issue: a strong man makes more declarative sentences than he asks questions. Creating a conversation in which you're asking too many questions will quickly become awkward or at least one sided. A woman will not have anything to react to, since she's mostly talking about herself for the conversation. It is up to you to ask some questions (in a statement sentence style) and then express yourself with additional statements, demonstrating your certainty.

It is often mentioned that enthusiasm is contagious and that much is true. Little do men realize that nervousness, awkwardness, and passion are just as contagious. Whatever voice you speak with, you spread to your audience, in this case a woman to whom you are strongly attracted. Naturally, if you approach in a negative frame of mind, the attitude becomes shared.

However, if you bring with you a new state of mind, a positive one, it is relatively easy to influence the other person following your lead. Case in point, if you approach a friend and become excited, describing something that happened to you, they will eventually share your enthusiasm.

Here is where tone comes into play. Tone is the secret "feeling" you impart through your words, your word choices, and the vocal inflections. It is similar to voice, except that voice is defined more by pitch, power and pace, whereas tone is all about the insinuation behind your words, which we very subtly communicate in everything we do.

When one deliberately activates a sexual state, it usually does not involve mirroring of the other person's state; that usually being one of nervousness, excitability, and so on. Rather a man *overpowers* a woman's happy state, with his own happy + horny state, by reducing the volume and the high-energy enthusiasm by 50%.

While you are happy and do wear a smile on your face, this comes from a feeling of calm and control. With your measured response, you can show a woman that you are sexually confident and thinking of escalating your dating behavior. Your stance is far more powerful and she will usually come out of her discomfort zone and into your comfort zone. She may actually mirror you, rather than continue to keep the same excitable energy level.

Tone is a powerful thing. With it, you can instantly pick a fight with someone, make someone feel good, put someone at ease…and you can stimulate in them curiosity and passion. In essence, make her feel what you feel. Most guys go about this sexual "tone" all the wrong way. They lose their smile and try too hard to show fake confidence and sexual interest. This is terrifying to a woman who has not been given an opportunity to become comfortable in your presence. Instead, the sexual state requires genuine warmth, happiness, calmness and tranquility. You match her enthusiasm but you temper down your interest and excitement to an alpha male's stage—she has to decrease her volume to meet you and when she does, you have demonstrated control of the conversation.

This all relates to what we are going to talk about in the next two chapters—the point where dominant social behavior actually crosses over and becomes subliminal seduction. Plenty of men are happy just mastering the "confidence" factor and learning how to talk to women.

However, if you want a little extra insurance, or are competing against too many other alpha males, or are interested in a woman whose shield you can't seem to break, this next bud is for you.

Chapter 6

Reprogramming The Way She Thinks

Once you start assuming the role of an alpha male who knows what women want, you enter the second stage of the proverbial male inferiority complex. You know what to do, and you know how to talk with women, but you still can't seem to figure out how to make them take you seriously as a sexual threat.

Maybe you have noticed you have a lot of women flirting with you, but are not sure how to escalate the situation. You might even say that it seems like women have a shield up, one that they never let down in fear that you may strike.

You are right, they do. If women are not actively looking for a partner, meaning they pretty much make it easy for you to come down and swoop them up, then they are probably keeping you at an arm's length. Is this because you are failing a test? Or are they simply trying to friend-zone you?

Contrary to popular belief, women do not just friend-zone the losers, nerds, and lonely hearts. They also try to friend-zone alpha males, and some alpha males never realize they are stuck in the friend zone, even if they try to break out using pickups and direct sexual come-ons. So what gives? How is it that a man can be unafraid but still not quite make a woman respond to him as serious dating material?

The problem is that her "shield" is keeping you out. It is not really that she's friend zoning you. She can probably tell that you are a sexual threat to her; she just does not lower her shield and keeps you in a controlled position. It is time for you to break this shield and see what she's really hiding from. It may be just a bad day, or it may be a means of finding only the strongest guy in the room, or it may be that she is cautious who she dates.

First things first. Whatever is up must come down, that is a physical law hard to argue. So if a woman's shield is up, that means it could in theory be brought down if you pass her test.

Detachment In Dating

One part of being the proverbial nice guy is taking an emotional perspective to dating, when in fact most of the people who date are leaving their emotions behind, carefully avoiding the investment of any real feelings too early on in the courtship. Maybe people call this game playing, maybe they call it heartless, or maybe they just call it being careful and not making any promises. Whatever we call it, it is clear that it is the opposite of what most people do when they see a relationship budding.

Instead of taking a step back, and enjoying the moment, they fast-forward the relationship and behave as if they are already familiar with the other person, already sweet, lovey-dovey and shamelessly enamored. It does sort of freak women out, especially since guys today are so desperate for female attention that they misinterpret simple politeness and cheerful behavior as flirty.

In general, detaching one's emotions is necessary in dating, and especially if you are a man encountering a woman with a major "shield", a.k.a. attitude problem and defensive stature. If you have ever dated before, and have met the "witch" façade of an uninterested women then you probably appreciate how difficult it is to flirt and act naturally when a woman is stoic, rude and seemingly non-responsive to whatever you come up with.

In this scenario, there is no other option except to take down the shield. It is the only way. Otherwise, the encounter will crash and burn all because of her sabotage. You could be cracking Conan O'Brien quality jokes, and she will probably still resist you.

The first thing this detachment does for you is protect you from becoming angry or depressed. Face it; if a woman reduces you to tears or sends you into a furious rage, she "wins". She loses interest and you probably end up causing a public scene, much to your own humiliation. Detaching yourself from the high tension of the moment is absolutely necessary for you to maintain your composure and let her know that you're not affected.

Additionally, detaching can also mean altering your perspective of the situation so that it does not feel like rejection. Rejection is causing an emotional reaction inside you and making you feel foolish and incompetent. Stop it! Reject that perspective and turn things around. This is for your own benefit and for the benefit of the woman, who will be forced to see you in a new light.

For example, if a woman puts up a shield and seems uninterested in you, what is your first reaction? You are not her type, right? Or, "Shucks I guess I screwed that up." Wrong. Here is an alternate perspective:

- Gee, someone is being a bratty little sister today.

- Oh, she is cheeky, that's so funny.

- How funny, she is playing hard to get!

- Wow, she has a major personality flaw, doesn't she?

You see what has happened with these alternative perspectives? You are refusing to let that shield stop you. You are moving forward, laughing off the threat she is posing—illustrating your greater power.

Now imagine her reaction when you say something patronizing, reinforcing this new perspective of the situation. A simple sarcastic comment or a "poking" comment like "Is your life really that miserable?" or anything that suggests she is the one with the problem is going to break her shield and either:

A. Force her to be nice and civil and let you proceed.

B. Turn her into an uber-witch and make her act twice as nasty, which again, is all only for your amusement. The more she flips out the better you look and the more she makes a scene.

Changing Patterns She Tries To Create

Of course, this is only one tactic to put down the shield. There is a possibility that she will continue her attack on you, or shall we say, her "defensive stature" by simply maintaining a negative pattern. You know what we are talking about here. When a woman does allow you to speak, to "try", but she inevitably answers negatively to everything you say.

She is winning the war. You may be coming up with great material but because she is resisting you consciously (and usually rudely), it feels as if you are not clicking and you are still not "special" enough for her. This is of course an illusion she is casting because she is obviously setting a pattern and a trap that you are falling into.

More to the point SHE is the one controlling the conversation. She is setting the tone and you are following her lead. You are failing on a completely different level. If you want to stop this woeful pattern, you must make a conscious effort to do so.

One of the best ways to do this is through validation. You can actually disturb her pattern in creation by asking open-ended questions, and then validating her as she answers. You still let her ask questions. However, instead of trying extra hard to impress her, to meet her approval because of a negative pattern she sets, you are reminding her that you are still higher on the "social value" scale. You "like her"; you admire her honesty even while you are reminding your "bratty little friend" that you are not so easily stumped, that you are still in complete control. The best way to usurp the flow of conversation from her, since she is using your answers to frame her own scene, is to say or do something surprising. This startles her and breaks the pattern.

Ultimately changing your perspective and detaching yourself only means that you are using her shield as a source of entertainment. You are laughing and enjoying yourself, and are not giving her the satisfaction of having won. The point is, she is not a horrible person, a mean woman, or any indicator of your own self-worth. She is just playing a game. Are you going to rise to her game or are you going to give up so early?

Demonstrating Value In Five Key Areas

This brings us to an interesting question though. How much is too much? Is there a limit to how much you can tease her, just how much "attitude" you can show? The real question is not "too much", but rather is it working? Now we come to the finer points of engagement. If you are engaging her, or reprogramming her perceptions of you then you are doing it right and need to stay in the course. If you are only striking at air, trying to be contrary and difficult, you can only get so far. One of the principles of engagement, beyond mere disagreement and teasing, is demonstrating your value.

We spoke of this earlier in the book but we are going to elaborate what it means. You understand by now that you have to demonstrate that you have high social value, you are an alpha man who is of special concern to her, and not just an ordinary fellow. So let's ask the burning question: why do women want men with value? Simple answer because women like how high value men make them feel. You might even say all women have the desire to please a man who is special in their mind—much in the same way men want to please a woman for looking beautiful and showing the smallest amount of attention.

So ask yourself; are you already attempting to demonstrate your value as a man? And how is she responding to this image you are portraying? Many men concentrate so much on the style of approach, whether it's the funny guy, the personal connection, or even the reinforcing of beliefs (which we'll talk about shortly) but they forget the most important factor: showing your value so that she sees you as a worthy sexual threat. Otherwise, you will fall into the friend zone, or the a.k.a. like-a-brother category.

Women usually do not feel attracted to a brother-figure in their life. There might be exceptions here and there, but ultimately what she prefers is mystery, soulful connection, shared perspectives, and similar backgrounds—coming from a man, she feels strongly attracted to. In contrast, the "nice guy" persona, which many men adopt (yet another façade they adopt, so don't think being "nice" has anything to do with being honest) in hopes of grabbing her attention is actually turning her away.

She might treat you like a brother, out of pity, eager to give you "something" for effort—sort of like the schoolteacher used to give you a C+ for trying.

So in demonstrating your value, remember these four tips for engagement with confidence:

1. Always make sure your voice has a smooth hypnotic quality to it when you speak. Sexy guys always have the voice that suggests sex, but of course, that refrains from being too cheesy or obvious. We talked about the sexual state earlier, but this time learn how to demand attention by using pauses effectively; manipulating a woman's curiosity whenever possible since they eat unanswered questions up. **This shows your value as an experienced lover.**

2. Echo her own voice. Now this may be a confusing lesson but break it down. We previously mentioned that it is okay to express disagreement. However, as you progress into the date or the conversation, your intention is not to constantly bicker, but to find common ground. She will admire your strength of character in the outset, realizing quickly you are an alpha male, and then look forward to finding common interests or feelings that you both share. Once you reach that point of agreement, ideally, she is hoping you will be her soul mate—that everything you feel will mirror what she feels. This is when it is time to echo her own voice, her own thoughts and feelings back at her. You don't have to be obvious about it, but subtle, implying that you feel what she feels without saying it—and more importantly, using the same words she uses. **This shows value as a good listener and as a man, she feels connected with.**

Example: One of the great master seduction techniques is "mirroring" a woman's conversation, actually going one-step past mirroring her body language. In this instance, you are borrowing the same words, images and feelings she mentions and using it to relate to her. Take the average guy. He is on a date with an Olympic gold medalist, one who has obviously seen and experienced different things in life than Mister Everyday Guy. He knows he cannot instantly relate to her life, so what he does is he allows her to speak. She describes the "raw power and heart-pumping emotion" involved in athletics and what she feels. Instead of changing the subject, he uses her descriptions and echoes it back. He asks her how she would feel if she could find the same "raw power and heart-pumping emotion" in a relationship. He borrowed her own imagery and gave it back to her. Not surprisingly, she responds to the comparison, expressing that she in fact DOES want to feel the same way emotionally that her body feels physically after sport. The point is, always use a woman's statements as "clues" as to determining what she wants in a man.

3. Always control the conversation. Earlier, we talked about how men lose control of the conversation after the shield goes up. A confident man's **instinct** is to dominate a conversation. His alpha personality is goal-oriented, successful and always offers a plan of action. You may think this is only in peripheral conversation like "I know where to go for lunch!" but it actually has more to do with you guiding her through the conversation, regardless of where you are physically going. You want her to feel safe, to feel comfortable in this new and interesting conversation. Experience is a great

teacher and will give you the calm and the foresight you need, to always communicate something important. If you do not have experience then you MUST make an effort to make every conversation meaningful AND to guide that conversation. Make sure your conversation has a point; think of it as a beginning, middle and end, with themes that stick out—facts and funnies that she can still remember hours later after the date ends. **This shows your value as a man who is in control and who makes women feel safe.**

Example: Think of a film director or writer, and how their job is to always stage scenes to reveal something important. The conversation always goes somewhere, and is important in character or in plot. Well think of yourself as the leading man of the movie, and your date as the "actress" who has to read your lines. This is an important part of dating dialog because most women want to follow a man's lead. It is almost like dancing. They want to reply, retort, flirt and banter with a man who has a wonderful "script". It is the least course of resistance since the lady's man makes conversation so easy. On the other hand, men who make women feel awkward and like they have to come up with something to say, are like a D-movie straight to DVD release. They don't get the girl. They are the same guys who waste so much effort on getting the woman **to talk**, to reply to them, to "give them a chance", when what they should be doing is guiding the woman through a conversation of their choosing.

Being a dominant conversationalist is not just about making yourself the focus of attention. It is about retaining power and value as the conversation progresses. For instance, men do not leave a conversation just because a woman seems like she is losing interest. They leave on a high note; they prefer that long-term positive association rather than simply staying with the woman and trying and trying and trying until she gets bored. Exiting at the peak of the conversation is not only a safe response but also grabs her curiosity, leading her to wonder why you would dare leave so abruptly.

Knowing where the conversation is going and "steering it" will protect you from those dreadful conversations that turn into un-fun job interviews. In these circumstances, you are not really steering the conversation but are hoping that she becomes excited about listing her favorite things, as if she is a Playboy Playmate—you know, minus the money and fame. This could be a means of validating her, but it does not feel like an actual conversation. It is not witty or flirty, but forced, and once again, putting too much pressure on the woman to be interesting.

- Conversation starters all have a point. If getting the woman to talk is your only goal, you are not going to get much further than this basic response. On the other hand, if your goal is to lead her to reveal information about herself, then you would focus on conversation starters that get results, such as "What's your story?" or even "What's the story behind that scarf?"

4. Avoid Fluff and Negative Talk. A natural inclination of some men is to go from self-confident and in control to overly critical, which essentially communicates negativity to a woman, who is mainly interested in positive associations. Some of these negative behaviors might include fluff conversations about personal problems, HER personal problems (thereby making you the brotherly friend), exes, and anything taboo or controversial issue conversations that are best left for the 6th date or so. Instead talk about interests (mainly hers); getting her story and the event itself so she can have something in mind about you to take home.

Body Sensitive Communication

You could definitely say that when you do reach a woman's comfort zone and do start communicating without any shield or resistance, that it's as much a conversation of bodies as it is a conversation of words. We reviewed the importance of receptive body language and confident body language in another chapter. Now we want to focus on reactive body language. You are not just posing or keeping a stance—you are dancing with your date, your moves are leading hers.

First, take personal space. When you begin talking to a woman, keep a safe distance from her since invasive moves will send the signal something is wrong. However, as you find yourself connecting throughout the conversation, your gradual goal is to slowly enter into her space, surpassing the usual 18-inch barrier that keeps you out of the intimacy zone.

This is as much a reactive move as it is a conscious one. You do not simply wait until you drift—you intentionally but slowly push into her space and then pull back, just to see how receptive she is to your presence. Eventually, if she is receptive she will crave your presence and will welcome you back in, probably by moving closer to you, as if giving you the hint.

Another aspect of reactive body language is mirroring touch. We discussed mirroring gestures, but kinesthetic mirroring is important in the **communication** of a date, and it works on a more conscious level than a subconscious level. When a woman touches you, on the shoulder or the knee, then she is probably sending "feelers" to see how interested you are. Respond in the same way, and when you do maintain eye contact since this sends a strong message and activates the sexual state.

Do not be coy or silent about the kinesthetic connection you are making. If anything, call attention to it, and blame her that she is putting the moves on you. This shows good humor, a guided conversation, and a fearlessness—a desire—to be intimate with her, all without the pressure of actually being overtly sexual too soon.

Reactive mirroring takes an even stranger step when a woman begins to mirror you unconsciously. Perhaps you start the procession, carrying her pace and posture. However, as you begin mirroring her, which she seldom ever notices consciously, she will begin to feel a kinship with you. When she is "hooked" and intrigued by your presence she will actually start imitating you, though unconscious of why. Subconsciously, she is trying to communicate with you, letting you know that she does feel a connection and wants to explore it.

As you gain more experience, and find a calm state of mind when in the presence of a beautiful woman, you may find even more subtle but visceral ways of mirroring her body; such as mimicking her breathing patterns, her blinking patterns and other subtle movements of head and torso. All she will know is that you seem to understand her, and that you seem compatible in a strange, unspoken way. It is deliberate action, and it is merely a bodily form of communication that works simultaneously with your verbal communication.

Learning To Read A Woman's Secret Thoughts

Up until now, you have heard some generalized notes on what receptive body language involves. Eye contact is always a strong signal, as is a head tilt, and even subtle gestures like a woman touching her leg, or touching a wine glass, anything that suggests further intimacy. However, none of these generalities actually reveal what a woman is "secretly thinking", which is why it is advised you "calibrate" a woman's reactions with some test questions; in other words you create a standard default reaction by which you can judge her future reaction.

For example, if you want to better read what negative signals she is giving, indicating disinterest or sensitivity in a particular conversational area, then the first step is to learn her normal face; then a face that indicates displeasure, then a face than indicates pleasure. Now once you gain a degree of comfort from a good introduction use these starter questions to gauge how she feels about certain topics.

It is almost like playing poker, you learn her face, her ticks and her "giveaways" as to positive and negative gestures. She won't realize she's making these gestures, as her body will be revealing moods and inclinations she isn't ready to share yet. They will be both positive and negative and you must react accordingly, taking it back a notch when she is offended, or continuing down the same route when she is responsive. This is actually the best way to gauge how much "is too far" when you are dating and teasing. Do not set a universal standard; just pay attention to her face and movements.

For instance, a woman who is interested but trying to hide it might:

- Show teeth when she smiles

- Shows her tongue

- Bites her lower lip or wets her lip

- Pouts her lips

- Blinks more than normal

- Pushes her hand through her hair or twirls it

- She grooms her outfit

- Exposes a bit of leg or her wrists

- Touches her cheek or her face

- Plays with her jewelry

- She "looks away" from you after making eye contact

- She mirrors your voice

- She tenses her muscles

- Her legs or arms rub together

- She rocks her foot or leg towards you

- Hip thrust forward and head cocked

These are just some of the gestures that men have noticed women giving "unconsciously", which are remarkable clues of how she is feeling. It is not necessary to memorize a list of movements, but rather learn to identify "congruous" gestures; that is multiple gestures or movements that are sending the same message. When a woman is interested in you, her body movements are not that subtle; she wants you in her space, she is showing you more of her, she is pointing her body at you in various ways.

As you offend her or disinterest her, these behaviors will cease and you will go back to the beginning of the date when the gestures were minimal and body language was almost non-existent. Adapt your attention accordingly.

What Does A Woman Do To Show She Is Interested?

When you finally reach a point of true attraction as well as demonstrate your value effectively, she will not hide her attraction but will go out of her way to show you interest. Of course, most women are not overtly forward in showing interest and will show it in more "friendly ways" that, naturally, she can later claim was NOT flirting. Or maybe she's subconsciously flirting and doesn't even realize it. In any event, look for:

- Compliments

- Arguments with a smile

- She claims that she can't hear you

- She laughs at you

- She waits for you or ceases from moving, giving you a chance to approach

- She touches you

- She allows you into her personal space and doesn't push away

- She talks too much

A lot of guys embrace the "push or pull" technique and may accidentally come off as disinterested in a woman and this is NOT what you're supposed to do. Women do like men that are interested; they just have to carefully balance healthy self-esteem with sexual interest. They are not dying to talk to a woman, but are interested in availing the opportunity. This means you do care about what she is saying, you are not trying to insult her, but are just "playing with her" and not taking yourself or her too seriously.

A good rule of thumb is to take interest in a woman's story. Don't fake it. Don't fake it with a nice guy act or with a Casanova act. Take a genuine interest and find something interesting about her to focus on.

61

A Melting Pot Of Emotions

This is perhaps one of the most confusing aspects of dating and seduction theory, the "push and pull" or "hot and cold" technique. The potential for misunderstanding this dynamic is always great and that is with both men and women. Let's start by discussing the theory before the practice.

In theory, humans respond to emotions more than logic. Logic is the rationalization process we go through to make sure that our instincts, our emotional wants and needs are met. Whereas men will oftentimes balance their emotional wants with their logical aims, women usually always respond to emotional motivations rather than logical motivations.

You may even be thinking of a woman from your own past right now who said she wanted a certain type of man that logically made sense, and yet only seemed to make emotional, perhaps even rash decisions with her heart. This is the human condition. We all strive for emotional fulfillment because a life of only logic does not really get us anywhere, or at least, it does not give us the "thrills" that make life worth living.

People today misunderstand this emotional need terribly, opting to suffer through abusive relationships or to become abusive because they think that is what the other partner wants. However, we simply want to feel emotionally attracted to a person. We want to defy logic.

So remember this when you "settle" in a conversation with a woman, who seems to find intellectual peace in you; she is connecting with you intellectually, and **waiting to connect with you emotionally.** This is actually phase two of the nice guy rejection cycle. A man passes the first series of tests and connects with her intellectually, showing himself to be a special male specimen, alpha, and supremely confident. Unfortunately, she still does not feel the animal attraction to him that she should. She sees him as a logical choice, someone she should feel crazy about, and yet does not.

This is because the man is coasting, using only his intellect, when what the woman desires is a courtship with a full gamut of emotions. She wants to experience positive emotions, passion, unpredictability, a tiny bit of negative emotions, and perhaps even a tiny bit of danger. This is why women are attracted to bad boys in general, because they give them the emotional stimulation that nice guys cannot.

Men who are overly logical and trying to "convince" women that they should give them a chance or feel something strongly, miss the joy of taking part in a relationship, and taking in all the unpredictable emotions. And in this tidbit comes a startling revelation: sometimes what women say they want (logically speaking) is not what they actually crave sexually. They are in a constant battle with their logical mind and their heart.

How Do You Emotionally Stimulate A Woman?

We reviewed how to stand up to a woman earlier, as a means to rile her up and activate unconscious attraction. However, stimulating her emotions in **engagement** (once you already have her attention and she wants to talk further) quickly becomes a matter of giving her a show, one that is going to stimulate all of her emotions and let her know that dating you is a memorable experience.

However, many thickheaded men out there think emotional stimulation only means aggressiveness followed by remorse. Wrong! There are many complex emotions that you can test with her, and the majority of them are positive. Think for a moment about some of the emotions you experience on a regular basis, or perhaps that you have heard of other people experiencing.

For example, consider emotions according to category courtesy of this Wikipedia table:

Kind of Emotion	Positive Emotions	Negative Emotions
Related to object properties	Interest, curiosity	Alarm, panic
	Attraction, desire, admiration	Aversion, disgust, revulsion
	Surprise, amusement	Indifference, familiarity, habituation
Future appraisal	Hope	Fear
Event related	Gratitude, thankfulness	Anger, rage
	Joy, elation, triumph, jubilation	Sorrow, grief

	Relief	*Frustration,* disappointment
Self-appraisal	*Pride* in achievement, self-confidence, sociability	*Embarrassment,* shame, guilt, remorse
Social	*Generosity*	*Avarice*, greed, miserliness, envy, jealousy
	Sympathy	*Cruelty*
Cathected	*Love*	*Hate*

Now remember what we said about positive associations. If you only offer a woman all of the negative emotions, it is only going to be a matter of time before she realizes you make her miserable (unless she has really low self-esteem). So instead of repeatedly stabbing her with negative emotions go for mostly positive emotions, like surprise, excitement, relief and self-confidence.

As far as negative emotions go, remember that you do not have to prolong painful experiences just to get her to "feel" something. For example, few men would think about scaring their girlfriends, or intentionally making them afraid. So a compromise would be taking her to a theme park and riding a roller coaster. It's "fear" in a way but it is fear you can easily change to joy, relief, and excitement. This is precisely why men take their dates to theme parks, horror movies, or any other event that intentionally stimulates emotion. This way a woman begins to associate powerful emotions with you and you seem like a much more enjoyable presence than the average logical guy.

If you do sense that she is becoming bored of the courtship, you could try a little more "push" rather than pull, and give her the gift of missing you. Or you could try de-validating her, (implying that something about her is not satisfying) which would be a way of manipulating negative emotions without going overboard.

Women love mystery and enjoy a little bit of curiosity in a relationship. This does not mean you have to literally keep secrets, but you can tease her, toying with her curiosity to give her the gift of mystery.

Whenever a woman becomes dissatisfied with something about you, pushing her away is basically a reminder, suggesting to her that if she does take you for granted you have no problem with it, and don't need anything from her. You don't need her forgiveness, her attention, or her approval. This is what is at the heart of push and pull. It is merely a man flexing his muscle and reminding her, just as we did in the beginning, that she is the one that needs validation from him. He is the voice of reason and the dominant conversationalist.

Some examples of pushing a woman away might include:

- Not returning her calls

- Canceling a date

- Talking to other women

- Not being as happy or trusting in body language, in essence starting her over on the intimacy cycle

Once a guy starts pushing an ungrateful woman away, she usually changes her tune quickly, seeing that he is calling her on her "testing" behavior. He takes one-step backwards in the relationship and goes closer to square one, where they were at the beginning of courtship. This is only fair, because she has already stepped back closer to square one herself, giving him less than 100% attention, or perhaps even giving him the cold shoulder. She starts the game and he plays along.

Also, giving a woman only positive emotions will cause her to get bored with you, feel dissatisfied with you, and lose interest in you. She wants to experience unpredictability and a tiny bit of negative emotions. By providing the woman with an emotional push-pull at least once when you are with her, you give her the full spectrum of emotional stimulation that she needs. You let her experience positive emotions along with negative emotions, which she craves. You can do the push-pull technique more than once like several times to generate in the woman even more attraction to you. The push-pull technique when you do it, it causes the woman to be attracted to you, because you are providing her with the emotional stimulation and unpredictability, which she craves. The woman will be attracted to you because of the emotional roller coaster ride you provide her with.

You can use the push-pull technique to emotionally pull her to you by using positive validation, or showing interest in her and her affairs by talking about them. You can emotionally push the woman away from you by using negative validation, or by showing disinterest. You would pull her towards you and then push her away from you even if she did nothing for you to push her away. You would do so to give her the emotional stimulation that she subconsciously craves, so that she is addicted to you.

A good rule of thumb when using the push-pull technique is to do more pulls than pushes. It is a good idea to have around 75% pulls and 25% pushes. In other words, for every three pulls you should have a push. You want the majority to be pulls because you want her to experience a positive experience, however you still want a few pushes because you want to provide her with the negative emotional stimulation and unpredictability she craves.

Remember people are in different moods at different times. So you could tell if you provided the woman with too much pulls when you feel she is becoming bored, and disinterested in you. That means you should quickly provide her with a push to keep her interested. You could tell if you provided the woman with too much pushes when you feel she is becoming bored and disinterested in you. That means you should quickly provide her with a pull to keep her interested. Gauge how many pushes and pulls to give her by determining her level of interest in you, and her level of excitement.

An example of the push-pull technique is if you are sitting with the woman and in the middle of the conversation, you tell her, "You are a good conversationalist, which is a good quality for a woman to have." (Pull 1). Then later on in the conversation, you could tell her, "Your perfume smells good, it has a stronger smell than what some other women wear." (Pull 2). Then later on in the conversation, you could tell her, "It seems you are a hard worker, more than a number of women I know." (Pull 3). Then later on in the conversation you could tell her, "You are talking too loudly keep it down." (Push 1). That is an example of one push-pull technique episode.

Examples of negative validation:

1) You are talking too loudly. (even if she is not)

2) You are talking at a very low volume. (even if she is not)

3) You are mumbling. (even if she is not)

4) You said that a hundred times. (even if she said it only twice, or you tricked her to say it a second time by asking her)

5) I had a pet hamster called (her name). (Even if it is not true)

6) I had a pet snake called (her name). (Even if it is not true)

7) Your dress seems uncomfortable. (Even if it is not true)

8) Your shoes seem uncomfortable. (Even if it is not true)

9) Your dress seems tight. (Even if it is not true)

10) Your shoes seems tight. (Even if it is not true)

11) How do your friends put up with you!

12) How did your parents put up with you!

13) We need to get you that guy over there as a boyfriend!

14) You have something tiny coming down from your nose. (even if she does not)

15) You have an eye booger coming from your eye. (even if she does not)

16) You should not have handled it that way.

17) You should not have said that.

18) You are talking too fast. (even when she is not)

19) Are you drunk! (even when she is not)

20) I saw that dress at the thrift store. (even if it is not true)

21) I do not like the style of that dress. (even if you do like it)

22) Hold on, I am talking to your friend.

23) Hold on, I am thinking, do not talk to me now.

24) Your hairstyle is not cut well. (even if it is)

25) Your hair is untidy. (even if it is not)

Ways to show signs of disinterest:

1) By looking away from her at something else

2) By looking at other women

3) Talking to other women

4) By not paying attention to what she says

5) By not responding to what she says

6) Going away from her to someplace else

Examples of positive validation:

1) You have a very beautiful voice, more beautiful than the voice of numerous other women. (even if it is not true)

2) Your dress looks more beautiful than other women's dresses I have seen today. (even if it is not true)

3) You seem to be more intelligent than other women at the party/work etc...(even if it is not true)

4) You seem to be a very good conversationalist, better than a number of women I know.

5) You seem to be a hard worker, more than a number of women I know.

6) You seem to be persuasive, which is a quality most women I know do not have.

7) You seem to be courteous, which is rare amongst most women in this area.

8) You seem to be responsible and mature, which is a good quality that a number of women do not have.

9) You seem to be sociable, which is a very important quality in a woman.

10) You look like (name of movie star). (even if she does not)

11) You look like (name of singer). (even if she does not)

12) You look like a model did you try modeling?

13) You look like a movie star did you try acting?

14) Your face looks unusually attractive, how do you maintain it?

15) Your parents must have felt lucky having you as a child.

16) Your friends must enjoy your company a lot.

17) Your hairstyle looks more beautiful than the hairstyle of the other women at the party, or work, etc...(even if it is not true)

18) You are very articulate when you speak, which is a good quality for a woman to have.

19) You handled it perfectly well.

20) You definitely should have said that.

While this is heavy stuff, this is still peripheral behavior. As we proceed into the next chapter, we're going to talk more about subconscious seduction, the truly subliminal things you can do to make a woman feel intrigued, perhaps even fascinated by your magnetic personality.

Chapter 7

Subconscious Seduction

Hypnosis is a dirty word in dating. Due to the sensationalism of the media, as well as overenthusiastic marketers trying to sell a book, a lot of people seem to think that hypnosis is harmful, dangerous or unethical. Sure, if you make it sound like guys are using hypnosis to bed unwilling women in a nonconsensual way, it sounds terrible. However, real hypnosis is nothing like what you have heard. There is nothing dangerous about it, and most of the clinical practices of hypnosis are quite productive. They help people stop smoking, stay calm, and cope with stress or depression, and overeating.

Hypnosis is also prevalent in entertainment, whether we are talking about "recreational hypnosis" (like past life regression mp3s) or even in the books we read, the movies and TV shows we watch, and the music we listen to. Hypnosis is merely an induction process that brings about an altered state of consciousness. The person is less inclined to take voluntary action and instead becomes highly responsive to what the hypnotist tells him or her.

We can obviously see this process at work in books. Without a strong narrative, a book would be boring and would drag. A strong narrative voice pulls us into the scene, hypnotically; you might say explaining to us what we see, what we feel and what we experience.

Now with that same logic, did you know that you could use this form of recreational hypnosis to better entertain a woman who otherwise does not feel any strong connection to you? To do so wouldn't be unethical, since what you are actually doing is trying to show yourself as a man who is more receptive to her needs, rather than simply, thick-headedly, focusing on only your own needs.

There are two parts to this form of dating hypnosis, conversational and sexual. We will get to the sexual element a little bit later. It is better that you focus on building tension in conversation rather than make an immediate "move" for sexual intimacy, especially if you are dating a woman who is not the quick fling type. (And believe it or not, a lot of them aren't!)

Eliciting Her Values And Your Own

In a perfect world, everybody would be a perfect match. You could just be yourself, land a beautiful woman, and not need any of this seduction or hypnosis strategy. Sure, that chubby little guy who works as a janitor and mumbles most of his sentences could date Angelina Jolie, just because you know, he loves her so much.

But it isn't a perfect world is it? Nobody is an automatic match. We all have to compromise, we have to investigate, and we have to play the game just a little bit (or a lot with some difficult women) to be able to "connect" with a woman. The sad reality is that if you wait around, be yourself, and hope that the perfect woman will come along, you are in for a lonely, miserable life.

In reality, upping your game, embracing the player's strategy, and learning female seduction and hypnotic tactics that work is a form of survival. Nothing else! Men must adapt to their environment. And for whatever reason, women are not interested in the lonely loser with a heart of gold. Not anymore. Maybe back in the days of Jane Austen, but certainly not today.

So are you willing to adapt to what women want?

We have briefly touched on what values are in earlier chapters. Namely, they are what define us as unique and individual human beings. Your values determine what you want out of life, who you want to end up with, or what kind of lifestyle you want to live. A person's values are closely tied in with his or her morals, ethics, dreams and ambitions.

Therefore, a love connection or a pseudo love connection that ends with a fling, both start with a dual reflection of values. So this is an easy way to reconcile what we find confusing in the dating world. How is it that opposites attract and yet women are still looking for a man that understands them and can relate to them?

Easy, because values are what we find in common. Peripheral differences are just the icing on the cake. Despite your superficial differences with a woman, the values you have in common are compatible. She immediately gets what you are all about, behind the peripherals that categorize you.

So let us say you really want to find love and not waste another second finding easy women to have sex with but with whom you are not really compatible. And many, many guys happen to agree with this perspective. Not everyone wants the player's life and you should not feel obligated to have sex with someone you don't want to. However, you absolutely SHOULD have the emotional capacity to be a player and to sleep with whomever you want. Because seeing dating from this new perspective will give you the self-confidence, you need to find the woman or women that you really do want.

So with that in mind, that men and women must share definite values, here is where it gets a little shady. A woman might EXPECT that you perfectly match her own set of values and that you want what she wants. However, until you literally have that negotiating process in conversation, she is silly for assuming anything.

It is a weakness that you can take advantage of. In order for a woman to have sex with you (you know, the Mr. Right, she dreams about finding as opposed to the cute lonely "friend zoned" guy that she doesn't want to get serious with) you must show her that you share her values. That you are, in fact, that special kind of guy that she is dying to meet.

Even if you're *not exactly that guy*.

Now is that unethical? Well, let's see. A woman spends two hours getting ready; putting artificial makeup on, artificial hair products, dressing up in ways she never would dress on a casual Saturday, and will pretend to be interested in men she really has no interest in if it benefits her in some way. All to impress a man she deems worthy of her attention. (And we're not even going to touch the whole "fake breasts" issue that some women have)

So is this woman being "herself?" Well yes…an "enhanced" version of herself. She is being the "perfect woman" that she expects guys want. In like manner, you are now going to be the "perfect guy" that she wants—the one who is worth sleeping with, dating exclusively, marrying or whatever.

One of the most effective ways to "subliminally seduce" a woman and to employ conversational hypnosis is to elicit the values that she is looking for in your own conversation. Now most guys make the mistake of "telling her" why they're so special. They talk and talk and try to convince her that they are not a risk, they are going to be a star, they are buff, and they are so amazing in some respect.

However, a man who is self-confident and suave "shows" her. He projects the values she wants. He drops hints occasionally and acts the part of the man who is all of these things. For example, instead of telling her, "Oh I'm rich." He will merely pass along designer names in conversation about fashion, or casually mention vacations he took in Paris, France or Disney World. He doesn't have to flaunt it. He just knows a woman will catch onto it naturally. He expects her to keep up. He does not feel the need to patronize by spelling it out.

Now there is a subtle difference between successful men and unsuccessful men when it comes to projecting. A man who gets it, who understands women, doesn't try to be "the perfect man." He tries to be HER perfect man. He purposely plays the part of her ideal man, and his prime qualities, all according to her suggestions.

This is why it is crucial to pay attention early on in the conversation. When she gives you this information, namely the traits she admires and finds interesting, you should be taking mental notes and should be *adapting* to this style of courtship behavior. She will usually tell you exactly what she's looking for; sometimes she'll be blunt about it (like when you ask, "What is your ideal type of guy?") and sometimes she will drop casual hints, whether it's admiring a movie or a celebrity, talking about her father, or talking about her career and hobbies.

This is where you play the part of an investigator. You might have to piece together some of the clues and gleam for yourself what particular quality she finds attractive. Let's say she gives you this information:

- My father took good care of us and made sure we had everything we needed growing up.

- I really admire Steve Jobs. He was a hard worker and it showed.

- So what is your career goal?

It is ridiculously obvious at this point, that she wants a man who is a hard worker and a provider, someone who is careful about career and life planning. Now are you "winging it" and talking about being unemployed and on welfare, or are you actually strategizing as you go along. Are you asking yourself, "What can I do to show her (not tell her) that I am a hard worker and a provider?"

Learning each woman and what she wants is an individual pursuit. However, there are generally life patterns that women follow. When a woman is younger, she often seeks emotional stimulation; as she grows older, she wants deeper emotional stimulation, eventually taking on her "greatest lover", someone capable of stirring her passions, both erotic and intimate. As she settles down, reaches peak child rearing age, she trades excitement for stability, and desires a material or emotional provider and strong father to raise children.

It does help to study the woman's profile and examine where she is in life and what qualities she prizes.

Re-Analyzing Her Words

There is another way to read a woman's mind besides her most obvious clues. It is in analyzing her seemingly unrelated statements. Take physical characteristics. Many women will tell you that they prefer tall men. Your first reaction might be to assume she has a "type" or a physical preference. Wrong. Everything a woman is attracted to is related to how she feels about a person.

If she tells you she likes tall guys, she's telling you she enjoys how that tall guy makes her feel. Protected and safe. The same is true if she says she likes funny guys. She likes to laugh. She likes a man who can converse freely, make her feel at ease, and cheer her up. Whether you discern these hidden meanings or directly ask her, ("How does this type of guy make you feel?") the cue is right there. This is the man she wants.

This is also the key to her heart; something that you must embrace to make a strong emotional impact on her. And it's not merely the type of man she wants, but also what is called her "desired state." This is precisely how she wants to feel in order to be turned on and opened to greater intimacy. Are you following these cues?

Here is an example from AskMen.com regarding the top 10 traits women look for in men.

1. Intelligence – She wants to be entertained, wants to be surprised and educated.

2. Power, Size, Money – She wants to feel safe and protected.

3. A Challenge – She wants to please him and to feel desirable.

4. Attentiveness – She wants him to always be thinking of her and to want her more than anything else in life.

5. Generosity – She wants to feel connected with someone motivated by altruism.

6. Sexual Experience – She wants to be led, to be educated, and to be wowed by a man who can tell her exactly what to do to feel sexual ecstasy.

7. Romance – She wants emotional connection and support.

8. Dominance (Goal-oriented men that are successful and leaders in society) – She wants to feel important, like she is truly special.

9. Class and Culturally Knowledgeable – She wants to feel worldly wise and smart.

10. Sense of Humor – She wants to feel excited, and be guided by someone who can make her feel natural without embarrassment.

Some other qualities women might find appealing include geeks/nerds, or "underdogs" that love completely and have a strong sense of fidelity, and movie star good looks, or what she sees as someone who has a movie star's charisma.

How Much Honesty Does She Really Want?

Now we come once again to the age-old question, does she really want you to be honest? Especially when she says, "Honestly now…" or "Be honest…" Is this a signal that it is really time to be yourself and forget all this seduction preparation. It might not be a good idea, not yet.

Because let's face it, just because a woman tells you something like, "Be honest…" that is not an invitation to confess your dirtiest fantasy. That is not an invitation to tell her that you are scared to death of women and hope she gives you a chance. No, that is her saying, "Be honest with me."

So ask yourself, what does SHE want to hear? Are you being honest with HER, for HER and about HER? Honesty really does not mean saying whatever is on your mind. Does that seem like a new thought to you? It shouldn't.

Let's say the worst case scenario was happening and your girlfriend thinks you're two timing her. She says in anger, "Be honest with me!"

Now is she talking about your honesty, or what SHE wants to hear from you? She wants you to confess to her and for her if you have been unfaithful. If you haven't cheated, you would tell her the truth. If you had cheated, you would tell her the truth. Because this is the honesty, she demands from you. (Yes, honesty means you never lie…sorry to get your hopes up there!)

And that's where it ends. The honesty that she wants from you for HERSELF is what you concern yourself with. Don't worry about confessing everything on your mind. Don't try to treat her like your own personal voice recorder. She says she wants honesty because she desires specific communication from you. Usually, when she says be honest, she wants raw observations concerning her and wants you to admit something she already knows.

Believe it or not, she doesn't really want to know what you think of the Green Pay Packers' defense or what they were really hiding in Roswell. Honesty is a woman's way of defining the communication she wants from you.

This is where the "seduction" element really comes in. From the time you get her "direct state", (what she desires to feel) you are being "honest" and presenting yourself as her ideal man (even if you are not exactly that guy). You are giving her the specific communication that she wants, **that she is asking for.**

Secret Desires

In addition to the desired state, and the secret trait list (values), there is also what we call "secret desires", which are experiences and accomplishments a woman wants—and will probably not tell you outright. These are her private diary type entries that she keeps locked away. But if you do take the time to review her list, ask her open-ended questions, and gather her desired state, you might find they are not nearly as difficult to learn.

Every woman yearns for something. Depending on her upbringing, genetics and personality that could be a safe family home, celebrity and fame, intense sexual experiences, children, a personal ambition, freedom, pampering, a career, a personal quest, and so on and so on. She usually does reveal hints about her ambition and in a few rare cases she may even admit outright, what she wants the most.

The question is, are you going to simply listen to this confession and shrug it off or are you going to fill in the void that is missing in her life and become the thing she yearns for? Are you capable of associating yourself with all of the things she wants? It might require some creative ability and some adaptability, but this is the surest way to create a strong emotional connection. Precisely what you need before the physical can ever happen.

Once again, directly stating your value is a miss. You must instead project mystery all the while making the same emotional connection with her desires. One of the best ways to do this is by telling stories about yourself, playing the role of her perfect man. Alternatively, you could speak your opinions about this "ideal standard" in passing, showing how your opinions indirectly show you to be a man who shares these values.

The one thing you don't want to do is lapse into an interview and cease commenting or stating anything; cease sharing your own personal opinions and stories that match what she's saying. When this happens, the entire conversation lulls and she feels interrogated.

One of the characteristics that truly makes hypnosis powerful to the point that it is clinically supervised (and set apart from casual entertainment hypnosis), is in the use of anchor words and trance words. Now because you lack the office environment and the years of experience of a hypnotherapist, you will never reach the point of becoming a master hypnotist —regardless of whatever they promise you.

However, you can still use "anchors" and "trances" in a limited way even in casual conversation.

Trances

In psychology, a trance is "a half-conscious state characterized by an absence of response to external stimuli, typically as induced by hypnosis or entered by a medium." This is the 'state of mind' you can put her in gradually , when she gives you undivided attention and begins to feel what you ask her to feel. (Remember, this is basically what hypnosis does; it makes someone else feel what you describe)

In the context of dating conversation, trance words refer to data she gives you. She can't help but repeat certain words or emphasize them, revealing to you the words that are most important to her and that are always a part of her subliminal mind. When you throw the word back at her she will respond to it emotionally and will find it easier to connect with you.

The same is true in sales and it applies equally in dating. You don't just repeat the word mindlessly but you repeat it in a slightly different way, rewording or emphasizing it in a different tone. But she still hears the word, a good two or three times in the conversation and sees that you're a good listener. More important, she feels a connection developing, as if, you know, in her own words, "Like you're reading my mind."

Anchors in psychology refer to what people use in decision-making, those small but significant pieces of information, in order to make a judgment. Once the anchor is "dropped" other judgments can be made by adjusting away from the first anchor.

Anchoring

Anchoring goes one-step further than trance words and actually adds an element of physical sensation to positive association and word usage. The premise is the same one first pioneered by the Russian scientist Pavlov. If you went to college, or even vaguely paid attention in high school then you might remember Pavlov as the dog guy, the one who showed it was possible to program a conditioned response in a mammal and on an instinctual level. Instinct…that is right, that means it would work in a human being as well. We are slightly more intelligent than other animals (err, usually, but we are not counting movie stars!) but what reaches us on an instinctive level is really an entirely different motivational force than what is logical and intellectual.

The Pavlov experiment showed that if you programmed a dog by ringing a bell every time you served him food, he would begin to involuntarily salivate when you rang the bell regardless of food serving. Pavlov programmed that dog to associate something with a sound, and it experienced a strong kinesthetic response after conditioning. The same is true of women, or men, (yes, who knows? Maybe women have tried to anchor you too!), who can be "programmed" to respond in a specific way by positive association.

We previously discussed the idea of making sure a woman's thoughts of you are always positive, so she can continue to think of you in an elevated state of mind. However, anchoring means you can program a physical sensation as well as a mental association. It works in a similar manner as Pavlov's dog, except that you replace the "dog food" with the positive frame of mind that you build inside of her. Once you see that she is happy, and that she is associating positive things with your name and face—and most importantly that she is "peaking" in interest—that is the right time to touch her in an innocent way and create a physical trigger for all of these positive feelings.

Just like a dog "salivates" when imagining the thought of food, so too can you make a woman mentally "salivate" by thinking about you and responding to your alpha male behavior. As soon as she is emotionally stirred, whether that is indicated by a smile or a hearty laugh, it is time to create that physical anchor.

The only problem is, she is probably going to notice that you are touching her, right? That is the key to making the tactic work. You must **distract** her from the obvious and not give extra attention to the fact that you are touching her. When most guys use the anchor technique they joke, or they ask a question, or they talk about the feelings they are experiencing (along with the women) of elation, laughter, joy and so on. They take away the attention from the touch so that the woman does not even realize it, or if she does, she does not give great thought to it. She is immersed in the conversation and hardly notices the touch, at least on a conscious level.

However, the gradual effect is that since she is associating all of this positivity with HIM, and because the touch seems to happen when she is at an emotional peak, she will actually learn to crave his touch. She will feel attracted to him on an even deeper level than just mental attraction. She will "salivate" for him and come to expect his charms, wit, and sexy allure—the wonderful way he makes her feel—whenever she thinks of him.

It is important that you stick to the same physical touch, including the same rate of pressure, timing and area of the body, to subconsciously emphasize a precise trigger. If each movement is different, it will not create an anchor emotional state. She will eventually realize you are just haphazardly touching her. So keep the move regimented and choose a spot carefully. When you get better at this stage, you can actually create multiple anchors for different reactionary moods, based on her behavior. For example, an anchor for horniness, for happiness, for laughter, romance, and so on. As long as you make each trigger unique and regimented, it will work.

The most common mistakes guys make in anchoring is

>A: Trying it too soon (without any positive stimulation)

>B: Over-anchoring and becoming annoying

>C: Not creating any consistency in touch or in "mood"

As you can see, anchoring is fairly complicated. Not surprisingly, most guys misinterpret this process completely and either believe that women can't stand being touched (not true) or that they just want a brave man to take a chance and touch them. (Also not true!)

The same is true of verbal anchors, and making her feel a certain way by repeating certain words when she is experiencing a heightened positive emotion. However, she is more likely to notice voice repetition than physical actions. She might not care, but if you suspect she might be disturbed at the realization that you are "training" her, go for a more subtle approach. For example, try simply saying something bold and romantic when you know she is feeling this way. She will learn to associate your "romantic moods" even without sensing the verbal anchor.

There is finesse and there is a recipe for success. Now you got it...use it wisely.

Using Hypnotic Language For Creating Attraction And Arousal

It is no coincidence that many men out there have great difficulty getting past the "swagger", past the bold introduction, and yet falter when it comes to actually connecting. Let us step back a moment and figure out why. It is because in courtship, in the dialogue of the date, you are communicating. What is hypnosis except a different kind of communication? Seduction, hypnosis, it is all a fancy way of saying, "Let's talk."

But this time it means, "Let's talk on a much deeper level than most people usually talk." In hypnosis, the idea is to communicate a feeling. That is all. Just a feeling.

So if you're happy, you may inadvertently find yourself trying to influence other people to feel happy. Nothing too scandalous there. If you are angry with someone, then you probably try to influence that person to feel your level of anger and frustration. You take the "fighting stance" and you begin speaking those "fighting words."

When you are dating, it is rather obvious you are feeling sexual, and desiring intimacy. So it's not so shocking that some of the smarter men among us do like to project sexuality into what they say and do, indirectly manipulating women to feel what they are feeling. The less intelligent men among us, or shall we say the less patient, do the same thing but without subtlety, without any restraint or filter, and not surprisingly they scare women away.

The funny thing is, women do want to feel sexual and they will insist on it before giving you the time of day. However, there is an art to stimulating a woman, and it is in a combination of words and physical actions, the "sexual state" we previously mentioned.

What does work is the power of suggestion. Now we are going to review this in the next chapter, when we discuss dating and sex etiquette. For now though, think about it from this angle: when you talk to a woman, do you just say things indifferently? Or do you say them in a sexual state? For some guys, that means making strong eye contact, speaking in a calm and passionate voice, or accentuating their masculine qualities. In effect, they are projecting sexual feelings by *being sexual.*

Now if you start acting like "the sexiest man alive" and become so obvious about it, you will cease being an alpha male and may actually morph into the grandmaster, which is a somewhat narcissistic "act" that just oozes raw sexuality at the expense of intimacy. It does not always work, but sometimes it does. Still, grandmaster is not what you are aiming for if you want to be a lady's man.

There is a subtle quality in being an alpha romantic. It includes the way in which he approaches a woman in the "sexual state." Knowing that he can only get away with so much in voice and mannerisms without being noticed, he instead chooses his words carefully, using what we are going to call sexually explosive words.

These words are not necessarily sexual in projecting, but are subliminally suggestive. Neurolinguistic programming is a more complex way to refer to this form of hypno-conversation, but the easier way to remember it is to call it, "Suggestive Words."

By using words that seem sexual, and that are usually used in the context of sex, one can actually elicit a sexual response in a woman, who will most likely not realize what is happening. For example, simple words like "I want" imply much more than simply stating a matter of fact. There is energy to this phrase, which implies character or even a state of mind in advance of the thought itself.

When someone says, "I want", they are actually saying, "I don't have, I am missing..."

Think about the phrase "to try", which implies an unknown outcome and a definite possibility of non-achievement. These are impressions that can be loudly communicated, and which are largely negative.

In contrast, an attractive man uses positive and powerful words which *seem sexual* and which produce the desired effect in a woman, if not instantly, then over an extended conversation.

It is not technically about the word usage, since linguistics has a lot to do with culture, vocabulary and other technical details, but it has to do with the "energy" of language, the images, and the feelings that words conjure up simply by being spoken.

Our memories are a collection of images, feelings, noises, statements, and impressions. When a person tells you a story, you experience the feelings involved and the images described. You may find in general that visual-minded people spend more time describing color, location, size, brightness and contrast, whereas audio-minded people prefer describing volume, sound, tone, and tempo. People, who are highly kinesthetic, will often pay more attention to pressure, texture, intensity and shape, not to mention feelings that the story described.

This is an important part of understanding hypnosis, since in order to reach a woman and persuade her, and guide her to a sexual state right along with you, you must tap into her "system" of processing information. It might not surprise you to know that women are usually not visual but a combination of audio and kinesthetic thinkers. They remember sounds, voice, and most importantly emotion. Emotion is the kinesthetic system you need to tap into in order to summon **desire.**

So if you're attempting subliminal seduction using only your own visual memories to describe something, you're probably not making an effective connection. You're not reaching out into her territory.

There are two facets to these surreptitious and provocative words. One, that you can simply describe an experience and summon emotion directly; two, that you can hint at something covertly that still feels like a kinesthetic connection. For example, there's the controversial "weasel phrase" invented by Ross Jeffries. He claims that you can put overtly sexual messages inside innocent sentences and open a woman's mind to sex. For example, instead of saying "below me", or "happiness" or "new direction" you could emphasize certain syllables and make the statement sound like something dominantly sexual. Even a phrase as soft as "your mind" could be pronounced, "You're mine," with clever emphasis.

Of course, it is highly debatable whether this works or not. And it's really easy to blow your cover (that's blow, not below) if you're sneaking sex words into casual conversation. If you can do it without drawing extra attention to yourself, it may be worth a try. However, it is far more important to focus on an eight-step plan to deflate a woman's subconscious resistance to you.

Remember it like this:

1. Build Rapport. This is the part where you show her that you are a good conversationalist, a confident guy, and neither a sleaze nor a weakling.

2. Mirroring is when the seduction technically starts, as you will begin to adopt her mannerisms, posture and mind focus.

3. Find her representational system, which she will point to herself, as she will focus either on kinesthetic, audio, or once in a great while, visuals. Now that you know what system she thinks according to, you can start creating a connection.

4. Visualization is the part where you intentionally stimulate her senses preparing her for the sexual state you want. This is what turns attraction into desire.

    Some visualization scenarios might include:

    •   Recalling a profound experience that happened to you and describing the details vividly, particularly the ones related to her representational system

    •   Telling a story of a friend, or the words of someone else

    •   Describing to her how she feels directly (which is a bit of an overconfident step that could turn her off)

•   Framing is the final step in the process. How you frame the situation is important in determining why she is feeling the way you are making her feel, and why she feels vulnerable around you. Therefore, you must infuse this situation with meaning, emotion, value and expected behavior, or how she is expected to react.

This is where the gift of storytelling comes in handy. If you are capable of telling a story, you will be able to get away with more because a woman's resistance is stronger without some sort of excuse, some way of framing the situation. Directly telling her you are trying to seduce her is obviously going to put up her defenses and she will resist whatever you have in store for her. Likewise, blatantly trying to hypnotize her with anchoring and other devices might seem very strange to her unless there is some guise of a story or a reason why you are doing this that seems innocent.

Resistance of any kind is bad for you. She might not totally shut down, but at the very least, she will think you are overly forward and you could be thought of as a pushy guy, who is just about as popular as Mr. Nice Guy. There is a huge difference in being pushy and being confident. What is the difference? It is in the framing, believe it or not.

A guy with no ideas pushes and pushes because he figures bullying a woman into responding is his only hope. A wiser man persistently tries to do or say the same thing in different ways, and the framing of the event is what a woman responds to in action. You can "frame" something to be innocent and conversation, whether as a means to prepare her for hypnotic suggestion, or simply to open her up to answering most questions—even if her shield is held high.

For example, a believable "frame" might be:

- A hypothetical approach: This usually leads to a more philosophical answer and longer pauses, as she is seriously thinking about your question. Therefore, you would either ask questions or tell suggestive stories that begin with phrases like, "If I were to tell you...", "If I were to do this...", or even "If you were to feel something..." This puts distance between her and the leading question.

- A curious approach: This asks a "survey" question, or simply wanting to know because of your curious nature. It often works because women and everyone really, love to be an expert and provide commentary on what they think about a situation. You would ask, "If I were to ask you, what do you value most in a man?" Although you are surveying her and she is providing answers, you also have the potential to work hypnotic and suggestive statements into your dialog when answering her; such as "I'm just wondering, since I seem to get different answers from a lot of people...what traits in a man really turn you on?"

- A self-aware approach involves simply doing what you want, and drawing attention to the fact that you're asking or saying something "proverbial" and then skipping all that nonsense. As in, "In most situations like this, the man is expected to ask about your weekend or day. But I'm not going to do that. Instead, I desire a deeper conversation. I am more interested in penetrating into your thoughts and learning something interesting." Notice also, the carefully placed sex words that may help to send secret signals to a woman following your lead.

- The Be Important approach bluntly, avoids the previous topic and focuses on what you want her to think and feel, since you ask, "I understand what you're saying. But you have to ask yourself..." It is almost a distraction sentence, since you guide her away from the previous line of question and answer and point a conversation you would much rather have.

- The explanation approach is a brilliant piece of subterfuge that asks a woman to explain herself, and why she has a strong opinion that you might disagree with. Simply asking something like, "I've never thought of it like that. Explain why you feel that way. Have you always felt that way?" Instead of arguing with her, you jump right into her logical and feeling process, asking her to explain what made her feel this way, what experiences brought her to this conclusion, and in doing so also discover a new way to explain to you how people persuade her.

- The boyfriend approach is another blunt tactic that has just as much chance of failing as succeeding. In this approach, you avoid all other pleasantries and simply ask her about her past relationships hoping to find a pattern. While this is hit or miss, if it works this will make her confess what she wants and she won't even realize she's giving you the cues on how to seduce her.

- The I Like approach: It is a very effective means of guiding her into a positive frame of mind, by stating what you like, and then letting her state what she likes. You are not simply focusing on aesthetics but are describing *experiences* that you enjoy and that you want her to experience and feel as well. You can start on a basic level by mentioning music or movies and then progress into daily routines, turn ons, and if you both are bold, sexual or dating preferences.

- Truth or Dare, minus the title. Naturally, you don't want to say it is truth or dare, since that's very preteen. But playing a game of 20 questions is a good excuse to make her feel something. When asking curious and "innocent" questions, do not blow the opportunity. Focus on her feelings and experiences, creating an emotional connection through the guise of a random question session. Another "game" to try is the "finish my sentence" game, where you begin a sentence and she finishes it.

Of course, some of these frames are best left until after you build some rapport, as obviously, jumping into a game of 20 questions might be too bizarre for an initial conversation.

Discerning Her Motivations

Clinical hypnosis is usually done with the intent of changing a person who voluntarily submits to the process, by changing his thinking patterns. During the hypno-session the doctor will actually spend considerable time giving affirmation statements; emotional statements that promote feelings of peace, which the respondent will say yes to. The hope is that the patient is gradually made comfortable through positive reinforcement so that when a dramatic shift does come, and new "programming" is put forth, he accepts the new programming and has a change in his thinking patterns.

In this special type of seduction or hypnosis, one concerned with influencing a person to feel a certain way, you are still going to need the positive affirmation phase—you simply have to go about it more subtly. However, you still want them to say "Yes" and to experience a relaxed feeling of peace, something they do not want to stop feeling. This is why we have discussed positive association thus far in great detail. If a woman is frequently saying, smiling, and encouraging you to talk more, you are handling the seduction phase perfectly.

Now comes the shift. In clinical hypnosis, this part is easy because you know the goal and the process to reaching that goal. In social seduction, you don't know the goal, beyond the basic "Get to know this girl." Therefore, you have to start positive affirmation while still undergoing the learning process about your date. The learning process should focus on **learning her value system,** since this is the unknown quotient. The "desired state" you hope to influence will arrive when you learn what the woman wants—what positive affirmations she wants to hear. They are not going to be to "relax", as in a regular session. They are going to be far more instinctive and basic in the beginning. For instance:

- What does she like in life?

- What does she want at this particular moment?

- What does she think she deserves?

- What has she lost before that she now wants to get back?

- What does she not want, because of bad experiences?

- What scares her?

- What makes her happy?

- What makes her laugh?

- What turns her on sexually?

Once you learn these values, you can focus on guiding her to the desired state. She is not going to answer these directly, unless you are already playing 20 questions; but she can be led into this discussion through emotive questions, such as asking her about her favorite memories, her job, her strangest experience, and all sorts of other minutia.

You might be surprised when she starts using you for wish fulfillment. It is actually kind of great that she gives you the benefit of the doubt and assumes you might very well be EXACTLY what she's looking for. For instance, if you ask a woman, "What do you think of me?" and the date is going reasonably well, she will give you limited feedback of what she notices, and in order to fill in the blanks of what she doesn't know, she will usually just imagine you as her ideal man in an ideal scenario.

If you have made her laugh, and that is a quality she is looking for, she will probably describe you as a funny guy. That is her wish, and the role she has given you. Use this momentum and do not say anything to disrupt her growing idealization of your personality.

You also have to be careful to not re-introduce awkward connectives in the conversation, since this literally breaks the hypnotic concentration. This is the positive reinforcement phase. If you abruptly change topics, rather than using smooth connectives, your chat will quickly deteriorate into the dreaded interview. That is why it is important to focus on proper connectives to use in a movie-like casual conversation.

Connectives include:

- Latching onto a word she just said and continuing with that word

- Latching onto a thought and identifying something closely connected

- Asking her a detail about something she just stated

- Imply something about what she says which she will either agree with or correct you.

- Go into your own story but make sure it's related to the thought she brought up

This is how you keep expanding upon the foundation you have built. This guides her along the path and makes it easier to influence, seduce, and persuade. Breaking her concentration by asking a series of disconnected, random questions will show her your poor grasp of conversational skills. It will also quickly let her know that she is overestimating your abilities. (Since we just learned that she is probably giving you the benefit of the doubt!)

Becoming Her Dream Guy

Now we have come to the part when you actively project the image of her "dream man", her Mister Right, her desired lover. Most guys know they want to be Mister Right but have no idea how he behaves. They might assume a macho identity, or even a perfect gentleman. However, these are merely peripheral performances and when you resort to playing "that guy" you are not actually delving deeper into her psyche to find out what she wants.

When a woman says, "Just be yourself!" she is actually telling a white lie; what she wants is for you to be yourself playing the part of her perfect boyfriend. Everything you project is about her. By now you have established that you are a confident alpha male and that she cannot easily control you—that builds attraction.

However, you cannot get by on flirting forever. Now it is time to start becoming the man she wants and showing her, in the most subtle of ways (which she will instantly identify with her womanly infrared radars!) that you are everything she is looking for. You elicit her values. You know the words she wants to hear and know how to physically and mentally manipulate her emotion to feel passion in your presence.

All that is left is to show her that this is the real thing and that you can deliver everything she wants. Of course, just telling her that you "love" (what she loves) is not the right way to communicate. It is patronizing and not quite believable. This is another instance where hypnotic suggestion will work wonders, as opposed to direct statements or questions.

The easiest way to continue seduction is to tell a story. Tell a story where you "show" (not tell) that you elicited her most important values. For example, if you know that she wants a man who can take her to fun places, and control the energy of the event, it would be smart to tell her a story about traveling to an exotic city and what you did while there—your take charge attitude that you demonstrated.

It is not a good precedent to lie. I know some players make a practice of this, figuring they want to project that illusion at any cost. However, it usually does not pay off. Because when you fib, you (A) Risk blowing your cover and will have to constantly think your way out of lies; (B) Are pretending to be someone you're not, which screams desperation rather than confidence; (C) are not truly owning the moment, because you're not speaking with natural charisma. Experience builds charisma. Lying is all about playing a part and not focusing in on your strengths as an alpha male in complete control of your life!

Remember what we said earlier about women describing things that represent their desired state. Do not be surprised if many women do actually want the same thing such as security and comfort. Once you identify her desired state it makes sense to insert carefully placed words in your story emphasizing the state of mind you want to put her in—and that she wants to be in—since she has already conveyed to you her desired state.

Finding out what she wants and then giving her all the "experience and emotion" of what she wants is the foolproof way to score, to win, to seduce—and it's biologically sure to work on concept. Since you are eliciting her values and becoming the man she has told you she wants, it is really just a matter of how you perform. If you do this right, she will feel a strong and impulsive attraction to you. If she does not respond favorably, it is likely you are not doing it right, or something is wrong with her, or she somehow senses you are a player— which probably means you're performing too well, and with not enough "real you" in your performance.

This is a universal strategy because seducing someone's mind involves a personal commitment to finding that person's values and desires, and giving them exactly what they ask for. This is the kind of seductive thinking worth millions, as it brings businesses millions of dollars in sales, which result from advertising and sales personnel who are trained to find values and provide product. In dating, it is much of the same formula.

Time Distortion

Time distortion refers to a technique used to ease a woman into hearing your stories, and lowering her defenses against your seduction. As we said, too much resistance means she does not fall for your hypnotic commands or even your attempt to find her state. She will resist you unless it becomes clear that you are making a personal connection and not just rehearsing all the right moves.

Time distortion is a clever way of expediting the process and jumping over hurdles like time, distance, and the long process of earning trust. This technique operates on the basis that a woman will feel what you tell her to feel, so as long as you provide a distraction. The distortion of time serves that purpose.

The way it works is by telling a story with emotions in the present, but with references in the future. As in, we will be _____ and you will feel _____. That is the formula, though a smooth storyteller has to dress it up just a little bit. For example, a man might start talking about where in the world the woman would like to visit, and after hearing "Ireland" or wherever, followed by what she wants to do there (which is eliciting her values) he can begin telling a story of what happens in the future.

"Wouldn't you love to see the rolling hills, and lay on the grass, perfectly content to look up at the sky and stars and then finish the day by a warm fireplace with someone special next to you. Feeling the fire warm the room, your muscles relaxing, and that special someone giving you a massage, rubbing your shoulders after a long, hard day."

With this example, we see that he is distorting time by making the future present, and by feeding her a dream or a fantasy that is solely stroking her own ego and appealing to her desires. Why would she feel defensive when he is only fanning on the fantasy she loves to entertain?

What makes the setting very effective is that the man does not even say that it is him. He eliminates that resistance quickly, telling her that it is not him (hence, bypassing all the "I don't even know you!" stage) and focusing only on what she feels during the experience. He takes her with him on a journey, eliminates resistance and distracts her of the necessity of time. What is now is then and so she is so enthralled with the experience she feels everything.

Every person, and especially a woman who is so used to awkward dating experiences with non-alphas, strongly desires to feel something amazing. Time distortion fantasies are a great way to give them what they ask for. Just be sure to find out her values beforehand so that you do not simply brag or tell a meaningless story she doesn't want to hear.

Another way to become her dream guy is to tell her you are her dream guy, but to do so in her own words, and with the gift of a few extra minutes on your side. For example, if you were to learn what her most important relationship quality is, and hold onto that, you could bring it up again later in conversation stating why the two of you might be compatible. "Because we have ___ and ___." (all of the values she told you). This is a way of using trigger words while also factoring in for time.

In essence, you TEACH her that you are her ideal man. She does not have to feel it if you give her a good lesson showing it, while of course not becoming too blatant or unimaginative during conversation.

Here is a powerful example, (forgive the unflattering illustration) but it emphasizes a greater point. Women who stay in abusive or unfaithful relationships rarely pay attention to what a man does, but focus on what he says. He programs her to believe that he is sorry, apologetic, making changes, and so on. She believes him, because he tells her what to believe—he uses those trigger words to emphasize a point to her.

This is an unfortunate situation and it teaches us one very crucial point that we as alpha-men must always remember. Women expect men to have power over their emotions. They want emotional stimulation. Some women with low self-esteem are so desperate for emotional stimulation that they will suffer with a lowlife guy who doesn't know how to be faithful or peaceable—rather than settle on a man who doesn't know the first thing about emotional communication.

So what are you teaching a woman when you begin dating? When you progress onto serious commitment? What are your trigger words? What fantasies and desires has she already given you? Lastly, what are you doing to expand on these and give her the fantasy romance she wants?

Women will tolerate a lot, maybe even too much, as long as you give them what they want. An emotional experience, which is exactly what love is supposed to be. Think of a woman's mind the same way a salesperson thinks of a customer. The customer has all the power since she has the money. The salesperson knows the best way to approach her is not to come on aggressively or in begging desperation but to sell a feeling, a need to her—the very thing she wants the first moment she walks into the store.

Seduction: that dirty word, that bad word that everyone fears, is nothing more than selling to a customer what that customer wants. Women want an emotional experience and with these hypnotic and persuasive techniques, you will be able to give the gift of feeling and will immediately pass into the VIP section of serious boyfriend material.

You will keep dating her, and dating her, and dating her. Until, maybe someday, maybe, she will sleep with you.

Wait a minute, what is missing in this scenario? How did you manage to come off so strong in the beginning but then falter just when you thought it was time to move into the bedroom? This is because there is a way to move from the emotional to physical stimulation process, and this is what we are going to talk about in Chapter 8.

Chapter 8

How To Close The Deal And Kiss Like A Dreamboat

Up until this point, we have discussed important matters of the mind and heart, but it does seem that women always seem to become defensive whenever it is time to consummate this attraction. Logically speaking, women should want to become intimate when they are emotionally stimulated. Whoever said women think rationally? If anything, most are irrational because they love the capriciousness, the unpredictability of love.

Therefore, what does appear to happen is that as soon as a woman really does start to like a guy, and does feel sexually attracted and interested in a guy, she puts up yet another shield. Maybe it is because society has engrained in women not to be easy, she has been hurt before in a bad relationship, or because she thinks you are seducing her.

Which might be the case, but as we said, seduction in itself is not a bad thing...it's a game, a little show that women enjoy. What matters is how you treat her afterward. That is exactly what a woman is thinking when a relationship approaches the red zone of sexual expectations.

Before we move on and discuss what a guy should do, let's attack our own instincts for a moment and figure out what most guys do wrong.

What is a nice, normal guy's natural inclination when dating a woman. Obviously, to be a gentle man. He wants to show her that he is kind, isn't a psychopath, and isn't going to be a brutish man perpetuating the rape culture we hear so much about. The last thing any man wants is to scare a woman he likes.

So yeah, the instinct is to be kind. To not be aggressive and to be patient until the woman is ready. That is exactly when she waves you in and says, "Let's do it!"

Sure. Well, you might be waiting a long time for that signal, since most women are not so forward as to ask for such a request directly. With a few exceptions of course, most women would die from embarrassment if they had to be the ones that took the lead. They would be showing themselves to be "easy", to be "aggressive", or a "man eater." And of course, the description every woman hates, the "prostitute" who has a reputation for being proactive and finding leads everywhere she goes with over-the-top behavior.

Believe it or not, there is such a thing as reverse rape culture, and no woman wants to be thought of as a pushy person who forces herself on a man! In the majority of cases, YOU have to be the aggressor, the instigator, the strong man who knows what he wants. You know that it is time. You are not afraid of making a move and you're going to guide her through this with a calm, powerful and sexy presence.

Ideally, she is following your lead like in a dance. She does not want to be embarrassed, so she is counting on you to know the moves. Herein lies the paradox. You have to be forward and edgy, without "forcing" yourself and scaring the woman to death.

Indeed, a slippery slope. However, the secret lies in understanding the physical signs as well as the mental signs. The moment has to be right, and it is a moment you should maintain control over. If not, you are the respectable gentleman who goes home with a hug, a handshake, or a reluctant gesture.

And all that means is (A) if she likes you, you will get another chance. Or (B) you failed and she's giving you the formal goodbye after the interview.

Rightfully so. Men are stubbornly linear in their expectations of a date. They think that since they have lasted the entire night without "screwing up" or making a blatant mistake, they earn a kiss goodnight, or a roll in the hay. They lasted the marathon. They earn the trophy.

WRONG! That is not how a woman sees things at all. Let us put it in science fiction terms for the TV fans out there: women are non-linear thinkers. If they want to kiss someone, they want to kiss him *in the moment*; when her sexual feelings and attraction has peaked, the high point of the conversation. If you miss this window of opportunity, well it is sort of like missing the proverbial "portal" that the action hero needs to successfully return "home." This is your portal and if you miss the chance, you can only hope she lets you start back at square one. To put it in a video game perspective, you probably only have three lives or so before she realizes she just doesn't quite connect with you like she should.

Yes, women want grand and passionate romance. As an experienced man, the man who knows how to push her buttons, you must learn to identify the physical and perhaps mental signals she sends you. These may be inadvertent, entirely subconscious or even blatant if she really likes you. (Which she probably will if you do everything else right)

These symptoms of unrestrained passion might include:

- She holds strong eye contact and then looks down and away.

- She opens up with responsive and "towards you" body language, usually changing from a defensive position.

- She starts mirroring your movements, posture, voice and conversation.

- Caresses herself or plays with her hair.

- She touches you, especially after a peak moment. She may even try to out-touch you, by touching more of you than you touch of her. That is quite the play, and if you blink, you could miss it.

- She laughs in an affected way, usually a throatier and slower-paced laugh.

- A shift in mood, a bit quieter in tone and voice, with a shy smile—especially if she was into you a moment ago.

The Kiss Comes First

Yes, the kiss comes first despite what you might see depicted on the net. In fact, kissing is probably the most important move, physically speaking. If the kiss fails, sex will probably not happen. If you do it right, she will be tempted to sleep with you and will have a moment of clarity; "Do I want to get involved with this guy or do I resist?"

She has not guaranteed to go through with it, because let's be honest—women are taught by their own female-centered seduction guides to avoid having sex too soon, otherwise the

87

guy loses interest. However, all you need is one kiss to test your chemistry and if you do it right, you WILL be on her mind for weeks and months to come.

How do you prevent the kiss from becoming clumsy, awkward, and a mood killer? Do not follow your instincts. A good kiss does not just happen. A good kiss is all about perfect timing.

To start, make sure all the other "stages" have happened. She has revealed herself to you; her desired state, her values. You have made her feel comfortable in your presence. She is enjoying herself and is experiencing a peak level of happiness. Remember one of the first few rules we learned in our confidence training was to move forward **without apology or fear.** A kiss is a dramatic gesture and must be done in want, and without the appearance of hesitation. As if, you cannot control yourself, as if you have to take action.

Of course, by this time you should have already altered your voice and slowed down your speaking and physical movements, matching her comfort level and fully immersed in the sexual state. You are ready to have sex with her, regardless of whether you actually do or not; this is the mindset you must have, to go through with this.

If your voice is naturally fast-paced and you just barely get through conversation without a big gulp (yes a lot of guys do suffer from this and experience talking to more women usually does help) then make it a point to pause more often and longer in your sentences. Make a deliberate effort to slow down and center your breathing.

You might say that a good kiss **starts with the eyes**. You do not just invade her spaces and jolt forward. Instead, you gaze at her making a triangle of her right eye, left eye and then down to her lips. Before you try to kiss her, gaze at her lips for a moment and make sure the energy of the moment is sexual, calm and in control. Change the mood if you have to, if there is too much laughter or a pause denoting awkwardness.

Up until this point, you have been prompting her to ask the question "Is this guy really interested in me?" This moment is where you do actually tell her how you feel, with your lips, and it is going to make her feel sexually desired, excited and even a little vulnerable.

The Push And Pull Method In Kissing

The vulnerability part is still a concern, even if you have your seduction move down. Sudden transitions from comfort to seduction (as in you moving in for kissing and presumably sex) have the potential to become explosive and send her running into retreat. As we all concur, most women do not want to be thought of as easy and realizing that you are pushing all of her buttons so adroitly will require just a bit of emotional foreplay. Yes, emotional foreplay precedes physical foreplay. Isn't dating complicated?

The push and pull method that we know by now in conversation is also an efficient protection against a woman's defense. You know the notorious hand that blocks your lips at just that perfect moment. Here is how it works.

- You want her to feel the sexual state and to feel the imminence of your approaching lips, so you perform the triangle routine.

- However, you stop short of actually going in for a kiss. You do not cower; you simply don't give her what she wants. You maintain eye contact, perhaps as if you are thinking about it, but are not sure you want to give her the satisfaction.

- You do it again, this time holding that imminent feeling for a long period of time, this time 5-8 seconds as opposed to the 3 seconds you formerly gave her.

- Keep doing this and teasing her with the feeling of assertively taking her, and she will begin to crave your lips. She will not feel that vibe of desperation, as in you literally cannot control yourself. She loves the idea that you are surrendering to her, but loves the feeling of waiting...and waiting...until just the perfect moment where she cannot take it anymore.

- By that time, she will be eager to feel your lips. Investing time in the emotional foreplay stage ensures that there will not be an abrupt "What are you doing?" moment, because she will already feel that sexual tension. She will not be able to say, "What?" because she knows what you are doing and she will be waiting for you to make a move.

Reading her signals is another part of the process, because depending on whether she was showing interest or is becoming more defensive or disinterested will determine if you have to spend more time in the comfort building process, in finding her desired state, and in generating attraction using the push-pull method.

The Right Signals: The right signals will consist of similar behavior she has been showing up until now, namely touching you and letting herself be touched, moving closer to you, or making her own triangle. She may also be teasing eye contact with you, by matching your intense gaze and then looking bashfully away.

The Wrong Signals: Wrong signals are not too subtle, actually. They usually consist of leaning back, making it difficult for you to reach her, folding her arms, or putting something in between your face and hers. (Like a glass) She may also lose eye contact with you and spend more time looking to the side, indicating her interest lies elsewhere.

These signals do not necessarily mean she doesn't want you, but do clearly indicate it is not the time to go in for a kiss, not yet. Follow her signals closely and you will not have to worry about getting the big and unpleasant "lip block."

How To Kiss

The first rule is do not ask permission but to take a leap of faith, after observing all the right signals and making it through the proper phase. Kissing is as much an individual art as lovemaking. Nevertheless, there are a few rules to take seriously even if you want to experiment with technique.

1. Have fresh breath. Bad breath will invalidate all your good work thus far.

2. Use your hands to touch part of her face, not a grab but simply a touch.

3. Take it easy and move slow with your lips lengthening the moment, as you want this to last longer so she will have more time to decide she trusts you!

4.   Eventually close your eyes. You can gaze at her for the first few moments of kiss foreplay, but as you begin the big smooch, close your eyes. Staring at her is fairly weird and invasive.

5.   Do not use your tongue too hard or at all for the first kiss. An overeager tongue is the sign of a boy, and one who has not quite mastered the control a woman finds attractive. After kissing for a few moments, and as you feel the heat building then you can gently insert your tongue just inside enough to push against hers. This is the proper way to French kiss.

6.   Do not slobber too much, keep the kiss dry. Your mouth should be just wet enough, as will hers, and there is no need to generate any extra saliva.

7.   Keep things soft, soft enough as if she were asleep. Think of kissing too hard and roughly as "waking her up", which is definitely comparable to snapping her out of the love trance. Your lips are merely caressing hers, on top and on bottom, tasting her and awakening her sexuality. It is just a hint of things to come and ideally should have a time goal.

Additional Hints On Closing A Deal

The next chapter will give some ideas on how to advance the stage to sexual foreplay. In the meantime, there are more "insider" notes about closing a deal with a kiss. The "closing" in a business transaction is always the most difficult aspect of a sale, and in like manner kissing a woman intimately **changes everything** between you.

A woman will typically avoid a man whom she figures is not worth any long-term investment, figuring he is beneath her level, or not quite boyfriend material. In other words, if you do not get through to the kissing stage in a reasonable period of time, you will be confined to the friend zone, and possibly for years to come.

As we said previously, dating is always goal oriented. In early courtship, you are after a phone number or a name. As you progress and are able to accompany her on a real date, or at least a time when you are both alone together, you will slowly build trust. In business, and particularly in real estate, closing a deal on a prime piece of property is so risky that it usually takes several meetings to close a deal.

In like manner for dating, usually the process takes a series of accomplished goals before you boldly move onto closing the deal with a kiss. These goals accomplished will also serve as the multiple "yes" statements that you need to put her in a better frame of mind, and more receptive to your wishes, as we learned in the hypnosis and persuasion chapter.

You are not always going to have the option for a fast kiss, so at some point and especially if you tend to see her in public places, you are going to have to settle for a less intimate goal. The best you may be able to do is get a name or a phone number and hope to contact her again for a more one-on-one occasion. While moving in on a woman in a public place is not impossible, it is just not very good momentum since your primary goal is making sure she is comfortable.

For more single women, being alone is the proper mood and setting for mating behavior, at least biologically speaking. This is why most men will try the "lone wolf" strategy, that suggests a woman is more likely to respond to a man's courting behavior if she is alone with him, because her focus is narrowed to him and him alone, and because he eliminates all other distractions, giving her the simple option of continuing communication or ending communication. Most women will respond to the lone wolf, so as long as they are allowed a high level of comfort.

Still, some women will resist being alone with a man, solely because it is so much easier to be seduced when all distractions are eliminated. So you might have to play the public place or even the "group" game, until she's ready to get serious about you.

There will always be exceptions to the rule; guys so confident that they can just waltz into a room, get a phone number within three seconds, and maybe even kiss her within three minutes. We will discuss this more in depth in the later chapters. However, these guys strong though they are, will take a big risk that might not pay off.

The seducer's angle is to spend more time building trust and reaching these goals of accomplishment by appealing to her curiosity, comfort and then her desired state. The simple answer on how to accomplish a dating goal is the same dynamic as in finding her life values.

You ask her what she likes to do, and you then use her idea to further the courtship. If you elicit from her that she likes classy restaurants, or Thai food, then you would work that information into your end goal. It is hypnosis, which she won't even recognize since it feels more like common sense at this point. "Hey, since we both like Thai food, let's go try that new Thai restaurant in town." It is a fairly reasonable proposal.

Although not eliciting her values is a bad idea in general--because why wouldn't you if you have that ability—you can actually entice her by either using the "boyfriending" technique, where you play the part of her would-be boyfriend and give a little preview of your dating personality, or you could give her an identity calling card to work with.

In the **boyfriending technique,** the game is as easy as just a matter of being nice, almost like children oblivious to the idea of a date. You could:

- Ask if she wants to tag along while you go shopping

- See a movie with the specific intention of analyzing an actor you both like

- Go see the museum exhibit before it closes

- Give her fashion advice

- Give her a free massage

- Get her a discount on dry cleaning.

- Go dancing or clubbing with friends.

And so on. In fact, the task itself is not really important. What matters is that you would help her preview a relationship with you, by fast-forwarding all the awkward sex phase and showing her what hanging out with you as a regular man would be like.

91

You would offer her the option to see you, to be your "friend", and to explore this new relationship without much of a commitment anywhere. It's not as effective a strategy as learning her, challenging her, and playing the conversational dance, but it's still a good move and when combined with other techniques we discussed earlier, it is a worthy end goal. Seduce her mind and then offer her a simple invitation to keep talking, and talking.

Another approach would be to give her a virtual calling card (not literally, as in online!) but as in something specific to remember about you. This has the potential to backfire, especially if she senses you are bragging about being something or having something. So instead of money or status, (or making an empty promise) focus on highlighting something about yourself that is FUN to remember, something that she will associate positively with you. For instance:

- A shared experience you both happened to enjoy

- A joke (that hopefully is not self-deprecating)

- Something you both like (and anything close to her values would be great!)

- Something about the location or the (happy) mood

And so on, and in this case she will have something to remember you by. Some guys even encourage the woman to give him a nickname, and of course to imply that her chosen nickname says a lot about him . This is "branding", and in business, it means that you take control of the public's perception. Yes, obviously you want to do the same to a woman! Do not ever let her decide what to think about you, since this is giving her power to decide your friend-zone fate. Instead, use this little nickname game to prompt her to give you an identity, one that you will presumably hint to her beforehand. You are the fun guy, you're the guy she associates with her favorite place, or in some way reflect her ideal man.

One of the best methods for getting her phone number is to use the nickname request, and to simply hand her your phone, letting her enter her number. Handing her your phone for her to enter her number and letting her enter it is the boyfriending technique. You are entrusting her, showing her that she qualifies for a lofty task.

Another method is to give her your phone number and imply that she should call you since she is obviously the one interested in you. A third method is to tell her that you both should meet up on a non-date to talk some more, or do some activity. If she agrees then you tell her to give you her number, you do not ask. For example, you could tell the woman, "We should meet up sometime this week over coffee to talk some more." If the woman agrees to meet then you could say, "Give me your telephone number, so that I call you and we schedule a time to meet."

These tactics accomplish the same thing: they take away the awkward nature of **asking her out directly.** What did we learn? That asking a woman for anything is just giving her a reason to say no, it is a man deferring to a woman and that is not what most women want in courtship behavior. So that brings us to a new closing strategy.

Eliminating The Option Of No

One of the best techniques for avoiding the big "NO" (although confident men really do not consider "no" the final word) is to eliminate the option of no. It is simple psychology. If you ask a customer or really anyone in any circumstance, "Are you sure you want to take this risk?", most people are going to want to say no. No one really likes taking a risk, and if you are asking her permission to date her, then there is really no strong motivational force prompting her to say yes. You will be lucky to get a yes based on good looks, or perhaps on your introduction, which was far better than your plea of "Please, will you go out with me?"

Even if you don't say "please", that's all she's hearing. If possible, you are far better off getting rid of the question and finding another way to accomplish your set goal. Some of the more innovative ideas guys might use include:

- Telling her where he will be, if she wants to tag along

- Telling her that he's going with friends and she's invited

- Arranging to meet up at the same place to continue a conversation

- Settling a bet or paying back a silly bet you made

- Suggesting a change of venue or scenery

- Suggesting you both quench your hunger or your thirst

In all of these cases, the dynamic avoids going into dangerous "dating territory" and this is mostly because women do get uncomfortable at the notion of **intense one on one dating**. As we said before, the lone wolf strategy usually works so well they just do not even want to be lured into that situation. So your best move is to downplay the "date" aspect, and eschew any feeling of strong romantic attention.

You would rather have fun than go on a date. You would rather hang out than go to a fancy candle-lit dinner, designed to provoke romantic feelings. She doesn't want romantic feelings stimulated until much later, so early "closes" must be short-term goals.

This is why most guys avoid asking a woman for her telephone number. Rather a guy usually tells her to enter her telephone number into his phone, or tells her to give him her number after she has agreed to meet him on a non-date. He assigns her a task that does not involve strong romantic feelings. A guy sometimes gives her his number but leaves the "ball in her court" so that she can decide that SHE likes him and wants to talk further. In this situation, the guy is also assigning the woman a task that does not involve strong romantic feelings. In all three situations, he assigns her a task so that it seems that she is investing time and effort into him, and that he is worth the trouble.

Always remember: **attraction is not enough**. Attraction gets her attention, but your goal is to push her to **invest in you**. This makes her think she likes you, because otherwise, she wouldn't invest anytime in getting to know you or making you happy.

Some women will actually call you and simply prefer to not give out their number. Ultimately, it is your choice on whether you want to send the message "I want your number and will not compromise on this..." or "I really like you, I hope you call me."

Perhaps the best way to gauge this situation is to make it more difficult for the 9s and 10s (meaning you demand their number or nothing) and a little more generous to the 6s and 7s who probably don't have great self- esteem. The choice is yours. Whatever you do, do not beg. If anything, it might be better to negotiate by giving her your number in exchange for her number.

This rule of avoiding the yes or no continues in courtship, even to the very end when you approach intimacy. When you do attempt to "lone wolf" it and invite her to some very special place where emotions can run high, hoping a kiss will follow, once again, the poor girl's defenses go up.

In her mind, she always has to rationalize that this is not a date, that nothing is going to happen, and that you are nothing serious. This resists awkward tension, intense emotional situations, and just about everything, she fears about meeting a stranger.

This is precisely why a lot of guys will give her an excuse free of charge. They might call it coffee, they might call it a non-date get-together, or just a simple invitation to see an old record collection or a movie they both love. The idea is that there is no date, no emotional commitment, and so she has nothing to fear.

She can always fall back on the excuse that she was just talking to a guy, just going for coffee, and of course, never let her guard down. She will appreciate a guy who gives her a good "platonic" excuse on why they are going off somewhere alone together. The less she has to think about it, and feel divided on whether or not she wants this, the better.

When She Closes Down Your Closing

Leave it to such an unpredictable "opponent" like a beautiful woman to throw multiple shields up, and usually at the time when you least expect it. What are you supposed to do when you are "closing" the deal and moving closer to lone wolf, kissing and sex (or getting a phone number in some cases) and she suddenly decides she doesn't want you after all?

This usually happens for simple reasons, a few of which are just a fact of dating life.

- She got a better offer.

- She was in the middle of something with a boyfriend or another guy and went back with him.

- The initial excitement she felt when connecting with you faded away. Your impact, while good, was not dramatic enough to merit further conversation.

- She caught herself liking you too much, only to realize that she really didn't know anything about you. The idea of meeting alone with you might even scare her, as she could figure you for a mastermind serial killer type.

There is a preventive solution as well as a reactive solution. The best approach is to make sure you make a more dramatic introduction and follow up so that she does not want to forget you. You can minimize the chance of her interest cooling by focusing more on eliciting her values, her dream man's characteristics, her secret desires, establishing the desired state, and not only delving into flirty, fun behavior. Another way you can minimize the chance of her interest cooling is by making her exert effort to get your attention or validation through the push-pull method. She has to get your validation or attention, because of your negative validation, or positive validation as a person judging her. As she tries to get your attention or validation, she will reveal more of herself to you. The more she is emotionally invested in the interaction, the more likely her interest will not cool off. You can use either method or both methods to prevent her interest from cooling off.

Most women have an uncanny ability to "fake" real interest in a guy; sometimes they are aware of this gift and sometimes they are completely oblivious. You may think you are making an amazing first impression when in actuality she is just humoring you pretty well, or is just giving you what you want so she can kill some time.

The best defense against underwhelming a girl is to focus more time on getting her to **reveal herself to you—her real self**. Women only think they are "connecting with you" if they are revealing something important about themselves, a side of her that most guys never get to see. This is trust building. If she does not trust you, obviously, you have given her no reason to do so.

Meeting with her again might be the only solution to a woman "cooling" problem. You could meet her again even if it is with friends or a tag-along sort of invitation. Something low commitment and safe so that you can work on establishing comfort. Since you have most likely made a good impression with alpha male behavior, the main intent is to show a glimmer of a sensitive side, suggesting to her subtly that you do have the inner qualities she needs, in addition to the alpha male qualities that attract.

After she identifies you as a confident guy she has to see her own values reflected in you, and this means sharing more of yourself, telling more stories, and giving her a reason to trust you as someone with "layers" of good qualities.

The Folly Of Online Relationships

This well may be the only dating advice you ever find that says, "Get away from the online chat!" While everyone knows flirting on social media or email is fun, these are avenues purely for introductions only.

Online flirting makes it possible for men and women alike to be more confident, entertaining and uninhibited. We get to engage in fantasies, do away with awkward social situations and explore virtual chemistry.

Unfortunately, this is like riding on the old "information superhighway" to **nowhere**. You are laughing, you are having fun, and the best-case scenario is that you turn all of this flirting into a real relationship, or at least real sex. Staying forever in cyberspace means you are virtually branding yourself as the "cyber guy" whom she likes, but is never going to work things out with in **REAL LIFE**. It is so rare for a woman to choose the cyber guy, the one who seems interesting, over the flesh and blood man in front of her who is stimulating her emotions, her sensations, her body AND her mind.

Women will oftentimes keep cyber guys around as ego boosters, as entertainment, but will eventually categorize them as relationships that are destined to stay online. Ironically, some of these women really will share something personal about themselves—maybe even a cybersex session. However, without the physical connection she will always be holding back something, and this means you are still considered untrustworthy when compared to real world men.

95

The best way to break out of the online prison is to take her away from the online world and spend more time with her on the phone. Then, it is a matter of arranging for a date. Accept (or better yet, come up with) a group event so that she doesn't feel unsafe or get the feeling of a "lone wolf" scheme. Simply getting to know her in person should be your main motivation.

If She's Playing You

It is not so uncommon that a woman might play you, letting you build up to a kiss, or another dating goal, but then send you mixed messages. Some men are content to ask, not if they can kiss the woman, but if the woman wants to kiss them. This reverses the process and avoids the big "no" brush off.

If she does say no, or go on the defensive at any point in the closing part of courtship, you have to stand strong and call her bluff. This calls for a neg-hit. She might be testing you or she might be trying to friend-zone you for whatever reason, but the worst thing you can do is to be a perfect gentleman and accept it.

You're not going to be aggressive, but you are going to remind her that you are still in control of the situation and you don't appreciate being played, disrespected, led on, or whatever she's doing.

So far, we have discussed kissing, closing, and moving in for some one-on-one romantic attention. Now we are going to cross that dangerous bridge that leads you from kissing to sex. A lot of guys would tell you that.

Chapter 9

Sex: The Undiscovered Country

Moving from sweet and innocent dating (well, more like dating and seduction) to hardcore sex, the likes of which men fantasize about constantly is no easy maneuver. Actually, the strategy for most men is not to bring up sex immediately (as with the grandmaster style, which we will discuss later) or not at all. Instead, they concentrate on making the woman feel comfortable and safe, and make her guess as to whether he is really interested in sex, love and all that jazz.

So for this chapter, we're going to assume you're dating a woman who doesn't want sex right away, and that you're not using a quick lay strategy, since that is counterproductive (and a bit of a risk) to some of the tried and true techniques we're going to discuss here.

The first rule is that you absolutely do not bring up sex talk at all, until she has displayed positive body language, based on a good rapport you have developed with her. This is the big difference between you, the alpha, and all the other jerks and "sleaze-balls" that she is instantly going to filter out because they are too dumb to think about anything else but sex. (Even though we are all pretty much thinking about sex the same...we are just approaching it in a very different way than the average guy!)

The Sex Test

Think of your initial mention of sex more like a "test" than a move. You want to first see how comfortable she is with the idea of sex, and with the idea of discussing sexual details with you. Rather than jump into an emotionally volatile setting, you simply want to gauge how she feels about the subject. Women will rarely state their sexual preferences upfront (and if she does, then fast-forward to the quick lay chapter), so that means you're waiting to elicit her sexual preferences, which will usually be a good while after eliciting her values.

Perhaps the safest way to test her is to tell her a story about someone you know, who has recently had a sexual experience. You could opt to simply ask her how she feels, but this may cause her to recoil. In fact, a lot of women do "recoil" or will appear shy when innocent conversation suddenly becomes sexual. This is a gut reaction and she will start to think, "Is sex what he wants? Is that all he wants? Is this really what I want to do?"

This is why most guys test her with a story about someone else, a friend or an acquaintance, who did something sexual or perhaps even provocative (like a one night stand or sex with a virtual stranger). Now is your chance to test her reaction. Does she laugh it off? Or does she seem offended at the idea of having sex so soon? Maybe that is an indicator that she expects you to wait a little while.

On the other hand, you are challenging her to drop her inhibitions and at least discuss the act, if not engage in it. What you are actually doing is summoning her erotic feelings by discussing these graphic visuals, but disguising the setting with a non-threatening "story."

She will probably not back off, because most women would be embarrassed to be thought of as a prude. They do not want you to "win" and to think you scared them into silence. So expect them to react positively, stating something along the lines of "That sounds fun," or

"That's her choice," the two extremes of answers possibly indicative of her level of comfort with pre-commitment sex.

What is important is that you deliver this story, this presentation, in a firm yet sensitive manner. You are not trying to shock her, you are simply relating the story as something that happened and sharing it with her. It's nothing so scandalous, and just in case she does object, then neg-hit her for being so uptight that she can't even discuss the subject

Here is the beauty of the sex story. It is not only hypnotic, in that it forces her to feel what you talk about, and not only an excellent testing procedure, but also it is anti-friend zoning. The moment you start talking about sex, even if it's about someone else, then you force her to think about having sex with you. It is not really optional; it changes the dynamic of the relationship, even if she's trying her best to friend zone you.

You have also managed to pass the filtering phase, proving you are not just a sleazy guy or just an asexual friend. You are a serious threat. It will move things forward, and if she likes you (and why wouldn't she at this point) then she will start echoing back the sex talk to you, showing that she's not an uptight priss.

Even if she does not respond favorably and tries to veer the conversation away from sex, then she cannot cancel out what has happened. She has thought about you sexually. And since you built rapport with her previously and made her feel comfortable, you will remain in her mind for quite a while.

Once she responds favorably, it is time to move to closing. However, play this one by ear. You cannot assume that just because she is open to the idea of having sex with you that she wants it immediately. She may be waiting to see if she likes you, or may even be playing her own strategy game on how to keep you interested. You cannot rush things if she is resisting you or you will undo all of the good techniques up until this point.

Determining What She Wants

Before making your next move, whether that is a first kiss or escalating a kiss to sex, you must know exactly what she wants. You do this by eliciting her sexual values, as well as her life values. During conversation, and particularly after your sexual story, she will probably admit what she is looking for, or will at least admit just enough to get you to decipher what she wants.

For example, a woman might admit casually:

- The other man in her life does not fulfill her sexually (or the other suitors she has).
- She wants to do something wild.
- She wants sex and passion.
- She likes breaking the rules.
- She wants love and commitment.

The next step after telling a story about sex is to actually feed her a sexual fantasy to further ignite her appetite, which will quickly conflagrate her resistance. A sexual fantasy goes further with the thought, and teases her about experiencing these sensations, a little more overtly this time.

She may get what you are doing, but she is receiving your communication loud and clear. You project to her, through your friend's fantasy (not your own, because you are not directly asking her!) what you want. Such as, "My friend is in a purely sexual relationship because she is free to experiment with no strings attached. To fulfill herself and what she wants, with no expectations. And the guy is cool with it."

You see in this sentence, you are not only continuing the fantasy but also telling her indirectly the kind of relationship you want with her.

Sure, you could exaggerate it and speak of love and commitment, but do not do that unless you really mean it and are willing to wait it out. Besides, projecting the wrong fantasy to the wrong type of woman does not work. A lot of women just want sex. They are not even thinking about commitment until long after sex happens. So give them what they want, by projecting the idea of a no strings attached experiment, one that does not end with you obsessively calling them the day after.

In your fantasy, encourage specific ideas that might appeal to both of you. Some men might volunteer sexual positions, sex in a public place, or even a threesome—something provocative. You can try this just to see how into you she is and how wild she considers herself. Some guys use this process as a way of filtering out the less wild women, in other words speed dating towards the exact type of woman you want. Why date the girls that do not exactly match you, right?

You do not want to "create the perfect girl" with this strategy, but want to attract the perfect match. This is why you should resist trying to tell her what kind of sex you want, instead help her bring out the kind of sex SHE wants that also matches your own desires.

Ultimately, you are going to be fulfilling her fantasies and so you need to know how to elicit her deepest desires and then play into them. Find out what she wants and give it to her.

The brilliance of this closing technique is that you will tease this woman so relentlessly that you probably will not even have to make the first move. A woman who has been properly stimulated emotionally and sexually is not afraid to make the first move, or at the very least, make it painfully obvious that she wants you. If you are not the natural "reach out and kiss the girl type", try this technique and watch her implode from desire.

What If She Doesn't Want To Talk About Sex?

The unthinkable! You mean a modern woman might actually not want to talk about casual sex with someone she hardly knows? Yes, it is possible, depending on the type of woman you aim for. Most women are not prudish, but you may find that plenty of women are unwilling to open up to you, especially if it is just a first or second date. (Or even before an official date)

It has often been suggested that there are two types of sexual female behavior, despite the myriads of sexual preferences or values that you have to learn. One, a woman wants a strong and assertive man who will dominate her, causing her to surrender to him sexually. The other is a more feminist-based attraction, one that demands the man cater to her, and be somewhat passive and cuddly. When she is ready, and only then, will she have sex with him.

99

It really depends on which type you are "hunting", as to whether you want an aggressive strategy (like what we just talked about) or a more patient strategy that goes the long term. Women who are wise to men will often postpone sex, as they have been prompted to do so. Your best bet for faster sex is a woman who is oblivious to dating "rules" and who is looking for a one-night stand just as much as you are.

That said, if you find an example of the second type of woman, the more patient and cautious type that does not want to talk about sex right away, you do have to adapt to this and take a different approach.

For some women, sex is not about the naughtiness or the emotional rush but about the feelings underneath; romantic thoughts, special memories and feelings reminiscent of love, not lust. They want a love story and so knowing this, it is time to exercise their **kinesthetic sense** (as well as their desire to feel touch, taste, smell, visual and aural stimulation). This way, the issue is less about being a sexual being (something a woman might have a problem with) and instead is about following the emotion of the moment. She should follow her heart.

In essence, you give the woman exactly what she wants to feel, rather than programming her to do your own bidding. You are the lady's man, a man intent on giving a woman pleasure on her own terms.

Missing Your Chance

Now here is where things get confusing. A lot of guys will interpret a woman's mistrust of a stranger as reason to play the gentleman. So it makes sense. She does not want to be an "easy girl" and have sex with you right away. She seems interested. She likes things comfortable and safe.

And then you wait. And she waits. And you stick in there and wait it out, right? Wait until she is ready and becomes the sexual dynamo you know she is—the perfect woman for you.

Not so fast. That all sounds good and romantic in a way. However, you may find in your own bitter experiences (and from many stories of men who have fallen down the waiting path) that a "special moment" NEVER comes. You wait and wait and eventually the feeling passes. She gets over you. Or she has sex with someone else.

What went wrong? Weren't you being the gentleman she needed?

The problem here is that you quite literally, very simply, **missed your chance.** Women have an internal timer when it comes to men, and if you are not immediately friend-zoned for making a mistake, waiting too long to make a decisive move will eventually get you placed in the friend zone by default.

Why women make you wait, while actually wanting you to make a bigger move, is anyone's guess. Maybe she wants it but is afraid. Maybe she wants reassurance after the fact, rather than you playing the role of patient parent. Maybe she is using you as therapy so she can sleep with someone else.

It does not really matter because a woman needs to know that you want her. This is all part of your alpha male identity. Once you are attracted to someone, you go out and try to win her. You try to have sex with her. Or if you don't want to be a womanizer then you marry her and be faithful forever.

But the point is you don't wait. You just don't do it. Sure, you can wait a few minutes in conversation. Maybe you can wait one or two more dates. But if you continually put off talking about sex, or making a sensual move on her, displaying clearly your desires, you are making a mistake.

The point is closing is everything in dating. If you do not "close" then it is all for nothing, and you are giving her plenty of chances to hook up with someone else. Ideally, you get to the close as soon as possible. Some women will take a little bit longer than others will, but what matters is that you make your move as soon as she begins:

- Displaying positive signals

- Showing signs of comfort in your presence

- Responsive to your suggestions of dating you, or a sex story, etc

- Giving more intimate gestures, showing that she's thinking about you making a move

This is the time to move and the only reason to stop is if she stops you. Maybe she will stop you and embarrass you, but at least she will know you are not afraid—that you are into her. When the opportunity arises, you must take it. A woman is an emotional creature and this is a victory of the moment.

Along the same lines, another reason to think "Close! Close! Close!" as they say in business, is because the more you make small talk after a HUGE emotional moment, the more opportunity she has to become bored with you.

This is another painful fact of dating. Every conversation is going to have a lull, even if you spike it full of good entertainment and great seduction. Your goal is to prevent this lull from happening by closing early.

The longer you take to move from a kiss to sex, or even to move from a hello to a date, the more awkward the situation will become. If you really like a woman the best thing to do is to look for that special opportunity where she is vulnerable and then pounce in the way she has suggested you ought to (according to her own values she revealed).

It is also advised that the more she likes you, the SOONER you should leave. If you leave early, you leave her wanting more. You fill up her positive associations of you and do not leave any more time for negative or less interesting banter. You leave on a high note.

This is not only to prevent the conversation from becoming boring and awkward, but also leaves her with the subconscious idea that **she wants you more than you want her.** This means it is not just the woman making you happy and appeasing what you want. SHE wants you. She is therefore willing to invest in you.

You have successfully communicated mystery and have painted yourself a busy and successful guy. That means she has plenty to admire about you.

101

So the best dating advice you can get is to go for the close as soon as she is willing and then say goodnight right after your "big number", just like any good performer knows.

This is also, why a lot of guys do leave first after sex happens. They may feel themselves weakening in bed, and may want to prevent becoming too nice and mushy, or perhaps even boring their date after a magical night.

The lesson is always leaving on a high note, whetting their appetite for more. The only time you can relax on this rule is if you get what you want and are satisfied. Such as, you go to bed with her. You really do not care if she calls again. Sure, why not stay an extra half hour or you convince her to marry you. Relax a bit after the honeymoon ends. Bore her with your stories. Take it easy a few months and stop thinking about dating seduction.

But yeah…if you're talking about dating and "closing" you can't really sidestep this point. You must have a strategy to immediately move in for closing, after she shows weakness, or you will miss your chance and complain about how fickle women are for years on end.

The Seven-Hour Rule—Is It True?

Many dating coaches believe in the seven-hour rule; namely, that it takes seven hours to thoroughly seduce a woman to the point of intimacy. This does coincide with the theory that a woman knows within a short time of meeting you, if she is ever going to have sex with you. Provided you make a first impression, you have seven hours to capitalize on initial attraction and create feelings of safety and comfort followed by sexual stimulation.

Now this may seem problematic. What if you just meet her coming out of a taxicab? What if you only have one hour before she has to leave? That is what dates are for, of course. The seven-hour rule means that you need seven hours of accumulated time to make a strong impression on her. So she may be able to forget you, and any sexual feelings you give her, if it is one or two hours worth of dating time. However, after she invests a full seven hours, which is practically an entire day of intense conversation, you will have made a strong impact on her emotions and on her long-term memory.

These are total hours, which you can break up into segments of time, as in introduction, date #1, phone conversation; friends hang out, and so on. Once the seven hours is up and you have not made any mistakes, much like college, you graduate to another level.

It is no wonder then that many experienced seducers report that they have sex with their desired woman within a week or even a few days. They know they have to close quickly or else be forgotten, so they spend up their seven hours rapidly, careful about not asking too much or being needy but also careful to monopolize her time when they do meet.

Since we have established that sexual seduction is a very basic process, the majority of these seven hours will be in making her feel comfortable and safe in your presence. You only need an introduction to show her your challenging and flirting side, thereby building attraction. So the entire trust building process is required to lower her resistance towards becoming more intimate with you. When the opportunity presents itself—when she is completely attracted, enamored and turned on and is showing signs of it—you make your move in less than a few minutes.

You may find that if you tamper too much with the natural seven-hour rule, you may meet with resistance. For example, if you go for a quick lay strategy on a woman who is opposed to casual sex, you will alert her that you are a master seducer and will probably be cut off because of her trust issues. Waiting a full seven hours, and making the time up in shorter implements, while focusing more on comfort-building and trust, would be the safer way to plan a strategy.

Even if you do have sex with her within minutes or hours, you may risk running her off, either because she feels ashamed that she was so easy, or she simply categorized you as a one-night stand and nothing more.

The seven-hour period should also be strategy-oriented, meaning you get something specific accomplished each time you see her. You share something, or you spend alone time together, or you tell a story. Eventually you make physical contact. All dating must be goal oriented and there must be a closing, even if it is a relatively small closing for the time being.

In contrast, if you happened to be trapped in an elevator with a woman for seven hours, you would have a full seven hours but it would be a dating marathon—and possibly a nightmare. No wonder guys make themselves scarce and leave frequently on a high note, rather than risk staying too long and exhausting conversations.

Psst. Here is a secret. You know how a lot of guys (maybe like you) feel as if they're not very good at conversation and can't think of funny things to say on command? Guess, what? We are all like that. This is precisely why we remind each other, do not wear out your welcome. No one can keep on the date personality for a literal seven hours. That is why men like to "wear themselves thin" so that they can be amazingly entertaining in short increments.

When those seven hours are up, she should begin showing signs of peaking interest and giving off gestures of vulnerability and sexual curiosity. When this happens, it is your job to put her in the lone wolf position—somewhere isolated and safe, where she can feel comfortable and there is an easy way to have sex without complication (i.e. taking her to your parent's house at the seventh hour is a bad idea. Very few women are going to have sex with you on the side of a building in public, for the first time anyway).

On the other hand, if you go well beyond the seven hour mark without making a move, you may progress into some strange place beyond the friend zone, a dating Twilight Zone, where you will either lose her interest or become one of these complicated guys whom she can't read—and whom she might very well dump for someone else.

If you have tried to bait her but she does not appear to be responding then it is up to you to make a move and to escalate it towards sex. In general, you should avoid making **unsure moves** since your hesitance will show. Besides, no decent guy likes to presume she's ready and just force his way in.

Therefore, make it a rule to not make a strong physical move until she has given you three signals. These might include excessive laughter, lots of touching, and perhaps starting conversations when you stop talking for just a moment.

One standard of kissing and really all of lovemaking is in the 90/10. You want it more, you advance 90% but not without her advancing 10% of the way to show you, she wants it.

If you are less confident about how she feels (but not in yourself, of course) then you can always taunt her to kiss you, with a mysterious question like "Would you like to kiss me?", or if you're escalating beyond a kiss, "Would you like to touch me?"

When you do this, she can either answer:

- "Yes!" which gives you no choice

- "No!" which she does NOT want to say

- Or "I don't know", or "Maybe" or "Why?" or any other chicken answer that you have permission to ignore and then can make the first move yourself.

One part of learning sexual strategy is understanding location change.

Location Change

Location change means you will be changing up the scenery of your date, based upon the shift in mood you are going for. Your first location is simply for arousing interest and starting attraction and it can be anywhere and with anyone.

The second location is when you progress onward to the comfort and trust building stage. You obviously need to take her into a lone wolf sort of environment, and with gradual trust, she will let you. The second location does not have to be isolated and probably should not be, or else she might become suspicious. Instead, make it a point to choose a location where you can talk one-on-one in comfort, such as a restaurant, coffee shop, mall, and so on. It is important you select the location so that you will be more comfortable in this environment.

"Jumping" refers to going from one location to another, usually on the same night you spend with her. This is a good method of clocking more of that proverbial seven hours without fatiguing at the halfway point because of familiar scenery. Moving from location to location keeps her attention, and may even encourage her to chase you, as you "invite" her from one location to the next—leaving it up to her to express interest in seeing you again.

Bouncing means, you leave the current location and invite her to follow you to a better place. This is a clever spin on the traditional "Let's date here and only here," which feels a bit too uptight.

Another variation of this jumping technique is time bridging, where you agree to see each other at a set time—sort of like an official date, except that you play it as a meet up and instead tell her to give you her number. It is a non-date sort of date, and you only use it if you must, namely because the logistics of the traditional bounce are too complicated. Ideally you only bounce, because it is in the "now" and that is what women like. However, a time-set appointment bridge is a last resort rather than risk-losing track of her. When you do make plans, do not ask permission. Simply assume she wants to go, as in "You must come!" or "I will pick you up at..."

Of course, a date is far better than just getting a phone number. After all, who really wants to talk on the phone unless you have to? It is nerve wracking and the pressure is on...and it is all for nothing except another occasion to talk on the phone. Much like the online charade a phone is simply another "bounce", something that gets you from introduction to in-person date.

At some point, you might have to settle for a phone number, but in the best scenario, you date because you are both here and because you are both interested. In other words:

- Do not arrange for next week because you are nervous and want to regroup.

- Do not keep her waiting, thinking this is building attraction.

- A phone number is not really a close. It is just a ticket to pick up where you left off; returning to the closing stage, you want.

So yes, it would be better to bounce around all night and then proceed back to your place or her place for a nightcap and a sleepover because then a phone number would come much easier and would really be a formality by then.

How To Choose A Location

As we said, you are the one that wants to set the location when bouncing around town, because this gives you a certain home field advantage. Furthermore, you want to give her the impression that you are not willing to go out of your way to please her. You are willing to meet somewhere close to where you are already going, to appear just busy enough to attract her. Excuses to meet with her are always good; as this shows that you are not one of those other guys who would bend over backwards just to fawn over her. She really has not earned that honor at this point. Remember that.

You do not brag to her that you don't need her, since this is patronizing. You simply live this philosophy. If she does not want to follow you, then go out and do what you wanted to do anyway.

One of the most important reasons to self-select the location, and especially the sex location (ideally your place so you can immediately feel comfortable) is so you can pre-acquaint her with your bachelor pad long before you ever reach the seduction phase. One common excuse for you to preview your home or apartment is to invite her to meet you at your place and then "forget something" so that the two of you can run up and grab the forgotten item.

That will give your date the opportunity to see your home (hopefully decorated artfully, interestingly, and neither boring nor dirty) and form a positive impression about your tastes.

This immediately squelches the "fear of the unknown" factor that is going to scare most women away from going back to your place later, should you directly ask them. They will know what your place looks like, where it is at in town, and feel secure enough to re-tour the premises. When you do invite her back to your place, keep playing it cool, and determine that you must get up early and that you do not have a lot of time. Strongly suggest to her that you are just talking and are not planning to have sex.

This will give her an additional illusion of comfort. Even if you do want sex, it will seem to her like a spontaneous and mutual decision. The idea is to strategize **each new location** as a specific goal, even something as mundane as going shopping for clothes together can have a goal-oriented purpose. You would do so to "boyfriend" technique her, showing her

105

what a domestic life with you would be like. Another example of a bounce goal might be to take her to a theme park, to further stimulate her emotions and have her associate you with these intense experiences.

To your date, all of this will seem spontaneous and that is what you want. However, a smart man never proceeds this far with someone he really likes without a plan.

Getting Her Relaxed And In Position

By now, the final seduction location will be familiar to her, since she previewed it earlier (Or at the very least you've described it to her). Understand that many of the locations you would choose for comfort building are probably not appropriate for first-time sex, despite all your public sex fantasies (If you want to give them a try, fast-forward to the quick lay chapter and hope for the best).

In most cases, choosing a comfortable and isolated setting is paramount. It must be catered to your mate's comfort, meaning it is private, and it is close to your previous location in distance. Meaning it is not a great feat to get from your living room to your bedroom.

As for the age-old question of "Your place or her place?" you have to determine this case to case, based on the "variables" involved . What could go wrong? When you go to her place, you have no idea what to expect, and what could throw off your game plan. Roommates, pets, parents, phones, passersby- all of these could be major distractions and mood killers for your night out.

When making the not so awkward transition from comfort and pleasure to seduction and sex, remember two things: laughter and intimacy. You already have them and now it is a matter of continuing them both to a higher, escalated level. So you've been laughing all day. For the evening's entertainment maybe you discuss photos or watch a funny movie, accelerating what she already enjoys. Right?

You have already shared intimate hand holding and touching so now you escalate it, perhaps by sharing something, or even sharing each other's germs by using the same cup or the same plate, etc.

From the kiss, which we discussed, and which you may have already enjoyed, you move onto foreplay. Before the actual touch and kiss, comes the decision to have sex. Which simply means, you lead her to the bedroom and you do it with confidence, charisma, sensitivity and firmness. You do it with a strong connection that you feel. You want to emphasize that emotional lock that you have together right now – so don't be overly smart or snarky when you're finally getting to the moment. Just focus on building the tension.

And yes, it helps a lot if you make the first time special. Some guys are really crazy about incense and making their bed look and smell nice. It may seem like a player-like thing to do, but let's face it, it's always going to be better than a woman coming home to a dirty bedroom that looks like a lonely bachelor's man cave.

Speaking gentle commands to your new partner and taking a ritualistic approach to your foreplay is also an erotic approach, one that will please her as it simulates a "couple" and how you and she might interact if you were always together.

106

Sexual Strategy

Quite a few dating books skim over sex because they do not want to go into any graphic detail about what sex is—they presume you're a big boy and already know what goes where. However, keeping a strategy in mind is a good idea.

Men tend to want to escalate sex, zoom past the foreplay and go straight to business like they do in the movies. Obviously, this is a mistake, as the woman wants to feel this is a special moment and wants it to last a reasonably long time—simmering her passion up through foreplay until it hits a boiling point.

Perhaps men are in a hurry because they figure they want to consummate the close before a woman changes her mind. Just for your information, very few women, if any, you are ever going to meet, are going to stop in the heat of the moment even if they do have doubts. They are locked in the emotion of the experience. They want to see this to its end. They might regret it tomorrow (which is something to consider if you are moving too fast) but they are not going to turn you away just because you are pleasuring them to the extreme. However, at some point you are expected to move past respectable kissing and then proceed on into the piggish, brutish and sexist XXX fantasies inside your mind—which by the way you should not be ashamed of...it's perfectly fine to desire a woman's body in a purely sexual way.

In general, you really should play it safe when it comes to foreplay, the exception being, if you share a mutual fantasy that you both have wanted to try. However, if there is no bizarre fetish on both of your minds yet, and you both just want to do the traditional mash up (or whatever you prefer to call it) then conservative is the way to go, and this means safe sex with a condom.

Remember the three C's of sex: Comfort, Casual and Connection.

Even though you are engaging in foreplay and doing the things the old fashion biological way, your goal is to not merely give her great orgasms but to make her STAY comfortable. Do not alarm her. Do not fast-forward to the "good stuff." Make sure she is comfortable with the pace you are going at it and with the setting (And turn off your phone, Dr. House. Seriously).

Next, focus on being casual. Do not make sex an ultra-serious, movie-like escapade where there are groans, moans, and serious eroticism going on. Keep it casual, light, and laugh if you want to, or if she wants to. Do not buy into the illusion that laughter is a mood killer, because it is not. If anything laughing together helps to build trust and take you farther into where you want to go emotionally.

Lastly, maintain the personal connection. Whatever foreplay you give her, you want to make sure it ENHANCES the connection she feels with you. That means that you follow the communication of her body. Listen to her voice, feel the way her body moves. What does she want you to do? Does she seem to respond more favorably when you caress one part of her body? If she is intensifying her moans in one area, that means you stay and you maintain. Sex for the very first time should not be a goal or a race. It is a memory that for your benefit and hers, should be extended.

(And hey, this isn't a book about stamina, but just know the longer you go about extending foreplay, the less you have to "give" in total minutes of staying power)

In general, it is highly recommended that you go for necking as soon as the two of you decide to become physical, because a woman's neck is among her most potent erogenous zones, and yet it does not feel as intense as a boob grab or a genital touch. Plus, it gives you even more time to stimulate her, making her say those all important "little yes!" affirmations before the bigger moves that are coming.

Let her be your guide and react to what she feels.

One note: Do not conclude that you have to lay 1,000 different women in record time to really enjoy your newfound hobby of casual sex (if that is what you want). Seeing the same woman more than once is not only better for sex (since the first time is usually not the most intense, believe it or not, given the newness and unfamiliarity), but there is also a certain eroticism in communicating with someone you've just had sex with, and whom you know you're going to sleep with again. The buildup, the phone messages, the knowing looks and smiles , it is all a unique joy. You should feel no pressure to cease the NSA (No Strings Attached Sex) relationship just because you could move on. The question is, do you really want to?

We will discuss a bit more of that later—that entire moral, ethical thing, and not to mention the pleasant side effect of love that is known to affect a bachelor or two.

Before that however, we know you are still clamoring for more sex talk. How do you have sex in record time with a woman who obviously is not going to keep you waiting? How can you make it without blowing it? And what are the mistakes men make?

Chapter 10

Quick Lays And Easy Sex

Here is the bottom line: do you want sex with anyone or do you want sex with a particular person—perhaps someone you have longed for a long time now? The idea that you can "seduce anyone at anytime" has some truth in it, but there are actually two different concepts within that one exaggerated mantra.

That is:

A: You can make your mind up to do whatever it takes to seduce (or fall in love) with someone, regardless of whom she is.

B: You can seduce a woman at any given time, using the hypnotic and attraction-inducing techniques you have mastered.

As you might guess, these are two very different situations because you may not be able to seduce just any woman within a restricted period, because of the variables in her personality, as well as the unique circumstances you have to deal with.

On the other hand, you could in theory seduce anyone if you were fully committed to becoming an important figure in her life, and dated her according to her own terms.

You also have the capacity to seduce a woman at any given time—but it might not be just any woman, as there are certain types of women who are more open to suggestion regarding casual sex and easy dating than others.

So lesson number one in speed seduction and quick lay strategies is; just how much time do you have and whom are you going after?

As we said previously, there is usually a seven hour (or longer) time commitment before a woman will consider becoming sexually intimate with you, and depending on the woman's own scruples and trust she may make you wait longer than the traditional seven hours of time.

The seven-hour rule usually applies to women that really do not have any dating criteria and are just following their emotions blindly. They are easy to seduce because they typically do not have any code of dating ethics or any "top qualities" they are looking for in a man. They merely want someone who knows how to stimulate romantic feelings. That is the "everywoman" or the common woman you meet, whom you can seduce "at anytime" and perhaps even in record time as we will discuss.

A woman who does have a dating criteria and who wants to see specific things from her date before she becomes intimate will not be as easy to lay on a first or second date. She may require more time.

Of course, not everyone likes to acknowledge this, but there is quite a number of women who do not believe in giving men sex early on, whether that's because of their moral perspective, or because they've read the "rules" which forbid women from surrendering so easily—even if they are turned on.

Smarter Dating, Faster Women

What you want to do at this point in time is learn how to maximize your dating potential and put forth less effort to have the most casual sex possible—that's your basic quick lay strategy. You find a woman who is interested in casual sex and you give her exactly the stimulation that she wants—whether it is fully aggressive or down to earth and patient.

This calls for more efficient date planning rather than meeting someone unique and then wishing that they were predictable and behaved just like the average woman. It is always possible that a normal woman just wants casual sex, just the same as an easy woman, and so your job in "quick lay" dating is to filter out women who are not going to sleep with you right away.

It might help tremendously to identify where exactly you are looking for women:

Casual sex dating is easier if you attend local dating venues such as bars, nightclubs, and the like. Searching venues like grocery stores, churches, or even libraries is going to be a 50/50 toss up or less, since these women have shown no social evidence that they are looking for sex. You will be able to turn them on and bring them into a sexual state, but that is no guarantee that you will sleep with them.

In analyzing the setting for casual sex try to think in terms of realistic sexual potential. What do you have going for you and what can women get out of you?

Most men who are into the playing lifestyle notice five trends when it comes to easy sex:

- Women who have high self-confidence and can handle no-strings-attached affairs, oftentimes "cougars" or older women who are only interested in short-term affairs.

- Women with very low self-esteem who want to feel good about themselves and think of sex and a relationship as personal validation.

- Women recently dumped by their boyfriend or who want to cheat on a significant other; a "rebound" relationship with little or no chance of succeeding long-term.

- Women see some sort of "incentive" in you that promises a future pay off in some material or intangible way.

- Women who have no particular mission or agenda and who are thus susceptible to seduction techniques.

As you might have noticed, you have polar opposite choices : insecure women and highly confident women, both of which want sex for different reasons. However, dating an insecure women can be emotionally difficult, and can be misconstrued as morally dishonest if you must promise or imply things to her you have no intention of fulfilling.

Most players prefer dating self-confident women, who are aware of what short-term relationships consist of, and will usually not play mind games, or try to guilt the player into making a long-term commitment he has no interest in. In contrast, of course, insecure women can be clingy, overly dramatic…or even dangerous in some cases.

110

The good news is that there are plenty of self-confident women and emotionally detached women "who go with the flow" and make sex easy—provided you have all the right moves.

Understanding the psychological dynamic is part of the battle. Many women balk at the idea of being a "slut" or being thought of as easy, and so will avoid giving into sex too soon—even if they don't want a commitment. They will take a wait and see attitude and will brush off one night stand sex if it turns out the guy is not compatible.

If such a woman has high self-confidence and can have sex without worrying about social "slut-shaming" behavior, you have definitely improved your odds.

Lone Wolf vs. Party Animal

There is another dimension to the great pick up location debate. Many men would tell you that it is easier to get laid in a bar or club, because of the physical experiences (dancing and such) not to mention alcohol which lowers a woman's inhibitions.

However, many more players do NOT prefer public places where sex and drinks are already on a woman's mind. Instead, they opt for the lone wolf scenario. They want to pick up women in a place where women **are not expecting it.** This means women are caught off guard and more susceptible to hypnosis and seduction.

In contrast, a bar or club is a scene where women expect to be hit on and are more wise to the game. They may resist a man who pulls off a perfect play, solely because they know he is playing them. They either like the guy's looks or play, or dismiss him right away. It is also a bit difficult to hear in a public place where music is loud and conversation is noisy.

Lone wolf mode favors quiet settings like bookstores, coffee shops, seminars and gyms. You can approach a woman casually, without the dating stigma, and without the rowdy atmosphere of a bar that is either hit or miss.

Niche Dating Online

In speaking of speed dating and casual sex it would be remiss to not consider niche dating, which is primarily an online arrangement nowadays (though a few private clubs might exist locally). This means that because of a peculiar or "niche" interest you share with the other person you are able to enter into a sexual and experimental relationship more easily and usually with less small talking and other preliminaries.

While the online world is littered with fake IDs, users and flaky types, this does help us to understand an important lesson about fast dating: when you are interested in somebody you accentuate your niche interest, perhaps seeking out clubs or public places where the niche interest is discussed. You can either approach the other person as a mentor or a student. Thus, giving the other person a role to play, making more sense of the relationship.

Seduction is made much easier when you share this interest, since you can use the hypnotic and seductive techniques previously mentioned under the guise of a normal conversation about the shared interest. For example, if you both like modern art, you could tell stories with embedded emotional commands about how certain art pieces make you feel, or what the artist was trying to make the audience feel. In this case, not only is the

111

other person relating to your art interest, but also is experiencing a rush of positive emotions with you.

The niche-dating situation is ideal because you really do not have to try very hard to come up with a new and exciting excuse to see the other person. You simply explore the mutual interest and try "bouncing" town to town for a sex strategy.

The Four Types You Can Definitely Score With

Although niche dating and seduction technique are all you need to know, would it really hurt to reveal to you the four types of women statistically more likely to enjoy a casual relationship?

They are:

- Cougars (Sexually experienced, often the aggressor, hesitant to commit)

- College girls (sexually adventurous, susceptible to new ideas and seduction strategies, low commitment)

- Women on the rebound (need reassurance, less interested in mind games and more need a confidence boost; but beware of commitment chasing types)

- Bachelorettes (Women engaged or even at their bachelorette party are far more likely to have an NSA affair because it's their last chance to act recklessly; ironically, while they are easy pickups they do tend to flock together in groups, so high confidence in the approach is required)

The 15 Minute Rule

You know how they always say that a woman knows within a few minutes of meeting a man if she is going to have sex with him? Well, in like manner you can know within 15 minutes if a woman is ready to sleep with you, or if you are wasting your time with quick lay strategies.

By reading her gestures and paying attention to her words, you can tell in less than 15 minutes not only if she's interested in you (short term or long term) but also if she has any major issues about sex—which would be a party pooper for your plans.

There are several factors to pay attention to during those crucial first 15 minutes.

These include:

- Her level of self-esteem

- Her general interest in you

- Her mindset

- Her ideal man (or in some cases ideal scenario)

- Her single status

Whether your date for the night is a good girl playing naughty, or a lifetime bad girl just looking for fun does not really matter. What does matter is her body language and how this suggests to you if she is ready for a casual encounter.

Some gestures are obvious; lots of touching, and even wearing provocative clothing sends a strong message of self-awareness and sexual readiness. It just depends on whether there are any alphas strong enough to move in for the challenge.

On the other hand, you must pry deeper to find out if a woman is merely interested (as in maybe real love or long-term attachment) or actually dying to have casual sex—and just waiting for you to turn on her triggers.

Accept that if a woman wants casual sex, you are not really going to be the "one special guy" she needs to meet—you are only going to be the **guy at the right place and right time**. This may require a shift in your approach. If you can adapt your technique to be "Mister Right Place" (A fun and confident guy to party with) instead of Mr. Deep and Complicated (meaning a long-term and intense relationship) that would prove more effective for a one night stand.

Another 15 minute play to quickly discover her sexual feelings is the sex shout out, or **talking about sex** in a third-person, off-handed manner. Telling a clean but slightly sexual joke, or telling a story about someone else you know, who had casual sex will quickly reveal her feelings towards the idea of a one-night stand. The more confidence she displays after you make the casual mention of sex, the better.

Pay her a sincere compliment. If you are dealing with a woman and a "shield" (as in she's a little reserved, not quite letting on how she feels about you) then measure your compliment and do not over do it. Say something nice and then take note of her reaction—this will immediately let you know her level of self-confidence.

For instance:

Level 1: She denies your compliment and insults herself, indicative of low self-esteem. Easy lay, but probably lots of emotional baggage.

Level 2: Seems embarrassed but takes it. She might blush and look away. Slightly low self-esteem, but not low enough to hurt her or you, maybe just inexperienced in dating.

Level 3: Returns a compliment; this reflects a moderate level of self-confidence, as she takes the compliment easily but still feels the need to reward you for it.

Level 4: She blushes but she keeps eye contact and smiles. Better self-confidence.

Level 5: She thanks you but does not return the compliment. Demonstrates high self-confidence, and probably a neg-hit type of girl who thinks highly of herself.

Level 6: Agreeing with you and not thanking is the highest level, possibly approaching arrogance or at least a major attitude. To some guys. this is a turn off and neg-hit worthy, but for others it demonstrates a woman who can be seduced as long as you play the game on her terms. After all, she thinks she is the star of the show.

113

Other indicators of low self-esteem might include:

- Always wanting a drink, this suggests an inability to relate to people casually and freely without intoxication.

- Wanting to have sex without a condom (Some women might actually suggest this, which is very risky and thus suspect behavior, indicating an over-eagerness to please a man, commitment-desirous, or just a woman who makes reckless decisions).

- Women who want sex with the lights off (Indicates low body image)

- Women who do not like being teased (This could indicate, if not low self-esteem then at least a defiance or uneasiness towards humor and casual sex, which could spell trouble for you).

Let's face it, if most women were okay with casual sex, men probably wouldn't have the "player" reputation. For sure, they would not feel the need to keep secrets, make up fake names, and do all of these other white lie activities.

If anything, you could say that player strategy encourages honesty, because although you are revealing the secrets to seduction, you are actually telling her that you are after casual sex only, you do not want to make any promises, and yet you are self-confident enough to enjoy the experience.

And yes, a lot of women have trust issues and will sleep with you out of "expectation". This is a bad move for you, even though the idea of seducing someone for purely selfish reasons is tempting. We will discuss the ethics of seduction in a later chapter.

What Speed Dating Really Means

Speed dating is not merely accelerated dating, but encompasses Ross Jeffries' teachings of neurolinguistic programming. This is the concept that suggests anyone can be induced or "reprogrammed" to act, based on pre-set conversations which elicit feelings and expectations.

The goal in speed dating is not to talk to a woman, and thus "learn her" as previously stated, but to guide her immediately into a vulnerable or altered state. This teaching assumes that all women are of more or less the same frame of mind. While this might not be true in your experience, it will probably remain true at least for a moderate to large part of the total number you approach. It is human instinct to respond to trigger words and actions, in essence reacting to an emotional "trap."

It is not really unethical—it's just more of a show you put on for her entertainment. It's anti-"connecting" since building a connection is secondary to saying the right words and doing the right actions so as to lead her down a path of logic and feeling.

The right set of moves a casual sex-preferring woman wants does include the following:

Patterning: Stories that describe a state of mind, forcing the woman to assume this state of mind and feel what you tell her to feel. However, it is not just describing exciting things, since this can easily become a spectator activity. In addition to an arousing story, you must also embed commands in your description. The embedded commands are usually direct sentences telling her what to feel—even if hidden under the guise of a neutral statement. Such as, "She could feel the excitement building." The additional words of "she could" were added in to disguise the command, which is "feel the excitement building."

Binder Commands: You can get as creative as you want when using carefully chosen words in your stories, such as binder words, which are more subtle and yet explicitly sexual commands. For instance, the sentence "That's the way to do it. Now with me, I think that…" at first glance appears to be innocent. However, the embedded command "Do it now with me" is perceptible, perhaps even on an unconscious level. The sentences, "Create an opening for it," and "That's a penetrating idea" would be other subtle variations of sexual commands. Pull this off correctly, and she will think she's the one with the dirty mind, which means she must like you.

Weasel Phrases: We discussed these previously and they are binder sentences with even more hidden structure. For example, "Below me" (Blow me); you can embed commands by emphasizing certain syllables of words.

Stacking Realities: Similar to patterning, this involves describing a hypothetical situation or experience and then making it double layered; as in you describing one reality, and then letting her feel that same reality.

Bear in mind, however, that the more open-minded and confident (and horny) the woman is, the less you will have to resort to making a long and complicated play via hypnotic suggestion. In fact, failing to speak directly to her, instead relying on quotes or stories could even paint you as weak. There is a natural "stepping off point" where you stop using the stacking realities or patterning plays, and just be yourself making a move.

According to legend, Ross Jeffries used the patterning technique to actually bring a woman to orgasm. He described a theme park description he saw on a TV documentary. For several paragraphs, he relates the story full of embedded commands telling the woman to feel sexual rhythms (as in, riding, freeing, letting go and others) until he climaxes the story with an orgasmic description. While there is no guarantee that you can literally do this it is safe to say that if you have the patience, the right voice, and the embedded commands clearly in your head, you can build a pattern to a peaking level of arousal and ready a woman for sex.

She will eventually realize what you are doing but will not care, provided you tell the story with passion and without any irony or self-deprecating humor. This technique requires a storyteller's confidence and poise, not to mention a resonating and explosive voice.

How Can I Memorize All These Lines?

A lot of men fear that they can't memorize all these hypnotic scripts and lines, which is a fair consideration. Ideally, you do not want to memorize the lines because it will sound too rehearsed, and you may even forget how the line goes. Ideally, you're going for extemporaneous delivery, not rehearsed material.

Remember these NOTES instead of an actual script.

1. Make your story natural sounding, which means no dramatics or perfunctory statements, as if writing a stage play.

115

2. Highlight the important parts with sincere intonation.

3. **Use your hands** for directional gestures. When you are embedding her to desire you, very subtly point to yourself or even your crotch. When you are embedding a command for her to feel, subtly point to her, showing her "This is your cue."

4. Always be vague rather than extremely specific. Yes, earlier on we spoke of the dangers of being vague when it comes to flirting with women. However, in hypnotic suggestion being vague about stories and logical details works, because now she can fill in the logistical "blanks" with her own imagination. You start off with a few details get increasingly vague in visual description and then focus on the emotions of the experience.

5. Focus not merely on emotion and excitement but on the positive physical sensations your story brings to mind. You start with visual and aural and as soon as naturally possible go into the kinesthetic description. When you describe kinesthetic pleasure, she has two choices: be seduced or leave you. It is very difficult, if not impossible, to listen to an intense story and not feel anything.

6. Adapt your story to her responses. Studying her face and hearing her voice will help you to realize if you are going in the right direction or if you need to alter your "chapters" in your story. Sense her. Do not worry about how you're doing. Follow her to that emotional state and guide her. The more you worry about your performance, rather than feeling comfortable and natural, the worse your story will read.

7. Be persistent with new patterns, if one does not seem to be working. A lot of guys will give up if the pattern doesn't immediately work, and so you have to prove yourself adaptive to her state. You can tell the same story but go into additional details if you see she's cooling off rather than heating up.

A Story Embedded With Commands

Using the previously mentioned guidelines you should tell a story about a sexual experience a friend or a stranger had. It can also be a sex scene in a movie, or a sex scene from a book or magazine article. You talk about a sexual encounter of other people so that the woman listens without resistance. This is one method in the quick lay strategy that is very effective. When you start telling the story you describe it in details using all the senses including the sense of sight, hearing, smelling, touching, and tasting. Also, you would address the feelings that would be felt in such a scene. As you tell the story you embed commands in the story so that the woman hearing it can vividly experience the experience, and feel the sensations that you are describing. You want to steam things up, stimulate arousal, and make the woman have sexual feelings for you. As you describe the story you would say seemingly innocent statements that command the woman to think or feel a certain way. Some examples of these statements are, " you could see", " you could hear", "you could smell", "you could taste", and "you could feel." When you say, "you could feel", you could describe the feelings of touch in the situation, or the emotions involved in the situation.

When describing the story you would say the command and the description after it loudly and with emphasis (louder and more strongly than other parts of the story). You would do so, so that the command sinks in and has an effect on the woman.   For example, when telling a story to a woman you would say, "You could hear her moan with ecstasy as she orgasmed." The command, "You could hear" followed by the description, "her moan with ecstasy as she orgasmed." should be said louder and more strongly than other parts of the story so that it has an effect on a woman and stirs her emotions.

An example of the "you could see" command is, "If you were in the room, you could see the man kissing and fondling the woman's breasts tenderly and with great passion." An example of the "you could feel" using the sense of touch is, "you could feel the soft tender skin of the man's chest as the woman touched it lovingly." An example of the "you could taste" command is, "You could taste the delicious taste of the man's nipple as the woman licked it slowly and erotically. She found the taste so delicious that she repeated licking the man's nipple several times." An example of the "you could smell" command is, "You could smell the appetizing smell of the man's chest flesh as the woman delivered a series of slow, soft, and mild kisses to his chest." An example of the "you could feel" command using emotions is, "You could feel the woman's intense arousal as the man started to penetrate her vagina with his penis slowly; you could feel her intense sexual pleasure as she was breathing heavily during sex."

Another form of command is when you are describing the woman in the story and you say what she is experiencing with her senses or emotions. For example, you could say "she could feel sexual passion", or "she could see the man licking her breast." When you say "feel" and the description that follows it, you are giving the woman the command to feel the emotions you are describing under the guise of an innocent statement, "she could feel sexual passion." When you say "see" and the description that follows it, you are giving the woman the command to see what you are describing under the guise of an innocent statement, "she could see the man licking her breast." Examples of other commands you could give when describing the woman in the story are, "she could taste", "she could hear", and "she could smell." In this situation you want to say the command like "feel" or "see" with the description that follows it loudly and with emphasis (louder and more strongly than other parts of the story). You would do so, so that the woman subconsciously hears the command "feel sexual passion", or "see the man licking her breast." Such commands affect the woman and stir her emotions.

When you are giving the "she could" command or the "you could" command you want to concentrate on the sensations that the woman in the story is experiencing through her senses, including the feelings that she is experiencing. You would do so because the woman hearing the story could relate most to the woman in the story, and not to the man in the story. However, you still describe the sensations and feelings that the man in the story experiences, but you do not emphasize it as much as the sensations and feelings that the woman in the story experiences. You would do so, so that the story is complete and not lacking.

A third method to employ when telling a story is to mention words the man said. Mention them loudly and with emphasis (louder and more strongly than other parts of the story), so that it has an impact on the woman and stirs her emotions. When you say "he said" to quote what the man in the story said, say "he said" softly and in a low voice. When you quote the man in the story this way it sounds as if you are telling the woman those stuff. For example, using this technique if you say, "the man said, 'I want to undress you and make passionate love to you.'", it will sound as if you are telling the woman that you want to undress her and make passionate love to her. You could quote the man in the story saying things to turn the woman in the story on, like terms of affection, or compliments. You could also quote the man in the story saying what he wants to do sexually to the woman in the story. A third way is to quote the man in the story saying things that he is feeling when he is aroused by the woman in the story, or when having sex with the woman in the story. You

117

should concentrate on what the man in the story says, because that is what will turn the woman next to you on. However, you should also say a little bit what the woman in the story is saying so that the story is complete and not lacking. Making the woman feel as if you are telling her stuff to turn her on, what you want to do to her, or what you are feeling when you are aroused or when having sex will make her extremely horny.

When you tell the story start off by describing it with great detail using all the senses. Also, describe the feelings that are being felt. Embed the story with commands as much as possible so that the woman vividly experiences what you are saying. Also, concentrate on describing what the man is telling the woman in the story. You start off describing the story with great detail, but you should become increasingly vague in your descriptions as you progress in the story. As you become vague in your descriptions, you should emphasize and focus on the emotions of the experience. When you become vague in your descriptions and focus on the emotions involved in the experience, the woman can fill in the logistical blanks with her own imagination. When you focus on the emotions involved in the experience the woman will feel extremely horny. She will realize that you are making her horny and will become lustful for you. She will start to fantasize about having passionate sex with you, and will be looking forward to being seduced by you. At this stage you can seduce her for a quick lay by telling her to come to your place to do some activity like watch television, listen to music, or talk.

Why We Must Tell Stories

The ironic thing about player strategy is that in many ways, it is INSTINCTIVE behavior that all men have in common. Consider as the nice guy, the former you, isn't it true that you wanted to demonstrate to a woman your value? You wanted to tell her what a great guy you were, and show her why she should like you.

The same is true in player strategy; the only difference is that you "sneak in the back door" so to speak, by indirectly stating these things through hypnotic suggestion rather than "overtly." When you say things overtly, there is far too much resistance. A woman should not sense you are selling yourself—whether as a nice guy or even as a cocky and arrogant womanizer. She should instead "feel" these attributes.

Overwhelming With Information

Thought binding refers to a process of embedding commands for a woman to open her mind. She is not only feeling something, but is being induced to accept new information that she may not be familiar with. This works on two levels.

First, she begins to learn and allows herself to be guided with your thoughts. This enhances the emotional process, since she is struggling to keep up with the new information you feed her. The more complex the logical process, the more she will adhere to the emotional experiences—meaning she is highly susceptible to your hypnosis.

Some master seduction players even make it a point to confuse the woman hearing the story in a logical context, so that her mind will be overwhelmed with information and she will have no choice but to focus on the emotional experience.

The three most important factors in hypnotic story telling are as follows:
Step 1: Setting up a pleasant scene, something indirect she has no objection to.

Step 2: Implying the mood, she ought to have and guiding her to expected states of mind and kinesthetic reaction.

Step 3: Ordering her to stay in the mood, and to focus on a feeling—not letting it slip away. What ultimately wins her attraction and desire is the fact that you keep her in the mood, the altered state, and do not let her out until you decide to do so.

And of course, never forget that **your own expectations and desire for a positive outcome** is what fuels your sincerity and confidence. Once you start doubting yourself, you fail.

Why You Should Dance

Here is a thought: maybe players who avoid nightclubs don't know how to dance! Because frankly, a man who doesn't dance or who dances poorly will undo any great seduction strategy he has up his sleeve. A dance is more or less a preview of a man's sexual skill and for generations on end, dancing has always been associated with lovemaking. It is a mating call, the roar you have to give that shows your alpha male status. If you plan on meeting women in clubs or bouncing a woman to a club after an initial introduction it pays off to invest in a few dancing lessons.

Dancing is as much an individual art as it is a science of memorizing basic moves. You cannot go too far outside the box where you confuse (and crack up) onlookers with weird dance moves. On the other hand, you DO want to look natural and sexual in your moves, rather than safely dancing a two-step and looking uncomfortable.

Dancing is not really about dancing the right moves like a disco movie. It is more about having confidence and playing with "kino" rhythms. You are not really aiming to dance all night. You are aiming to have:

- Intense eye contact

- The chance to touch her and have her touch you back

- Subtle brushes against her body

And the like. So the ultimate ideal here is to dance just enough so that her interest is piqued and then **get her off the dance floor**. After all, you can't get laid in public or at least not in a "respectable" club. Your goal is to move her off the dance floor and into a more lone-wolf friendly position.

The one exception is great news for the quick lay strategy. Women who are highly responsive to kinesthetic stimulation love to dance. They love to touch you and be touched in return, especially in public, and they are fairly easy to spot. If you can get your dance moves down and maintain confident eye contact with a few "kino" moves then you may be able to have sex with a woman immediately—as in, a car, a bathroom or somewhere close by.

Kino women are not that interested in talking but want aggressive confidence. If you find one of these ladies, you won't have to invest much in storytelling.

119

Grandmaster Approach Explained

We have not spoken in great detail about the Grandmaster Approach because it's not actually a "player's technique", but is more easily defined as a monster aggressive move that occasionally works and sometimes falls flat. In terms of quick lay strategies, it is more likely to work in a club and in a crowded venue than in one on one connection and seduction.

It is comparable to dancing actually, except that you dance with words. You make a "spectacle" of yourself. (More on this shortly)

The Grandmaster strategy however is extremely sex-centered. There is no finesse in it. You simply overwhelm the woman with sexual innuendo. You do not hint—you tell her that you want sex, with her, and you are excessively bold about it.

You are not mean-spirited or lecherous about it mind you, as in an anti-social sort of way. Rather you are funny, likable, smiling and beaming with confidence. However, yes, you only want sex with her and you enjoy shocking her with that news.

The problem, as you can figure, is that a lot of women will take offense to this and decide you are breaking the rules. You will be deemed unworthy and may be slapped or at least rebuffed with a condescending remark.

And you don't care. Because you are "high on life" and your confidence is unbreakable. Your humor and aggressive sexuality may even attract another woman that night—perhaps an insecure woman or a woman who's equally vain and wants to challenge you.

The advantages to the Grand Master play are that:

A. You are extremely confident.

B. You are having fun and women just love to be entertained.

C. You are always in control of the situation. You do not let their reaction affect you.

D. You are not really embedding anything—you are just telling her to think about sex with you directly.

E. You use a lot of kino, meaning touching and perhaps a story telling experience with of course, heavy sexual overtones.

The disadvantages are obvious. Even if a woman is not offended and amused, she will probably only sleep with you as a one-night stand and not take you seriously as a real relationship possibility. Furthermore, even some one-night stand women will avoid you because they NEED emotional connection. Grand Master avoids emotional connection. He is practically distant and wears sexual innuendo as a sort of "guy shield".

How Do I Know If GM Is Working?

Obviously, if a woman is still listening to you, and has not walked off in a huff you have a chance. However, she might be waiting to see if you calm down and go into "seducer mode." This is probably not going to work. Reaching up from Grand Master confidence to

"Seductive Lone Wolf" territory is such a huge jump you might eventually be a disappointment to her.

Needless to say, if you want a quick lay and you're using GM, don't back down. Continue the act until you score or go home with a bruised face. You cannot change mid-maneuver and become someone else. It is not showing "commitment" to the role.

You will notice if it works because the woman will react bashfully most of the time, unless of course she has extremely high self-esteem. (In which case she will probably think you are hiding and unworthy of her) If she does appear shy and blushing that may be a sign that your aggressive moves are working.

Grand Master Advanced Stage

A lot of guys fail to realize that Grand Master doesn't just end the night with the same act, behaving like a brat and demanding sex. He "progresses" onto another stage. Whereas the goal of the seducer is to bring a woman into a comfort zone, the Grand Master has the opposite goal: to take her out of her comfort zone and work her into a sexual rage that she simply has to release.

Besides your preferences for wild sex and jokes, here is your arsenal:

Neg Hitting: You neg-hit her when she says something negative. You train her to respect Grand Master by giving her backhanded or subtly insulting comments, reminding her you are still in control. Do not focus too much on her looks, but instead criticize (in a funny way) her behavior and negative attitude towards you.

Be Vain: Believe it or not, complimenting yourself (even to an absurd degree) is okay in Grand Master style. The idea is that your humor and vanity is so over the top, it's just a performance. She is too busy laughing to be offended. You can also remind her that you are so good, that you could sexually satisfy her in profound ways. There is programming going on here, obviously, but there is nothing too subtle about it.

Story Time: Yes, despite the fact that Grand Master and Seduction Master are two different strategies, when it comes to storytelling hypnosis, the rules apply to both. You can, while in GM mode, tell her a story full of kino or even sexual feelings of these other characters. Be sure to maintain strong eye contact as you reveal all of the details.

Pick Up Lines: Of course, the GM loves pickup lines because they're cheesy, over-the-top, and sex-obsessed. Some classics are "I'm organizing a threesome party for my friend later tonight, want to come?", or "Ever tried one of those extra large condoms?", or "I've named your legs, Christmas and New Year's. Can I see you between the holidays?" It does not really matter if you memorize pickup lines or if you just say a bunch of sexually offensive (but not personally offensive) things to her.

You WANT her to be shocked and to be thinking, "I cannot believe he had the guts to say that to me." You are basically guiding her into an altered state, one that she will eventually enjoy—provided she doesn't run away in terror.

Turning Her Into Your "Slave": For lack of a better expression, you can make this girl into your "slave" (that is the subordinate lover, following the lead of the dominant) by pretending as if she's the one acting sexually aggressive and trying to pick you up. In other words, you

121

are allowed to say she is a "slut" even though you are not actually slut shaming her. You are simply giving her the role of love slave, while you continue being the Grand Master. This master-slave dynamic can be taken to absurd but funny heights, as you program her to think she is the one showing interest in you, all the while you are simply telling her what a slut you want her to be.

Dirty Jokes

Longer stories that end with a sexual punch line work just as well as pickup lines and hypnotic storytelling, especially the longer they are. You lure them into listening to the long story and this gives you a chance to settle her down into a listening state, and then suddenly you deliver a whopper of a punch line, of the dirty variety, and one that usually ends with the woman having sex with you. If you're good you could even work some embedded commands into these silly stories.

For example, the age old telepathic watch joke:

"A man walks into a bar and takes a seat next to a very attractive woman. He gives her a quick glance, and then casually looks at his watch for a moment.

The woman notices this and can't help but ask, "Is your date running late?"

"No," he replies, "I just bought this state-of-the-art watch and I was just testing it."

The woman is intrigued and asks, "A state-of-the-art watch? What's so special about it?"

"It telepathically talks to me," he explains.

"What's it telling you now?"

"Well, it says you're not wearing any panties..."

The woman giggles and replies, "Well it must be broken then, because I am wearing panties!"

The man taps on the face of the watch and explains, "Damn thing must be an hour fast.."

As you can see, there aren't a lot of rules to remember since you can break the rules for this act. You are programming her directly, breaking down her resistance through humor and always approaching her from the sexual state, forcing her to think of you in a sexual way—whether she likes it or not.

Do You Tell A Woman She's Beautiful...Ever?

This leads us to an interesting question. Since you're going all out in GM mode and saying whatever you feel like, should you tell a woman she's beautiful? Usually not. That is not the GM way. The Master would rather tell a woman she is horny and talk about himself rather than flatter a woman and tell her something so emotional and sincere as "You're beautiful."

Why?

It is not necessarily because pickup artists never use the word "beautiful." It is simply that "beautiful" and other images and feelings associated with intense love and longing seem to recall to mind monogamy, commitment, and marriage. Simply put, you should not use these words right away in dating. They will make you sound too much like other guys who flatter and extol women for simply being perfect rather than making her EARN that compliment.

A pickup artist simply knows that "beautiful" is a word he reserves for someone special. She wants to feel special to you before she accepts such a major compliment.

One exception to this rule might be in insincere flattery. Some natural players use terms like sexy and beautiful so mindlessly, that women know not to take them as serious compliments. Guys might use these words as mindless flirting, perhaps even playing a mind game with the woman, complimenting her and then neg-hitting or ignoring her, making her wonder just how interested he is.

The point is, don't ruin quick lay strategies by throwing around "sincere words" you don't mean. It is confusing to a woman who either wants to do you, get to know you, or be entertained by you. And this all goes back to the very first chapter—stop treating strange and attractive women like they're special. Get to know them and start seriously dating before you flatter them beyond all reason. Have some fun first.

The Quality Of Being Excellent

Grand Master is a rather crude interpretation of the old adage "Be excellent in her presence." If you were to guess on what kind of man could make a woman instantly horny and forgo all of this dating seduction theory what would you say?

Gee, if the guy were famous that would probably be the best aphrodisiac. And you would be right.

We discussed having social value earlier on, but for this section we want to focus on "being excellent." If you can demonstrate to her your proficiency in something (tangible or intangible), and something beyond what other men are capable of, you do stand a much better chance of a quick lay. Musicians know this, which is why they invest so much time in their garage bands. Even older and distinguished professors can be excellent in presence by demonstrating their knowledge.

The question is...after you show them your amazing education and alpha male status...what are you doing to transition from Excellent Performance to Sexual Tension? If you do no such transition, then you will make no impact. However, if you can wow them with your alpha male knowledge and then follow it up by using storytelling and summoning up her emotions and passions, you will get laid quickly. Even Grand Master mode coincides with an excellent display. You have performed well...now you want sex. She may oblige you if you really tickled her erotic senses with that performance. You might even say you are playing the celebrity in this instance. You let your art and skills do half the talking. Your art skills are the "dance" you need to rile her up. All that is left is lone wolf, kino and sex.

The Ideal Guy, Not The Nice Guy

Remember when we reviewed eliciting a woman's values and becoming her ultimate dream catch? Well there is a "quick game" for that maneuver too. Instead of taking the time to learn her and reflecting these qualities, you would focus on asking her directly for her "ideal guy." Rather than patiently waiting and eliciting values, simply induce her to give you more details. Make her describe her ideal man in excruciating detail and start revving up her sexual appetite.

Then accelerate it further by asking her what he would do to turn her on, or even what she would do to turn him on. This further fuels her fantasy and hypnotically suggests that she is experiencing this fantasy right now. She will feel everything she describes, in essence, hypnotizing herself.

All that is left is to project this attention onto you by talking to her in her emotionally aroused state. Within a short amount of time (within a minute or two), she will realize that you are the one stimulating her emotions and may even blindly think of you as the "Ideal Man."

At this stage you can seduce the woman for a quick lay. However, you can intensify the quick lay chemistry between both of you by asking the woman what turns her on in bed. As she describes what turns her on in bed, you could ask her more specific questions about what she said. This way she describes in greater detail what turns her on in bed. You would ask questions using the five senses and the feelings she likes to feel during such an encounter. When you do this you could use commands for the five senses and feelings.

The commands are "you could feel", "you could taste", "you could smell", "you could see", and "you could hear." For example, "You could feel the soft skin of his fingers as they touched your breasts tenderly?" Also, you could repeat what she said in more detail as if you are clarifying what she said. When you do this, try to engage all of her senses and feelings. Use commands such as "you could smell", and "you could feel". When she is describing what turns her on in bed, you could make assumptions about other stuff that turn her on in bed so that she corrects you or agrees with you. Also, when making assumptions you want to involve all of her senses and feelings. You should use commands such as "you could feel" in your assumptions to stir her emotions. In any of these instances, when you use a command followed by a description you should say the command and the description louder and stronger than the rest of the story. For instance, "You could feel sexual passion as he touches your vagina.", you would say "You could feel sexual passion" louder and stronger than the rest of the story. You would do so, so that the woman hears the command and it makes an impact on her, stirring her emotions.

You can ask the woman what she likes the man to tell her in bed to turn her on. When you repeat what she says you could repeat the woman's statement loudly and firmly. However, when you say "when he says" to quote the man you say it softly. Let us take the statement "You get sexually aroused when the man tells you, 'I want to be inside you.'" as an example. When you say the statement, you can say "I want to be inside you." louder and stronger than the rest of the story, making it sound as if you are telling the woman next to you that you want to be inside her. The part of the statement, "the man tells you", you would say it softly so that it really sounds like you are telling the woman next to you, "I want to be inside you." in the present. You could mention other phrases to the woman and assume or ask her if they turn her on in bed. This gives you the chance to tell her stuff that you think are erotic and will turn her on, under the guise of an innocent conversation. When you do so you would say the erotic words louder than the rest of the sentence as mentioned earlier, so that it sounds that you are telling her these words.

You could also discuss what she says and does to turn the man on in bed. That will also make her horny, but not as horny as discussing what turns her on in bed. Nevertheless, you should discuss it so that the discussion is complete and not lacking. However, you should focus on what the man does and says to turn her on in bed, since she can relate to that and that makes her extremely sexually aroused.

Doing all these methods will make the woman extremely sexually aroused. At this stage you should be able to seduce the woman to a quick lay, by asking her to come to your place to do an activity like grab a bite, get some drinks, or talk.

This works like a charm for certain types of women, i.e. insecure women who deeply desire a fantasy come true, just as the GM strategy seems to attract party girls.

The main point to remember about the quick lay strategy is to "program her quickly" in the way she best responds to. You won't always discern what that best way is right away, but if you can quickly adapt your strategy and maintain a high level of confidence (all the while pursuing women who actually want casual sex) you will find that women are very often much hornier and indiscriminate than we give them credit for.

Chapter 11

Seduction In A Nutshell

Once you understand seduction, it is no longer mysterious, nor complicated, but simple. Once you practice your seduction skills, they become second nature to you. As a result of practicing your seduction skills, you can do them more effectively.

Where To Meet Beautiful Women To Seduce

Many average guys wonder where they should go to meet beautiful women to seduce. They believe that beautiful women exist at places that they do not have access to. When they see a beautiful woman on the street, or doing a daily activity like shopping at a supermarket, they believe that this woman has to be picked up in a special setting that they do not have access to. For example, if they see a beautiful woman at the supermarket they believe that the only way to pick up such a woman is to meet her at a party, dating service, or be referred to her by a friend or relative. Many average guys fail to realize the truth about where they can meet beautiful women to seduce. The truth about where a guy can meet beautiful women to seduce is anywhere there is beautiful women. It can be in the street, mall, supermarket, liquor store, bar, nightclub, bookstore, park, club, organization, school, or even work.

Well, how can you tell if the woman is willing to be seduced?

Which Woman To Approach To Seduce

There are several ways to pick a woman to seduce when you are walking in the mall, street, or anywhere else where women exist. If you are walking in the mall or street, the best way to pick a woman to seduce is to glance at her eyes when you see her walking towards you. When she glances at you keep looking into her eyes, while smiling a half smile. Try to maintain eye contact, without looking at her from eye to eye, and without glancing away. The smile is not a full smile where your teeth show, it is a half smile where your teeth are completely covered with your lips. About half the time, the woman will not notice you. She will just keep walking, and you will look for the next woman. About a third of the time she will maintain eye contact with you for an instant and then look away. If that happens you should keep walking. In a few cases, the woman will actually look into your eyes and hold eye contact, while returning the smile. If this happens that means you have found a woman that is most likely interested in being seduced. You have just established a direct connection to her brain and emotions. You can proceed with your seduction attempt.

You can use the same technique if you are sitting and women are passing you by. You can also use the same technique if you are walking and you are passing women that are sitting. In addition, you can use the same technique if you are sitting in a room and looking at women that are sitting down in the room.

A second way to pick a woman to seduce is to go after a woman that wears revealing clothes, where her skin shows. The reason is a woman dressed like that is most likely horny and looking for a guy to date. A third way to pick a woman to seduce is to go after a woman that has a good amount of cosmetics on. The reason is that she took time to look good; that means that there is a big possibility that she is looking to attract a man.

Not every woman that maintains eye contact and smiles back to you is looking for a man to seduce here, however there is a big chance that she is looking for a man to seduce her. Also, not every woman that wears revealing clothes, or a lot of cosmetics is looking for a man to seduce her. However, there is a big chance that she is.

What If She Is Looking For A Wealthy Or Handsome Man?

What if you illicit the woman's values, or try to establish her desired state and you find out that she is after a man that is wealthy, or handsome, and you do not have either characteristic. Rather, you are on welfare, unemployed and very ugly. To make the situation worse, what if she wanted a guy that drove an expensive car like the Lamborghini, and you do not even own a car, but ride a bike? Do you just give up on the woman, and say that she is out of your league? Wrong! Experts in female psychology know that looks, fame, and money are insignificant factors for most women. What does matter to a woman is how you make her feel. This is so because the woman makes her decisions based on her emotions.

Therefore, when a woman tells you she is looking for a wealthy guy, what she is subconsciously looking for is to feel safe and protected. So if you make the woman feel safe and protected by establishing the desired state in her by recounting stories that show you as a person that offers protection and safety to others, you will fulfill her subconscious need. She would not care even if you were on welfare. Also, if she told you that she wanted a guy that drove a Lamborghini, if you ride a bike do not sweat it. Subconsciously she is looking for a guy that makes her feel important. So if you establish the desired state in her and make her feel important she won't care that you ride a bike. If she says that she is looking for a man that looks like a movie star, and you are very ugly do not worry. Subconsciously she wants a man that makes her feel comfortable. So if you establish the desired state and make her feel comfortable she won't care even if you are ugly. If she makes it clear that she wants someone that is successful and you are not do not worry even if you are a failure who filed bankruptcy, and are unemployed. What she is looking for subconsciously is a guy that has passion for life. So if you establish the desired state in her and make her feel that you have a passion for life she won't care that you are a failure. If she tells you she is looking for a short guy, she wants to feel comfortable. If she tells you that she is looking for a thin guy she wants to feel comfortable. If she tells you, she is looking for a muscular guy she wants to feel protected. If she tells you she is looking for an athletic guy, she wants someone that has a passion for life.

Relate To Her Wishes

If you find out that the woman you are with is looking for a man that is wealthy or handsome and you are not handsome or wealthy, there is another way to generate chemistry between the both of you. The way to do so is to relate to her desires. You could tell her how you always wanted to be wealthy from the time you were a child, but uncontrollable circumstances prevented you from attaining that goal in adulthood. You would describe in detail the wealthy lifestyle that you had fantasized about, including a detailed description of the expensive possessions you had fantasized of owning. Then you would describe in detail the uncontrollable circumstances and events that lead you to be in your current financial situation. When you do so she will be able to relate to that and feel a connection to you. This connection that she feels to you will make her more attracted to you. It will make her attracted to you despite the fact that you are not wealthy.

127

If you know she wants a handsome man and you are ugly, you can relate to her wish. You could tell her how when you were a child you had always fantasized about growing up and looking like a movie star. You would describe in detail the looks that you had fantasized about, and the lifestyle that those looks would have brought you (like lots of dates with models, and lots of fans chasing you). You would describe how as you grew up, you had to accept reality that you were not going to have such looks. You would describe how you fantasized about getting cosmetic surgery to improve your looks. Then you would describe how you matured and came to the realization that looks are not important. What is important is a person's qualities, who he is. Then you would describe some positive qualities about yourself. A woman will be able to relate to that and feel a connection to you. This felt connection will make her attracted to you despite the fact you are ugly.

Relating To Her Values & Secret Desires

When you are eliciting the woman's values and secret desires if you find some of her values and secret desires you cannot mirror, then you should focus on the ones that you can mirror. Doing so will make her feel a connection with you and very attracted to you. However, the values and the secret desires that you cannot mirror you should relate to them so that there is nothing giving her second thoughts about you.

For example, if the woman is an Olympic athlete that has won gold medals in the past and she really values winning another gold medal in the upcoming Olympics, and you are not an athlete and cannot mirror that value by saying that you want to win a gold medal then you could relate to her value. You could tell her how you always wanted to be an Olympic athlete and win a gold medal, and how events and circumstances prevented you. Then you could tell her how you exercise regularly, and what a fan you are of the sport that she plays (you watch it on television, read about it in magazines, watch it live, play it, etc.). You could tell her what a fan you are of the Olympics and how you admire its athletes. You could tell her how you watch the Olympic athletes train from time to time.

By doing so you relate to the woman's value of winning a gold medal, even if you cannot mirror it. If you mirror her other values and you do not relate to her value of being an Olympic athlete and winning a gold medal, there is a possibility that she might have second thoughts about you. This is because she might want someone that relates to her value of being an Olympic athlete and winning a gold medal. If the woman was an Olympic athlete and never won a medal and her secrete desire is to win a gold medal, then you would relate to her secrete desire the same way. By mirroring or relating to all of the woman's secret desires and values, you make the woman feel you are her soul mate.

Establishing The Desired State

When you watch a horror movie your state of mind changes. You become afraid when you see painful things inflicted upon the characters in the movie. You become afraid despite the fact you are in the cinema with no reason to be afraid. Likewise, if you watch a movie with a sex scene in it you become horny. You become horny because you see the characters in the movie having sex. You become horny despite the fact you are in the cinema with no reason to be horny. The point that I am trying to make is that your state of mind changes based on what you see others are doing to each other.

Therefore, you can establish the desired state in the woman by telling her stories of what you did to other people. (Remember the chart with the 10 traits women look for in men in chapter 7) If the woman wants a wealthy, powerful, or muscular man you can establish the desired state in her by telling her stories of how you made other people feel safe and protected. It does not have to be great exceptional stuff. It can be normal, trivial, and everyday stuff. For instance, you could tell the woman how you made your neighbor's baby feel safe and protected by carrying him in your arms and singing to him when he was crying. Or you could tell the woman how you made an old woman feel safe and protected by helping her cross the street.

If the woman is looking for an intelligent man, you would tell her stories of how you entertained other people. If the woman is looking for a man that is a challenge, you would tell her stories of how you made women feel desirable and how they wanted to please you as a result of it. For example, you would tell the woman about your fat neighbor and how you made her feel desirable by complimenting her on her body and personality. Then you would describe how the woman tried to please you as result of that by baking cookies for you.

If the woman is looking for attentiveness in a man, you would tell her stories of how you always thought of the women that you were dating. If the woman is looking for generosity in a man, you would tell her stories of how you were motivated by altruism. If the woman is looking for sexual experience in a man, you would tell her stories of how you led and educated in bed the women that you previously dated. If the woman is looking for romance in a man, you would tell her stories of how you made the previous women that you dated feel a connection and how supportive you were of them.

If the woman is looking for dominance in a man, you would tell her stories of how you made other people feel important. If the woman is looking for a sense of humor in the man, you would tell her stories of how you made other people feel excited and be their natural self. If the woman is looking for a culturally knowledgeable man, then you would tell her stories of how the women you dated previously you made them feel worldly wise by appreciating their knowledge and discussing worldly wise topics with them. If the woman is looking for a handsome man, you would make her feel comfortable by telling her stories of how you made other people feel comfortable. The more stories you tell to establish the desired state in the woman, the stronger the attraction she will have to you. You would tell stories until you feel you have generated enough attraction in the woman.

She Is Looking For The Best Possible Partner To Reproduce

Evolution put into the female mind a subconscious selection mechanism to help her find the best possible partner to reproduce. This means that a woman's subconscious mind is pushing her to find a man who she believes can protect her, provide for a family, and is worthy of her level of beauty. Remember a woman wants to feel that you are that man. Well, how do you make her feel that you are that man?

It is not by beating up other guys, or bullying other guys. The way you make her feel that you are that man is by showing her that you are a challenge to her. You do not show her that you are easily acquired, because she will quickly grow bored and lose interest. You do not show her that you are completely unattainable, because then she will also lose interest and give up. However, you show her that you are interested in her, but leave her unsure if she acquired you or not. If the woman knows you are interested in her, but is not sure if she acquired you that will make her extremely sexually passionate for you. She will be extremely attracted to you because you are a challenge. A woman values a challenge; she does not value that which comes too easy. It is human nature to want what you cannot have.

129

You make her feel that you are a challenge by using the push-pull technique. By using the push-pull technique, several times during a seduction attempt, you make her feel that you are interested, but leave her unsure if she has acquired you. Using the push-pull technique several times during a seduction attempt allows you to build a lot of attraction with the woman. This is because you activate a full spectrum of powerful emotions in her, in a way that most men never will. The attraction is accompanied with strong sexual tension, because you are activating in the woman a strong sexual drive in a way that most men will never trigger.

You could use the push-pull method at the beginning of the encounter, in the middle of the encounter or at the end of the encounter. You could also use the push-pull method in the middle of trying to establish the desired state, or mirroring values if you so choose. You could also use the push-pull method in the middle of eliciting her secrete desires, or ideal man characteristics if you so choose. The more you use the push-pull method in an encounter the more attraction and sexual attraction you generate in the woman towards you. The push-pull method, if done in a playful teasing way by the man is extremely effective in generating attraction and sexual attraction. Even though an outsider might look at the evening between you and the woman using the push-pull method and think that you were difficult, or challenging, at the end of the evening the woman you are with will go home with a deep, profound feeling of inner satisfaction, and deep attraction to you.

When a woman starts to test a guy by throwing down a challenge, most guys act incorrectly. They just crumble and lose energy. They tell her, "Ok, whatever you want." This makes her bored and lose interest in the guy. What an alpha male should do in such a situation is challenge her back twice as hard, so that the attraction, sexual tension and chemistry in this situation escalates. The woman will find the man a challenge and will be extremely attracted and sexually attracted to him. If you do not understand how to handle a woman when she tests you by throwing down a challenge, you will miss all opportunities to amplify the sexual tension and attraction.

A second way, you could show that you are interested but leave her unsure if she acquired you, is by eliciting her values, her ideal man characteristics, her secrete desires, or establishing her desired state. Either you could use these methods, or a combination of them to show you are interested in her. But you do not show her that she acquired you by not saying things along the following lines: "I am yours.", "You captured my heart.", "I will do anything for you.", "I need you.", or "This is love at first sight." You just show your interest in her and leave her wondering if she acquired you or not. You can use either the push-pull method, or this method, or both methods to make her feel that you are interested but leave her unsure if she acquired you.

You never should be easy, or too "head over heels". You should never show that you are needy, or clingy to a woman. You should never show you are not a challenge to the woman. Doing any of these things when you are trying to seduce a woman will only drive her away from you, making your seduction attempts futile. You always need to present yourself as the prize and a challenge. Doing so will awaken the sexual animal in her, that will want to pounce all over you to satisfy her sexual desires.

What Is Seduction

The average guy sometimes compliments a woman expecting it will bring him closer to sex. It will boost her ego but she will rarely, if eve have sex with him. The average guy sometimes converses with a woman for a length of time talking dull and mundane stuff thinking that will bring him closer to sex with her. It rarely does. The average guy sometimes buys the woman drinks expecting that she will sleep with him for that. It rarely happens.

In fact, there are some women that go to bars with no money accompanied by their female friends, expecting to be wined and dined by the men there. After that, they either give the man a fake number, or ask for his number and never call him. Some might be courteous and give the man their real number, but they will never return his calls. They move on to the next guy that will wine and dine them for free.

The average guy sometimes buys the woman gifts expecting that she will sleep with him for that. She rarely does. Some women ask the guy for gifts seeing how much they can get out of him. They try to get as much expensive gifts as they can from him. When they feel they cannot get any more gifts from him, they do not return his calls anymore. They move on to the next guy that they can suck. The poor fellow ends up with a hole in his pocket and no sex. The average guy sometimes keeps self-depreciating himself in front of the woman expecting that will lead to sex with the woman. It rarely does. A guy sometimes tries to please the woman, doing and saying whatever she wants, as if he is her servant, expecting this will lead to sex. It rarely does.

What is seduction? Seduction is when a man with confidence approaches the woman and takes control of the encounter. He starts with an introduction followed with a conversation. While doing the conversation he tries to create chemistry between him and the woman by either establishing an emotional connection with the woman, or by using the push-pull method. He establishes an emotional connection with the woman by mirroring her values, establishing her desired state, relating to her secret desires, or relating to her ideal man characteristics. He can use either one of these four ways to establish an emotional connection, or a combination of them. The more ways he uses the stronger the emotional connection. If he establishes an emotional connection with the woman, he will be looking within the woman instead of just looking at the surface of the woman. He will be having the woman reveal important stuff about herself, a side that most guys never get to see. This alone will sweep the woman right off her feet and into the man's bed.

The push-pull method if used by the guy especially in a playful teasing way, will activate a strong sexual desire in the woman for him. This is because he will be triggering in her a full spectrum of powerful emotions that most men will never trigger inside of her. Using the push-pull method alone will enable the man to get the woman into bed, and addict her to him. The woman will be addicted to him because he takes her on an emotional roller coaster ride with the push-pull method. She will also be addicted to him because he lets her experience unpredictability with the push-pull method, which is an escape from the humdrum of her everyday life. If the man uses either the emotional connection method, or the push-pull method he will be able to attract and seduce a woman regardless of his physical appearance or financial situation. This is because either method lets the woman feel, and the woman makes her decisions based on her emotions not logic.

If the man uses both methods simultaneously in an encounter, his seductive ability will be greatly maximized. He will be able to seduce and addict a woman to him, regardless of his physical appearance or financial situation. That is why you sometimes see a guy who is a loser with no money, and bad looks with a very pretty and financially secure woman. He is unconsciously using one of these two methods or both to get her attached to him.

131

Although using anchoring, or trance words alone will not lead to sex with the woman, using them with the emotional connection, or the push-pull method will make your seduction attempt more effective. In a nutshell, establishing the emotional connection with the woman, and using the push-pull method are the two most effective ways to seduce a woman. Anytime the man is having resistance from the woman in seducing her, he should try to establish a stronger emotional connection, or to use the push-pull method, or both. Then he should continue trying to seduce her. He should use either method or both methods until the woman does not resist him anymore.

A man should get the woman to emotionally invest in the interaction as much as possible so that she does not flake on him later on. He can have her emotionally invest in the interaction by having her reveal important stuff about herself. He can have her reveal important stuff about herself using the mirroring of values, establishing the desired state, revealing her secret desires, or revealing her ideal man characteristics. The stronger the emotional connection the less likely she will flake on the man. A second way that the man can have the woman emotionally invest in the interaction is by using the push-pull method. Using the push-pull method the man gets the woman to exert effort to get his attention or approval. The more effort she exerts in getting his attention or approval, the less likely she will flake. She has to get his attention and approval because of his negative validation, and positive validation as a judge of her. She has to reveal stuff about herself to get his attention and approval. The more stuff she reveals about herself, to get his attention and approval, the stronger the connection between both of them. The stronger the connection between both of them, the less likely the woman will flake on the man. In conclusion, establishing an emotional connection, and using the push-pull method are the core of seducing a woman.

Quick Lay & Easy Sex

A quick lay is when you have sex with a woman the same day or night you meet her. You are not picky about the woman that you have sex with because it is just a onetime thing, or just casual sex over a period of time. Therefore, you do not bother getting to know her intimately. You do not bother with mirroring her values, establishing the desired state, or learning her secret desires. Your main concern is to quickly find a woman that is after a quick lay like you. You do that by going to a place where your chances of finding quick lays are high like a bar, or nightclub. Then you talk to each woman that you find there that does not have a man with her.

When you talk, your concern is talking of a sexual nature. You should talk about a quick lay experience that a person (friend, relative, stranger, or character in a movie) had. If the woman responds negatively to the story just quickly, move on to the next woman . Do so until you find a woman that responds positively to the story. She can respond positively in many ways including relating to the story, smiling, laughing, or touching you. Other positive ways she could respond to the story is by asking questions about the story, or telling you a similar story. If the woman responds positively to the story that means that the woman most likely is interested in a quick lay, and most likely she is interested in you.

You can create chemistry between you and the woman in a quick lay situation by talking about sexual experiences of other people. You could also talk about sexual scenes you saw in movies, or read about in magazine articles. You could describe sex tips you read in a book, or a magazine article. The more you both talk about sexual experiences of other people (including sex tips you read in a publication or sex scenes in movies or magazine articles), the stronger the quick lay chemistry between both of you. When you talk about the sexual experiences of other people you should embed the story with commands, and engage the woman's five senses and her feelings.

A second method that you could use to create chemistry in a quick lay situation is the Grand Master method. The third method that you could use to create chemistry in a quick lay situation is asking the woman to describe her ideal man. Then you would ask her what her ideal man would do to turn her on, and what she would do to turn him on. At this stage you can seduce the woman for a quick lay. However, you would continue by asking her what turns her on in bed. When she describes what turns her on in bed, you can ask her more questions or make assumptions so that she describes stuff in greater detail. You can also repeat to her what she said in your own words with greater detail and emotion, stirring her emotions. As you talk to her to get her to reveal more details you want to engage all five of her senses and feelings. You want to embed your discussion with commands.

The Grand Master method is not a reliable method, since it does not always work, and sometimes alienates the woman. The two effective methods in creating quick lay chemistry are talking about sexual scenes of other people, or talking about the woman's ideal man, what he does to turn her on, and what turns her on in bed. Both methods are extremely effective, so a person has to decide when he is seducing the woman which method works better on her.

However, the most effective method in creating quick lay chemistry between you and the woman is using a combination of both methods. In the combination method you start by talking about sexual scenes of other people, however once you feel there is enough comfort between both of you, you continue by asking the woman what turns her on in bed (also, you discuss a little bit what she does to turn the man on in bed). When you are having this discussion you engage the woman's five senses and feelings using embedded commands. This method is the most effective because it is filled with sexual talk, and this sexual talk is personalized for the woman towards the end of the discussion. This method creates intense sexual feelings in a woman if done properly. However, one method might be effective on certain women, but on other women another method might be more effective. It is important that the man when seducing the woman he sees which method works better on her.

If the woman resists your seduction attempt in a quick lay strategy just build more chemistry by using the method or combination of methods that you find appropriate. Do so until you feel you have built enough chemistry between the both of you and then try to seduce her again.

What is that? Do you have a less than common scenario and you can't seem to crack the case? Relax....your problems are most likely not that unusual. Consider our next chapter.....

133

Chapter 12

Groups, Sticky Situations, And Other Troubleshooting

Up until now, we have discussed ideal scenarios and somewhat common scenarios that men will statistically encounter. For this chapter, we are going to bring up some unusual situations that may confuse novice players, and perhaps, even more advanced pickup artists. Of course, none of these situations have a perfect answer, only what has been observed to work for others. Let's consider a few questions one by one.

What If She Only Travels In Groups?

If she resists lone wolf strategy, do not be intimidated. It is more challenging to flirt in groups but it also comes with its own advantages. Men who flock together in groups demonstrate social value and paint themselves as fun loving, desirable alphas. So if she wants her flock around, find your own pack of stags and date in groups.

Make sure your group of guys are each successful in their own right and that you're not actually creating a gang of losers. Next, designate a primary and a wingman. The primary initiates conversation and has first dibs on which girl he likes. The old crass saying "bros before hoes" essentially means that once you select the woman you want of a group you don't abuse the trust of your wingman by switching up on him.

As a primary, the man makes it a point to compliment and direct attention to his wingman. You may find that dating in groups is actually far more comfortable than lone wolf dating, since you can always fall back on rapport with your wingman, if the dating conversation doesn't go perfectly well.

You can also use your wingman to give sneaky compliments, passing off your own flattery as the words of your wing-man. Another idea is to discuss your wingman's dating problems ("He just broke up with his girlfriend," or "I want to set him on a blind date") as an excuse to start flirtation dialogue with your new friend.

Women may or may not see through this, but what matters is positive association and non-awkward tension. You can even start touching her when passing on your "friend's compliment" and start flirting early on. Last but not the least, you can even create a bit of a white lie and claim your friend is rich, famous or talented in something. There is lots of "rehearsed" fun you can have, when you have living props to work with.

Dating in groups is a lot of fun, and can work to your advantage if you have multiple friends all looking out for you, and trying to help you get laid by making you look good. (For which you will return the favor later) You can even strategize together, discussing in advance bouncing locations or stories to tell.

One thing to remember is that group dating favors "party animal" conversation. You are either going to approach this as Grand Master (a risk, admittedly) or Mr. Talk Show Host and keep everyone laughing. Group dating is about fun, not serious lone wolf conversation. Do not waste time trying to corner her alone or you will spoil the comfort of the scene.

If she is attracted to you, she will motion for some alone time, or you can try to arrange for a bounce and some "get to know you" alone time later on. For now, enjoy the group dynamic. Also, that seven hour rule still applies. If you consistently see her for seven to ten hours after meeting her, she will begin to crave some one on one attention, at which point you can break up the groups.

You can also opt for some dancing or performance work to stir up her desire for you without long conversation.

How Can I Use Jealousy As A Weapon?

Jealousy works wonders in group settings. Whether you are talking about clubbing with a female "wing-man", or pivot, (a platonic friend who immediately shows you have value as a friend of all women), or hitting on one girl to get the other girl's attention, jealousy is a powerful dating motivator.

Some men even ask along female wings on their dating adventures with the specific goal of inciting jealousy. Women are naturally jealous of each other and will often start "wanting what they cannot have", as soon as they perceive another female threat and your social value. The fireworks are volatile here. By paying attention to subtle displays of jealousy, you may even start to fan the flames and get a little more attention from the woman you like best.

How Do I Approach Groups?

Two main ways: either by focusing on the most boring or least attractive member of the group, or more challenging, trying to appeal to each woman individually. The best way to infiltrate a group (and worry about selecting one later) is to simply get one on your side so that the entire group approves of you. Trying to entertain them all at once is an uphill battle, and essentially, you are performing for an audience—so you have to make it good.

The idea is that you single out one girl to whet the jealousy of all the others in the group. You do not even have to pick the one up, so as long as you grab the group's attention. A group may even assign one of them to you, particularly after you ask which one of them is ____ (the "most" at something). This is a great way to simply earn a place inside the group and break down barriers.

Group dynamics is a great place for humor. Skits, jokes, and one-liners but not GM dirty can go a long way in making the entire group laugh, and thus welcome you into their circle.

Why Not Just Chase After Your Desired Woman In The Group?

Because you want to befriend "the group" first; otherwise, you are allowing obstacles to separate you from the object of your affection. If you single out one woman of the group, that jealousy we spoke of will soar and will actually work to your disadvantage. The group might turn on you and start cutting you down, ruining any chances of your romantic union. Even if your singled-out person does like you, facing the criticism of the group may be too much.

135

Your best bet, as mentioned before, is to befriend one "weak" member platonically or entertain them all, essentially eliminating obstacles by turning them into friends. You are also advised to quickly identify the "alpha" female and befriend her first, so that she doesn't end up not liking you and neg-hitting you (or just blatantly acid-tongue striking you) in front of everybody. The gang leader is usually the mouthy one, the negative one, the most beautiful or the most intelligent.

Why Befriend The "Lesser"?

Simple—because the prettiest women expect to be hit on first. So if you hit on the least attractive member of a group first, the prettiest girl will be provoked and intrigued. She will quickly see you are not like the other guys and will be curious to know why you chose the less beautiful one instead of her. What is it that you are looking for, she will wonder.

How To Turn A Group Into A Lone Wolf Moment

You are correct in assuming you can't do the full seven hours in group therapy. You will eventually have to separate your favorite pick from the group, as too much jealousy is a bad thing and being romantic with one woman as the rest of the group watches is a jealousy-provoking move. This is where having an extra wingman comes into play. He can provide the distraction needed for you to separate your favorite female friend from the rest of the group. You could also tell her that your friend wants some alone time with her friend and thus further paint the illusion that it's time to separate.

It is not a good idea to let her return to the group once you have made some lone wolf progress. The group generally does not respond well to breakups and you will lose all of your momentum by letting her ask permission. Simply reassure her that leaving her friends will not be a big deal and that they will all be okay with it.

You can also take a more direct approach to the situation and simply explain to your preferred date of the group that you want to tell her something in private. When you do get her away from the others, or at least in a one on one conversation with the others nearby, give her a sincere compliment—but fall short of telling her you like her or that she is beautiful. Intrigue her curiosity by giving her a decent compliment favoring something specific about her skills, personality, fashion, or whatever.

What If More Than One Woman In The Group Likes Me?

Play this one carefully because as stated, once you "choose" and decide you like one girl more than the other, this creates a festering ball of jealousy within the group and it will work against you.

The simple answer: entertain and flirt with them both. They will both compete for your attention until one of them relents and goes back to the group, while the other one (usually the eager one) stays with you. You may have to neg-hit or be assertive if both of them try to leave, but you definitely want to hold onto one and not let opportunity pass you by.

What If I Want A Threesome?

Threesomes are possible and if you are in GM mode it's perfectly acceptable to shock them both and say such a line—and risk being slapped and abandoned by both women, as is the GM lifestyle. However, when it comes to "safe seduction" it is generally a bad idea to try and make threesomes **out of groups of female friends**. There's a good reason groups of female friends don't have orgies; they are platonically connected to each other and will typically not have an interest in such a thing. They are more like family than sex friends, and could even be sisters or cousins.

If you are serious about pursuing a threesome, it is better if you:

    (A)   Filter out straight women and instead aim for bisexual girls.

    (B)   Choose two women that do not know each other.

    (C)   Let them know that you do see other girls and are a ladies' man. You can even demonstrate this and activate some jealousy.

    (D)   Introduce girls to each other, essentially making your own gender-neutral group.

    (E)   Flirt with them both, letting them know you are interested in a threesome.

    (F)   Ask if they are bi-curious (which you should at least suspect by now) and escalate sexual tension by playing into a group fantasy. Recall visuals and kino to mind by sending them lesbian and threesome fantasies, in third person if necessary.

    (G)   Bounce to a more comfortable location, or several if necessary.

    (H)   Discuss your shared sexual fantasies outright.

    (I)   Hope for the best, because honestly, this is harder than seducing one woman at a time!

What If She Doesn't "Feel" Anything On My Stories

If you are giving your best hypnosis story and she seems oddly cold or distant, the problem is either that she is consciously resisting you (less likely) or that she simply is too inexperienced to understand the feelings and experiences you are talking about. If you sense this happening you may actually have to find a more common and relatable activity that she can follow along with. Ultimately, hypnotic reprogramming can only be achieved if she understands the premise and does not have any resistance to your set up.

Help, I Can't Talk To Women!

Many men will lament the fact that despite all the good ideas they read in books, when it comes time to actually go and talk to a woman, they seem to hyperventilate, or can't remember any great lines. They are simply too nervous to even start a conversation and no alpha posing can make them unafraid.

Don't sweat it...this happens a lot, and is actually part of the growing up process for men. Unless you were raised in the city and were a janitor at a saloon or brothel, you probably have NOT been exposed to lots of sexy women.

This is fairly normal and most men are a little nervous if they haven't had experience in talking to sexy women. The only way to conquer this phobia is by creating your own gradual exposure therapy to what you fear. You do that by talking to lots of women especially sexy women.

If you seem to have problems thinking of something to say, then do not worry about hypnotic suggestion or player techniques right away. Simply make it a goal to approach a woman in a completely platonic context (which you are good at, right?) just for the **experience** of talking to her.

Step 1:

Do not waste this opportunity. Make up something innocent and non-sexual, such as, telling a woman she dropped something (if she did) or asking for the time. When you do this, make it a point to **look her in the eyes.** Do not run away in terror. Maintain strong, steady eye contact. Smile sincerely. Become accustomed to the experience of talking to a woman just as a friend or even a stranger. Break the fear of the unknown. Try to do this a few times a week, whenever you go out in public.

Step 2: Next, make it a goal to have half of a conversation, or even three-fourths of a conversation with a woman. Do not be content with one question or one sentence. Make it a goal to have a beginning, middle and end discussion of approximately 30-90 seconds. While this will be difficult with random people in a busy location, you can try for longer chats with waitresses, cashiers, librarians and so on. They have to listen to you...and you have to learn how to make small talk with people. If you have trouble with this step do the same thing with men, older women, or younger girls that you have no sexual interest in.

Step 3: We are fairly sure you do at least have a mom, aunt, cousin or some other female relative or friend that you can practice with. Relax, we are not telling you to "pick up" your relative that would be gross. However, maybe it is time you start practicing:

A: Being assertive and saying no, when everyone expects you to say yes.

B: Start having fun and teasing people in general for laughs. You could do that even with family members, and various guys you know. The teasing doesn't have to be sexual. This innocent and non-sexual banter can prepare you for being more comfortable and less "formal" around women.

Step 4: Practice your player strategies online if you are too nervous to try it in person, or if you need a little more experience. Do NOT become a recluse who only plays online. This is just a stepping-stone to better things coming. Typing with a text messenger or email allows you to release inhibitions, think over what you are going to say, and try whatever player technique interests you without the chore of appearing "alpha."

Step 5: When you have successfully managed to talk to women platonically and are becoming accustomed to the idea of regular conversation, it is time to adjust to "player vs. player" mode, to borrow a metaphor. However, rather than approaching a 10, try approaching a 3 or 4, or as low as you need to go for practice. Flirt with someone that you probably would not have any real sexual interest in, just to see how the experience goes.

Note how your voice reacts, how your eyes move, and the reaction of the other woman. In general, it is easier to have sex with 3s and 4s but don't feel obligated. There is no golden rule that says you cannot mindlessly flirt for fun. Just don't go breaking any hearts asking out grannies, okay?

Step 6: Now it is time to up your ante and start talking to better-looking women—7s and above, all the way to 10. Some men just take the band-aid approach and rip their jitters away by going out there and totally improvising. You can say something lame like you are taking a survey about dating, or that you're a shy guy trying to conquer your nervousness about talking to a beautiful woman, or whatever. The point is not so much picking her up but simply going out there and getting used to the idea of talking to a woman—and **controlling the conversation.** Make it a goal to start the conversation, do the most talking, and then finish it with a date possibility or just as friends. The results do not matter...your coming of age experience does. It is time to face your fears.

Step 7: Last but not the least, it's time to get rejected. So many men fail to take a chance because they are desperately afraid of being rejected. We actually did cover various strategies earlier in this book to avoid giving a woman the power to reject. However, for this present moment, we advise you to not be a player but to simply go out there and ask a bunch of women out. Simple action, requiring no thinking. Tell a woman she is beautiful and ask her on a date. Or play the Grand Master role and fail miserably. Or neg-hit some hot blonde and have her yell at you and insult you. It does not matter but you need to get over the fear of rejection. The fear of rejection is actually much worse than the rejection itself. Do not let fear of the unknown multiply and become something truly anti-social and pathetic—like a 50-year-old virgin who cannot talk to women. It is time to grow up!

Help! I Can't Do The Hypnosis Part!

All right, this is a legitimate problem, because let's face it—most guys are not poets or writers, and even fewer guys have lots of experience in public speaking. It is one thing to think up conversation and act super-confident. What about storytelling, reframing and other hypnotic techniques? Would it be embarrassing to try to tell a story and flub your lines?

Well yes, it would and it happens. Ultimately, though, you can learn to practice and perfect any conversation, even if that conversation is telling an interactive story. Let's cover some basics first of all, to try to help you calm your nerves.

A. Do NOT try to come up with some amazing, Oscar-winning screenplay. It is better that your story be commonplace and not feel "made up" to impress her.

B. Do not think of a scenario that would confuse her. Ideally, you want something that she can relate to, that the two of you have in common.

C. Instead of trying to lie your way through an adventure, which is really making it hard on yourself, try to think up stories that **actually happened to you.** If you can recall an experience, during which you felt strong positive emotions that will work just fine.

D. If you have to improvise and tell a story about a situation that is not familiar to you but familiar to her, try your best to empathize with what she feels based on your own experiences in similar but not identical situations.

139

E.   Try to make the story somewhat short but concise and packing a punch. The shorter the story the earlier you can use it.

F.   Lastly, remember that your natural inclination is to think in terms of facts. This is not how a woman thinks. Focus on sensation of the moment and the emotion caused by the experience. Suspense also goes a long way, especially in a story designed to stimulate kino or sexual desire. Think of it as an emotional journey you are taking this person on, not merely an exchange of facts.

For example:

Good Idea: A long time ago, I visited the beach in Galveston and tried to relax for a little while before the sunset. As I began to doze off, I felt a tingling sensation at my feet. I looked up at…

Bad Idea: Yeah, I went to the beach last year. It was cool.

In the "bad idea" example, the man simply tells a fact, not a story. He does not build up to anything. He does not share THE MEMORY. He shares, instead, a factoid about his life. Not nearly as interesting.

Special Story Types

Sometimes the type of story you tell makes all the difference. We already discussed framing (a good way to involve her own feelings and emotions in your interactive story) as well as third person "friend" story, which lowers resistance.

However, other types of stories might be appropriate after you establish some rapport. For example, the "conspiracy" story works as not only a distraction and emotive experience but also lets the two of you share a secret together. This form of shared reality lets her invest in you and feels like she has something special with you; you can create nicknames, inside jokes, and keep exclusive secrets about other people you know. These "endearments" you create together then can help solidify your budding relationship.

One popular variation on the conspiracy story is the "murder-marry-shag" game. It is a player favorite, where he asks his "date" to identify three strangers and then say which of the three she would murder, marry, and shag respectively and the reasons for doing so. This seems fun for her and is a huge clue for you on figuring out her values. You can also customize the game to your own preferences; perhaps even "telling stories" of other people you are watching, based on their behavior.

The vulnerability story is a "type" but also an important factor in all stories you relate to your subjects. The intent is to tell a story that not only produces strong emotions but also paints you as a vulnerable man, something that women will instinctively want to nurture.

Understand, of course, that nice guys jump the gun and may paint themselves as overly vulnerable before ever establishing confidence, power or value. Stories of your vulnerability should follow a rapport building session.

Some popular vulnerability story settings include:

•   Embarrassing stories

140

- First love (childhood regression)

- Pet memories, especially death

- Family members' injuries or the death of major figures in your life

- A secret

- An insecurity that you overcame (Notice, not weakness just emotional vulnerability)

Naturally, this is easy to fake, but you may find you tell a more effective vulnerability story if you search through your own memories for true emotional experiences in your own life. As you will NOT be telling stories of your own weakness, do not bring up ex-girlfriends or other stories that would make her question your ability to cope and function as a strong man.

Jealousy stories, particularly ones in which you involve another woman physically somehow (such as a wing-woman) are very effective. You can tell emotionally evocative stories that **establish fear of loss.** A woman who fears losing you to someone else, as you have value, will be far more motivated to make a play for you—or at the very least keeping you talking.

Ultimately, a girl wants to know that you are choosing her over another contender. It's competitive on a subconscious level. Telling stories of jealousy, hence, is a very effective play, but not until you have already increased her attraction and investment.

Practice Story Telling: It might help if you make it a goal to start telling short stories to women as practice. If you are nervous start small, but talk to someone you are not attracted to, and focus on stimulating emotion. You might even challenge yourself to work in certain "trigger words" into the story to see how the subject responds. Remember when doing any hypnotic talk:

- Slow down and don't rush through the story

- Recall something you know well, so that you don't look for information while summoning emotion

- Speak in a natural but firm volume so you can be heard

- Practice your pitch (tone of voice), power (increases and decreases in volume), and pace (the speed in which you talk) all of which can be varied for effectiveness. The tone is especially effective; remember the "Sexual State", which is to be passionate about what you are saying and to feel the emotions you describe vividly, so much that you pass along this enthusiasm. If you are having sex with a woman, naturally, your voice is not going to be a growl, a monotone, a rasp, or a "public speaking voice." It is going to be slower than normal, guttural and deep-voiced, and tempered with a warm feeling, as if consoling someone in grief. However, keep your smile so that your "state" comes across as positive and intense rather than overly sentimental.

Why Don't Women Like My Job?

Have you had the experience where things seem to be going fine but then she asks you what you do, and then seems disappointed that she asked? This is because you just failed a particularly sneaky test. Women do not really care what you "do", although they might think they really want to know.

They only want to know what you "do", as in the image you want to project to them. Just telling her the unimpressive job that you have, or that you are unemployed is not going to pass her highest quality filter. This is because she does not know how to relate to that, because there is no "story" or projected image. Instead, what you should do is take the opportunity to tell a story, explaining what you wanted to be as a child (regression) followed by the events that happened in your life that led you to be in such a job, or unemployed. If you do so she can understand what your dreams were and how your circumstances led you to such a job or to be unemployed. She can relate to that and feel a connection to you. The connection she feels to you will make her more attracted to you.

If anything, view a woman "asking what you do" as the chance to tell your first story. Get used to the experience and make sure she's eating every mysterious word that comes out of your mouth. Soon enough, you are going to tell her an even better story that's going to make her feel something far more profound.

What If I've Been Friend-Zoned?

Being friend-zoned by a woman you have a sexual interest in, really "sucks" for lack of a better word that conveys the disappointment and frustration you feel right now. It is so easy to run away from these embarrassing memories and those dreadful conversations where your crush shatters your ego.

However, you should know that it is **never too late to try again.**

Here is the problem. Up until now, you have been "friendly" with your crush, probably afraid of introducing any sexual tension because of the fear of rejection. Ironically, you got rejected anyway, so there's really nothing to lose at this point. Your ex now associates you with a certain image, an asexual projection that she simply does not find sexually appealing. You haven't challenged her, you haven't attracted her, and all you've done thus far is try to manipulate her into feeling something you haven't stimulated in her.

Your new goal is to reprogram her to accept the "new you" and challenge her views of what the old you was like. It won't be easy and she will resist re-categorizing you with all she's got. However, you can do the impossible and break out of that friend-zone by following these tips.

- Start dating someone else and let her know. Sometimes simply being sexual, even with someone else, will force your friend to look at you in a new light. Tell a story about your exciting dating adventures and she might become a little green-eyed and actually start thinking about you in a sexual context.

- Stop being nice and asexual in her presence. Be a little difficult, unpredictable, and alpha male, making her aware that "something" has come over you and that you are not going to be the same Mr. Nice Guy you have always been to her.

- It may help to relate your "new personality" with a major event in your life. For example, maybe you just got back from vacation. Maybe you experienced something profound and now see relationships and life in a different way. Share your new wisdom.

- Toy with her curiosity while projecting mystery. Tell her you had a dream about her, and begin pushing/pulling her emotions, making her question whether you really do like her or not.

- Make a conscious effort to talk to her in the sexual state, even if you do not hit on her blatantly at first; stop being afraid of eye contact, touching her, and other kino techniques.

- Invite her out for platonic friend activity, or in groups, and begin a new "seven hour" standard with her, letting her see a new side to you.

- Do not accept any offer to be her "friend." Say you already have enough friends and cut off communication. A time later (approximately two months), you can start over.

It is not easy to rewire a friend's attraction, and many men have failed to do so, since first impressions are so important. However, it can be done with a strategy and a commitment to destroying the patterns that the old you set in motion.

Help, This Woman is Getting Wise to Me!

Indeed, a woman who begins to see through a player's techniques is oftentimes the most intimidating adversary. After deflecting the "witch shield" a girl might put up to scare off lightweight guys, you may be surprised to see her shooting down your neg-hits, hypno-stories and teasing scenarios and instead saying:

"Why are you asking all of these questions?"

Or

"Are you trying to pick me up?" or even worse, *"Are you a player?"*

Whatever your instincts are, they are probably incorrect. No, you do not admit you're a player. No, you do not deny you're a player, nor do you go on the offensive then this shows weakness. You don't explain the "rules" that you've read, because that's like admitting you need "Cyrano" to win Roxanne…and you're the clumsy Christian de Neuvillette (If you need a literary reference!).

This is obviously a move of aggression so if you are thinking a neg-hit is the best way to play it, you're on the right track. However, stick to the subject at hand and don't needlessly insult her. As to the question, "Why are you…?", simply explain that you are trying to get to know her (an innocent gesture) and want to know if she is the type of person worth getting to know. (A neg hit and a means of giving validation)

If you don't want to neg, or even better yet want to just follow up a neg with a compliment, explain that you enjoy talking to women like her who _____ (a sincere compliment, preferably about her "positive" personality traits and not just her looks).

143

At this point, she will both accept your answer and move on, or she will continue her defensive attack and ask if you are a player or are trying to seduce her. (Or any other variation on the question/comment, showing that she knows you are a womanizer)

Once again, do not answer her question. Instead, continue the flow of conversation. This is a good time to be mysterious and to not reveal that you are either a womanizer or a shy boy. She might want one but not the other. A lot of women have major issues with players...then again, a lot of women are intrigued by the challenge of a player. So rather than commit to one of the two, it's best to simply throw the third degree back at her, and ask why it's wrong of you to just get to know her—an altruistic thing to do.

A neg-hit (Are you worth my time here?) and a compliment later (You seem interesting...) are usually enough to calm her defenses. Women who are wise to player strategy are either cool with it or they're psychotically paranoid and mistrusting.

If you are really committed to winning a woman over, reaching the heart of an anti-player will be a long and arduous process of building comfort and trust and assuring her that she is the only one you want. Naturally, most players do not waste time with a woman who hates the game so much—it is just trouble waiting to happen.

If the woman is rejecting your story every time and turning your open-ended "Have you ever..." questions into yes or no responses, then try reframing the same story but in the third person—as in a friend of yours. Sometimes women become very defensive when you talk in second person or first person.

But The Woman I'm Interested In Is Older Than I Am!

The problem only occurs when one of you has a problem with the age difference. Provided you are acting like an alpha, you are not ashamed of your desire, the older woman should be flattered at your attention—even if she is not ultimately interested. The idea that May December relationships offend some people may be just the bad boy game you need to entice an older woman into a fun relationship.

You may find more difficulty picking up younger women actually, who oftentimes have an inflated sense of self-worth and are deserving of some neg-hits. What works even better though is reframing her "concerns" about the age difference and telling her a hypnotic story, or giving her a second-person conversation about the pleasures of dating an older and experienced man.

If the younger woman continues to hold up her shield then neg-hit her back down, suggesting that it's her flaw that she doesn't have an open mind, and that frankly, she doesn't qualify in your mind because of a lack of intelligence, maturity, experience, and so on. If you remain confident and showcase your positives (in fact you turn all negatives she says into a positive for you) you may find that younger women are remarkably naïve after voicing their initial concerns—they just need to learn some respect, that is all.

What If I Exaggerate The Truth (White Lie) When Mirroring Her Values, Becoming Her Ideal Guy, Relating To Her Secret Desires, Or Establishing The Desired State, Won't I Attract A Person I Am Not Compatible With?

When you are mirroring her values, becoming her ideal guy, relating to her secret desires, or establishing the desired state you should do your best to use experiences and qualities that you do possess since you can describe them more convincingly than made up ones. However, if you find that you need more qualities and experiences that you do not have to form an emotional connection with a woman it is okay to make them up. However, make an earnest effort to sound convincing when you relate them to the woman. Also, make an earnest effort to remember the qualities and experiences that you made up so that you do not make a mistake while speaking later on and contradict yourself coming off as a liar.

 If you can remember the qualities and experiences you made up and there is no way for the woman to find out that you made them up then it is ok. You should not worry about attracting the wrong match if you do so since if you are looking to find someone 100% exactly like you, you may never find such a person. What matters is that you want to be with that person and are willing to do whatever it takes to be with that person. That is the stuff that a successful seduction and a successful relationship are made of.

 (By the way people are always changing. For example, a stingy person can become generous, and a rude person can become polite. Also, people are always experiencing new experiences. For example, you can help that old lady across the street anytime in the future, or you can fly to Paris anytime in the future.) (Never lie about physical things she can find out the truth about, like your wealth, health, who your family is, etc....)

When To Call Her?

If you got her number and you did not have enough time to chat and use seductive techniques on her (like creating an emotional connection and the push-pull method) you should call her the same day. You should call her the same day if you met her in the afternoon or morning. However, you should call her the next day in the morning if you got her number in the evening. The reason is you want to call when she is still in that positive state of mind towards you. You do not want her to cool down towards you.

However, if you met her and spent a lot of time together talking and using seductive techniques on her (like creating an emotional connection and the push-pull method),and then she gave you her number, then you should call her by the third day. You want to call her by the third day or before so that she is still in that positive state of mind towards you. You do not want to wait more than three days so that she does not cool down towards you. You should follow this three day rule until you have slept with her. After that call when you see fit.

When To Have Sex?

In a regular seduction the general consensus is to have sex by the third to fifth date. A significant number of women have sex on the first or second date from time to time. After the fifth date if the woman does not have sex most guys give up on her. However, you can wait more than the fifth date to have sex if she is worth it. In a quick lay scenario you should have sex that same day.

Who Pays On The Date?

The general consensus is that the man pays for the first date, and after that the couple goes dutch. (dutch means that each one pays for himself) You should pay for the first date, however from the second date onward go dutch. The fact that the woman is paying

145

for her share makes her more invested in the relationship, and enhances your ability to seduce her. If you pay for her on the second date and onward it will make you seem as if you are supplicating to her and not a challenge which will work against you. If you make her pay her way from the second date onward you will seem a challenge, and an alpha male.

Do I Buy Her Drinks?

If you met a woman at a club or bar you do not buy her drinks if you have not had a chance to talk to her enough and have not had a chance to use seduction techniques on her sufficiently. If she asks you to buy her a drink tell her that you will buy her a drink after you know her more. You do so because if you buy her drinks before you have talked enough with her and used seduction techniques on her sufficiently then you will be like the average guy that is supplicating to her. That will hinder your ability to seduce her. If you tell her that you will buy her a drink after you know her more that will make you seem like a challenge, like an alpha male. It will make her attracted to you.

If she has to leave before you have a chance to talk enough then tell her that you both should meet sometime this week at a bar, over coffee, or at a restaurant and that this time it is your invitation (meaning that you are paying for both). Then you could tell her to give you her number so that you both schedule a time. (Try to do at least one push-pull, mirroring of values, becoming her ideal guy, relating to her secret desires, or establishing the desired state before attempting to get her number. The more you can do the better. Doing at least one of these seduction techniques before attempting to get her number will increase your chances of getting her number.) You tell her that the next time it is your invitation because you want to show that you are willing to pay for the first date, and that you are not a miser. If she does not give you her number that means that she was after free drinks, you did not miss out on anything.

After you have talked to the woman sufficiently and used seduction techniques on her sufficiently then you can buy her drinks. You do so because this might be your first date that could lead to sex that same evening. Even if it does not lead to sex that same evening that is your first date if you spend enough time together and you buy her drinks.

Dating Committed Women

Whether you are talking to a woman with a boyfriend, a bunch of "guy friends" or even a husband, there are some players who stay clear of a taken woman. We will discuss a little bit about ethics in the next chapter. For now, we are simply going to explain how you do it, you know, for educational purposes.

First, understand why women are taken in the first place. Not all women are "happily together" with someone. Sometimes a woman dates a nice guy and gradually settles on him, figuring it's the best she can do. Sometimes she marries a guy who is persistent but who does not really do anything for her. Sometimes she is just horny and wants to cheat on her man, or maybe she is thinking of breaking up with him and you are in the right place at the right time.

There are two basic strategies to picking up attached women:

A.   Hit on her and ignore her when she says she has a boyfriend, showing you really do not care.

146

B. Prove to be a superior man than her boyfriend and win her over.

Most players do not even ask if a woman is taken because they don't care. They are locked in the moment and want a date. The woman is usually the first to bring the subject up and instead of actually saying, "I'm not interested...", she usually says it as a shield, hoping you'll leave her alone. What she is actually doing is friend zoning you, and filtering you out. Little does she know you are an alpha male and know the perfect way to put down shields.

Technique 1: **Ignore her yammering about her boyfriend.** She may be doing it out of instinct, or simply to warn you. If you ignore it, she may drop the subject entirely.

Technique 2: Become her friend. This is tricky, because ideally, you don't want to be her friend, and you're not going to be. However, giving her the illusion that you don't care if she has a boyfriend—because you're just getting to know her platonically—is a great defense. What kind of crazy person doesn't want another friend, anyway?

Technique 3: Use some comedy to lighten up the moment. You can mock-complain that she is telling you all her problems, or hitting on you, or whatever. The idea is that you're downplaying the "dreaded confession" and laughing it off. It is not a big deal and it is not the point of your conversation, or so she thinks.

Technique 4: **Make her question her loyalty.** Putting doubt in a woman's mind about her loyalty to her man is surprisingly easy. Just think of how many women are in relationships right now because they think they "have to be" or they just rather evolved into a relationship. How many of them really have passionate romances? How many are actually in lust or love with the man they are with? You may be surprised at how few of them are that excited about their status. You could raise doubt by simply asking if she's *really happy* with the guy, or far more subtly, ask her about him and let her explain—usually in very bored, generic terms—what an interesting fellow he is. (And he's usually not, and she knows this)

Technique 5: Question the *commitment* of her relationship. You do not have to question her boyfriend's prime quality if you don't want to—who knows, maybe she's dating a millionaire celebrity, which is a pretty big deal. On the other hand, you can raise the same amount of doubt by simply asking or assuming that it is **really serious**. Now watch in amusement as she downplays how serious it is. By simply joking that she's getting married or is seriously committed, she will feel trapped and be reminded of everything she doesn't like about the guy.

Technique 6: Reframe the situation using subtle hypnosis to tell her how "happy she is", and explicitly remind her of how complete and satisfying the relationship is for her. Once again, as you describe the perfect relationship, she will be reminded of just how lacking it is and how she wants to find something better.

Technique 7: Befriend her guy. This is not a great move, but some players have found success by actually befriending the guy and the girl and then subtly criticizing the guy in front of the girl, making her see all of his flaws. When a woman has a man, you not only become her ideal man, but show her why her present guy is not right for her.

Technique 8: Alienate the boyfriend. This brutal move works well, since your primary goal is to change her perception of her man into a villain. This works very well when her significant other is not present, and is often out of the picture. You can accuse him of having negative qualities (raise her paranoia by telling her he is probably cheating). This raises doubt immediately, as every woman has a jealous streak.

Technique 9: **Use some friendly fire on the boyfriend.** Coming on too strong will alert her to your womanizing ways, and will probably be a mood killer. This is why most guys criticize the competition very subtly, pretending as if they are making excuses for him and are on his side (You SHOULD stay with him!), even though they are actually planting seeds of doubt into her mind at every turn.

Technique 10: Finish her off with storytelling. Namely, a third person hypnotic session talking about a friend who found out her boyfriend was cheating, and how devastated she felt. In this story, you are actually programming her to feel great doubt.

Technique 11: If she still wants to spill let her. Ask about her ex-boyfriends and previous relationship and find out if there are any patterns. For example, does she tend to chase after cheaters, or get with guys who don't complete or challenge her. You can add fuel to the fire by talking about positive experiences, hers or your friend's, in which breaking up was the right thing to do. Associate positive things with leaving him, or cheating on him, and assign negative feelings to waiting and remaining loyal.

Technique 12: Continue embedding commands and keeping the feeling going. The best way to do this might well be to recall a past relationship and how satisfying it was, in comparison to what she has now. Perhaps an ex-boyfriend, or if she has none, just speaking about grand romances like she sees in the movies. Talk about the intimate and intense positive feelings she enjoyed, and get her to recall them as if they were happening now. The general idea is that women remember things in the past far more intensely and positively than the current. Furthermore, a lot of women want what they can't have, and so the idea of a hot ex-boyfriend Is oftentimes more appealing than a current boyfriend who is boring.

Technique 13: Begin touching, right after summoning up volatile feelings. Try kino moves like a massage, backrub, hand holding, or whatever it feels like she needs from you. She will already feel attracted to you, but will be waiting for you to make the first move, going from emotional storytelling to physical sensation. You never really have to tell her that you want to steal her away—it just happens. Just like she wants it too.

How Do I Know If She Likes Me?

Of course, not every woman is going to fall for this routine, especially if they DO have a boyfriend that completes them. There is a good chance that no matter what you say, she will reject you because she is not looking to cheat, breakup, or entertain doubts in her relationship. So gauge her reaction carefully to see how interested she is, when you give her the routine.

Note her:

- Positive and encouraging body language

- How eager she is to talk about her guy

- How willing she is to open up about her problems and treat you like her therapist

- She subconsciously creates the opportunity to spend time with you (she may invite you somewhere or remain open to the possibility to see you again).

- She admits to cheating in the past, or that she has thought about it. (Or breaking up with him) This may very well be foreshadowing for what she is trying to find the courage to do.

The very idea of seeing you again will be highly erotic to her and in many cases, she will be highly aroused at all of the visuals and thoughts you feed to her. Committed women oftentimes fall into sexual routines and may be sexually frustrated with their lover. They already have a boyfriend, and so are ONLY interested in sex—, which may even be a catalyst for breaking up with the other guy. This is your ideal situation because most women, who are committed, are probably not going to want a firm commitment from you. They only want sex, and so they are more interested in performance than your "ideal man qualities."

Of course, the entire relationship lives or dies based on the illusion of friendship. She may even "hit on you" first, bragging that she has a boyfriend. However, she will never actually tell you she wants to cheat or would be willing to cheat. She wants it to be YOUR move, to seduce her and give her no other option.

She may even say she has a guy already as a means of releasing her culpability in the situation. She told you she had someone, was attached, and so it is your fault for pursuing her even though you knew her story. It is weird female logic but it is usually what happens.

This may also require that you come up with excuses on why you want to see her again, that are not blatantly sexual. As we said in the earlier chapter about sex, a woman must always be able to rationalize that she's not dating you, not going to have sex with you, and that she's still the good girl everyone thinks she is.

If you help her with the excuse, (inventing dumb reasons to see each other again) you will probably have an easier time securing plans, as she can always make excuses to herself and feel okay about her new friendship.

Essentially the formula is inspire doubt and then give her the (sexual) ideal boyfriend that she wants. You assume the good boyfriend's characteristics. You are always there. You are fun. You are available. You are easy to talk to and adventurous.

Why, it is so easy...you might as well just start seducing everybody! Married women, friends of friends, your buddy's friends, lonely women, women who just broke up...

Wait a minute now. Is there such a thing as ethics in dating and seduction? What a coincidence—that is the subject of our next chapter.

149

Chapter 13

This Thing Called Love...Take It Or Leave It

Love means many things to many different people. Some people think of love as perfect "soul mate chemistry." Some believe love is just lust and that it is a lie we all tell to ourselves. Some people expound upon the qualities of love beyond romantic affection—as in agape love, or the love of your fellow human being.

Indeed, there are different categories of love. What you feel for a woman whom you truly are compatible with, and learn to respect and desire to take care of, is going to be different than "loving" the feeling of quick lay sex with a hot girl you met one crazy night.

And this type of love is different than the love you have for family and for your friends. You will find as you mature in life that different people merit different kinds of love. You may meet people you will never speak to again. On the other hand, you may also meet very special friends—some of whom will be women, who you still want to be friends with even after the romance ends.

Life is a bit unpredictable and so people continue to define love for themselves, interpreting what they "want" from dating in very different ways.

Are You A Male Slut?

Isn't it interesting how you hardly ever hear about guy slut shaming. Slut is an offensive term that is often used to demean women who are sexually active. However, it seems as if men have a free pass to sleep around until they finally decide to settle in with just one woman.

The truth is that all of this shaming talk is ridiculous. No one should be forced to be sexually celibate, nor should anyone be forced to be sexually active against their will. We all have highly individual preferences for sexuality based on our genetics, environment, and experiences in life.

One of the first things you realize as you mature is that the more people you meet, the more bizarre sexual stories you hear about. If you really do make plans to meet a lot of single women you may be surprised to learn that some women are:

- Waiting for marriage, and they do not want sex. (Yeah, really)

- Some women are insatiably horny and are natural born cheaters even when they are with somebody.

- Some women don't want to be seduced at all. They want to meet someone that is compatible with them.

- Some women only date players, even though they may harass you for using seductive techniques.

- Some women will expect commitment from you, immediately after sex.

- Some women will forget your name despite doing terrible-wonderful things to you in bed.

And the list goes on. You cannot really group all women into a single category, because although they all do think similarly, very different backgrounds produce different variables. One of the points we made very early on is that a womanizer does not memorize strategies, as much as he learns a woman's personality, adapts to it, and uses basic seduction principles to guide him.

So the question is, now that you are aware of your power as an alpha male and master seducer...are you going to sleep around and score with all sorts of women? A lot of men surely do want to, and make it a sport. They figure, they have learned the magic combination and are now having sex with all sorts of beautiful women...

Why settle down now? Why leave the party just as you are having fun? Suddenly, the prettiest girl they once thought was the most intimidating girl in the world is JUST a person—nothing out of this world. The morning after, the guy might even feel a bit commitment phobic.

After all, what does the girl have to offer HIM, now that he has had sex with her, and does not feel that extreme attraction that he felt before? Now she has to measure up to his high standards. And they may be too high for most women.

It is a reversal of the typical dating process, and to some men (especially ones who have had difficulty picking up women before seduction strategy) it is comeuppance, fair play, and perhaps even "revenge."

Other men, however, may see all of these mind games as pointless. They still use the seduction strategies and flirting techniques, but it is with a different aim than just "conquer all women." They might realize:

- Now that they have power and charm, they do not want to sleep with every woman they meet.

- They may only want to attract a certain type of woman, one who has the ideal criteria.

- Getting sexually involved with a number of women is not always the great fantasy they envisioned at one time. It's emotionally vexing for them.

- Logistically, they want to be careful about getting involved with unstable women; i.e. giving out real names, home addresses, phone numbers, and so on.

So what we often tell people is that BEFORE you date, and before you put on your game face to "seduce" a woman's mind and body, decide what you want out of this experience.

Decide if you want casual sex or a relationship, and do not meander after the fact. It is natural for some guys to have sex with a girl then feel guilty or vulnerable, and then jump into a commitment with her —a commitment they might not even want.

151

On the other hand, some men take it way too far—to even misogynistic levels and they actually prey on insecure women and treat them abusively. It is a very ugly motivation and not at all what dating should be about.

Dating should be about mutual pleasure. Everything a player does is for **a woman's pleasure.** A lot of guys still don't get this. They figure, they want to be a jerk who is successful with women and not a loser nice guy. What they do not realize is that players can be "nice guys" who just happen to know **how to play the game.** They know what women want and what they don't want.

Why Do People Hate The Player And The Game?

This brings us to an interesting point. If player strategy is giving women what they want, why do women "hate the game and hate players?" They may actually hate the idea of seduction only because so many media sources have given it a bad reputation. As in "Men hypnotizing women to have sex with them!" which is ridiculous. All seduction techniques, even the most sneaky and subversive, are merely evoking feelings that a woman already has—**and that she has perfect control over.**

There is no hypno trance you can pull to force a woman to have sex with you against her will. Not even Sigmund Freud could pull that off, since all of his hypnosis patients **volunteered** to undergo his experiments. Forced hypnosis is the stuff of science fiction, honestly.

So at the heart of seduction strategy is the fact that a woman WANTS to be seduced. If she did not want it, rest assured, she would end communication with you. This is precisely why we have to admit, it is not possible to have sex with any woman at any time, because such a thing would be illegal and immoral.

Another reason why women hate the "game" is because quite frankly, they resent the fact that smart men have taken power and control away from beautiful women. Of course, women want to stay in control of every situation. They love the filtering process and friend-zoning guy after guy who doesn't meet their high standards. It is an ego boost for sure.

So the idea of an alpha male that comes along and breaks through a woman's "shield" and acts confident and cocky, as if he's doing her a favor, sure it provokes a lot of women. They resent that men can LEARN these techniques, rather than just naturally have the power to please a woman. But hey, information and knowledge should always be free…to the "elite" and to the common man.

Is Seduction Offensive To Women?

What about women who say that "patterns" and stories are manipulative and offensive? That depends. "Manipulation" is merely what EVERYBODY does in dating. A nice guy "manipulates" women by buying them gifts, and trying to sell them on what a great, asexual, non-threatening presence he is. That is one form of manipulation.

Manipulation is ultimately communication, and one person trying to persuade another person to see his or her point of view. It is called "sales" in the business world. It is called evangelism or persuasion in religion and politics. And guess what…it's just part of human nature. We all want to persuade other people to see things from our point of view.

As far as seduction being "offensive", that would only be true if the other person was **offended by sex**, which is what a player wants…and ultimately, what the woman wants who has sex with the player. If a woman is offended by casual sex, why is she having casual sex in the first place? If anything, she resents the idea that even a geeky looking, or slightly overweight guy can make the same sexy moves as a hot movie star and get laid just the same. It is sexual discrimination against less peripherally satisfying men. That doesn't seem fair, does it?

Seducing a woman is not a crime—it is a gift. You are giving her the gift of an exciting, erotic and unpredictable relationship. Believe it or not, she will thank you for it long after the relationship ends. Women love those "once in a lifetime" affairs that are purely sexual.

What about the idea that seduction theory reflects badly on the guy—as if he can't win over a woman by just being himself? Well, frankly very few people are completely "themselves" when they start dating. They usually put their best foot forward and project the image of success, happiness and excitement. That is just what we do naturally.

A player goes one-step further than just being himself. He becomes the man **the woman wants to be with**. He fulfills the role, not lacking in his own life, but what is lacking in HER life. She is the one who wants to be entertained. He is entertaining her. What is the problem?

What about the common complaint that you are "Talking at a girl and not to her?" Here is the beauty of it all. While one can argue that patterns are "scripted" and not real connection, you have the OPTION to really connect with the girl or just feed her the patterns she wants to hear for casual sex. The choice is yours and hers. You both have the option to really connect, or if one or both of you decide it is not real compatibility, you simply have sex and forget about each other.

What seduction theory is, is basically leveling up the playing field. She has a beautiful face and body, and has the potential to "cast illusions" to a guy making him think she really likes him. Likewise, he has the potential to cast illusions to a girl and make her think he is Casa Nova himself. Women use their beauty wisely. Men use their brains wisely.

Lastly, understand that there are going to be rude and unscrupulous people who use seduction principles for selfish and mean-spirited purposes. That is just life, and that applies for both men and women. We wish everyone could be kind and respectful of each other, but it does not happen in the real world.

This brings us up to the next point…

Respecting Women The Player's Way

You DO owe women a certain level of respect when it comes to dating and seduction. There will be many players who disregard these rules of etiquette and will reflect badly on the whole game. They give seduction a bad reputation because they treat women badly. This does not have to be you. You can still be a respectable man who women like, even though they cannot "catch" you and marry you on a whim.

The rules of etiquette are simple:

153

- Do not lie, ever. There is never a need to lie or to pretend you are somebody you're not. Frankly, the whole "I'm an agent from Hollywood and can get you modeling work!" is not very ethical either, even though some guys use it. A true player and ladies' man does not need to lie to score. He is upfront about what he wants, and knows the triggers and buttons he needs to push to score on his own ability.

- Do not make promises or implications you have no intention of keeping. This is not quite lying, but a lowdown thing to do anyway. If you are a true alpha male with the capacity to turn on a woman you do not have to promise her anything. All you have to do is show her a good time. You do not have to promise commitment or imply that you are the perfect husband she has been waiting for. Players who disregard this simple rule often discover that insecure women can be a major headache and may even become violent when they are spurned.

- Do not prey on drunk women, who may be unconscious. While it is not illegal to have sex with a drunk woman (and it IS illegal to have sex with an unconscious woman!) most players won't do it. One, they want to seduce and enjoy the fruits of their labors—they do not want to take advantage of a woman when she is acting stupid and inebriated. It takes the joy out of the experience. Besides, a hung over woman could turn vicious in a hurry when she realizes you took advantage of her drunken state of mind, and that is a mess you do not want to step in.

- Do not prey on insecure or rebounding lovers. Now this is not as black or white as the above situations, but most alpha still won't do it. It is almost too easy, and too cruel, to sleep with a lonely woman who is so desperate for love and attention that she will surrender sexually within hours or even minutes of meeting you. These girls have major issues, and are just dying for a man to love them. That is not you, let us be honest. So do not get her hopes up for a "real relationship" if that is what she really wants. It is much more enjoyable to date women who are self-confident and want no-strings-attached sex like the one you do. The less drama you get wrapped up in, the better.

Showing Respect To Other People You Meet

Besides the aforementioned areas, there is another aspect of "morality" to consider. Should you seduce anyone, at all times? Just because a woman might be sexually interested in you does not mean she is going to want to have sex with you. She may regret a one nightstand, and particularly if she has a boyfriend or even a husband.

Some men will not chase after girls who are attached because they consider it a betrayal of the man she is with. Consider it a sort of karmic consequence, that if you choose to become involved with somebody who is attached, you are already telling her that you can't be trusted, that you probably don't want a long-term relationship, and that you don't care about the consequences of this action.

Cheating with a married woman may actually cause her great guilt, and result in a broken family, a broken marriage, and all sorts of negative reactions. The fact that married men often become enraged when they find out about an extramarital lover might be enough to turn a player's attention away from a married woman.

It's not merely protection for your own well being, but it's the idea that you would be responsible for causing stress and pain in a committed relationship. Many world champion-caliber seducers out there simply will not compromise their morals just because they can. There are plenty of attractive single women out there, many of which want casual sex, or want to take things super slow and carefree for the time being.

Before you decide you want to score make your own checklist of red flags, which means it is best to avoid a troublesome situation.

- Your date is single and unattached

- She doesn't seem clingy, needy, or insecure

- She isn't harping about her ex

- She isn't a vulnerable single mom or a crackpot in therapy

- She believes in safe sex (no exceptions to this until you both get tested)

- She doesn't have a temper, a psychotic stare, or mention strange incoherent things that seem out of place in the conversation

- She doesn't expect anything from you

Morals And Ethics In Dating

The last item is particularly important. Among sexually active "educated" members of society, particularly in sexology and therapy, there is a strong belief in the need to be honest. The A person who is confident about his sexuality, his value, and his sex appeal has no reason to lie, deceive, or even imply anything insincere. To do so would be to take advantage of the other person, essentially letting her mind "fill in the blanks" of all her relationship questions.

Women tend to do this by nature. They may even idealize a man they like, assume the best of him and figure he is their perfect man. Obviously, you can't go around terminating their delusions and telling them that you're really a player and just want sex. That is honesty to the point of rudeness. Women may well want the illusion of romance, even if **in their heart, they know this relationship is all about sex.** Some women want romance, some want sex. What are you going to feed them, fueling that fantasy?

You do not have to lie or promise to be the perfect guy. All you have to do is follow the techniques, tell stories with a point and sex will happen naturally. Most women know that they have to sleep with a guy before he gets serious about them.

The complication occurs when a woman purposely resists sleeping with you, despite your best efforts, because she has her own list of seduction strategy. If she is making you wait, and wait, and wait…is it an act of selfishness to seduce her and go after that "peak moment" we talked about without letup? (If you wait a moment too long, the mood will pass and she will change her mind.)

No. Because as we discussed, a man really only has a short period of time to reach out to a woman who is sexually peaking in the conversation. The bottom line is that if you are two consenting adults, you both have the right to decide to do this, to go and follow the emotion, wherever it may lead. By agreeing to go on a date with you, she assumes responsibility for her conduct, which may include casual sex.

Your own only obligation is to avoid dishonesty, avoid implying something that is blatantly false, and make sure that she feels the passion of the moment. Almost needless to say, if a woman says "No." she really means "No." You would think this would not be a problem now, but unfortunately, rape crimes are still being reported all over the world even in the most civilized countries.

The whole point of being a player is the power it gives you to please and attract women, so by all logic they should be begging you for sex. You should require no pushing or coercion at all, not if you do these techniques correctly.

How Do I Know If It's Real Love?

There is only one final notion to consider, and that is whether that special feeling deep inside of you is a swelling of your heart or your lower extremities. There is no question that lust satisfied feels very much like love. You find that you love sex, you love women (all sorts of women), and the feeling of having sex with a woman in an impulsive decision is a magnificent experience. And so you might also confuse an infatuation for your new crush as something deeper than it really is.

This actually happens more often than you might think. Guy figures out the secret to getting laid. He decides he wants to date the entire city. However, the first or second score he has, he finds a vulnerable side to the girl he likes. He starts to wonder if maybe he was meant to meet her all along—maybe she is his soul mate.

But is that true love talking or is it just guilt? Do not underestimate the power of guilt. Having a woman fall hard for you may be an awe-inspiring experience. And no, it's not always easy to tell a woman who really likes you that you just want to be friends. Sure, the shoe is on the other foot this time, but you still may have lingering doubts about how you really feel.

The first thing is to figure out if you really feel something for this individual person or if you're just experiencing a rush of emotions, as indeed sex is a positive activity that one can fall in love with—apart from an actual person.

When analyzing the aspects of love, it's important to consider the logical side of it. While you are a man and do tend to think logically in general, remember that men can be sensitive and emotional, especially after sex, and so you have to guard against feeling or thinking anything too impulsive.

And this means:

- Not telling her you love her just because you feel awkward

- Not telling her this was a mistake

- Not freaking out or doing anything else, besides just calmly accepting what has taken place

156

Not only should you avoid wearing your heart on your sleeve and putting your foot in your mouth so as not to entrap yourself—but even if you like the girl, it's just not a good idea to be so honest so soon.

Now that you understand player strategy, you have VALUE and have the same social pressure and high standards as a beautiful woman. And guess what women are taught about dating! They are taught to filter out bad ideas, protect their vulnerability, and not just follow their heart or do anything rash.

That is right; women are taught to know **in advance, what they want out of a relationship**. This way, they won't fall for any random guy they meet, and they won't waste time with bad idea relationships. The same can be said of you. Before you decide to date anyone, decide what **qualities are important to you.**

We talked about valuing yourself earlier in the book, and will reiterate the point. However, this is not just about being selective and being self-confident. This is about telling the difference between a fling and someone you could really learn to love.

What Makes A Fling?

There is nothing wrong with having a fling. And here's a tip to remember: sometimes the best flings are the ones that FEEL like love. It is not a big deal. Not every one-night stand has to be about sex, detachment, and anonymous mind games. Sometimes you can have very intense, dare we say **loving** affairs with a woman whom you have NO REAL FUTURE WITH. And that is okay, provided you don't intentionally hurt anyone.

Sometimes affairs continue for a while but eventually fizzle out. So taking a relationship you do have an interest in, extra slow, and concentrating solely on sexual experimentation is a smart move. You may find that after weeks turn into months, her attention or your attention may be distracted. The two of you may feel for someone else, or may just get bored of the same old sexual shenanigans.

Gee, a good thing you don't promise to marry her, right? Take things slow and take the time to experience the joy of an ongoing, no strings attached affair.

If the relationship does have a future, it will keep going and you will not become bored of her. You will find something intriguing in her and that may draw you in closer, so that you desire even greater intimacy and discovery with this person.

What Makes It Real Love?

As you are going to learn in the next chapter, real love means **staying together** because it is very possible to love someone, and yet not be able to forge a relationship with that person. This may be due to nagging flaws, their immaturity (or your own), or difficult circumstances. So while you may explore a variety of relationships that seem to be "love at first sight", don't expect them all to go the distance.

Therefore, knowing that love starts with an open mind (meaning you do not fall in love just because a woman sleeps with you) it is important to consider three different views of love.

Love: The Idealistic View

The idealistic view of love assumes that love is based on chemistry, and perhaps even a "soul mate" that is meant for you if you want to be romantic about it. In simple terms, this means that you DO have a criteria. You are not just looking for a pretty face, a hot body, or even someone nice, funny, and interesting. All the usual things girls are!

Instead, you're looking for very specific qualities that you find intellectually and emotionally fulfilling. If you were to find this "ideal woman", you would desire sex. However, sex would not be the primary goal. You would be attracted to her personality and her fine qualities that define her. Sex would be just one of many things that you would love to do with her.

Not all guys like the same thing. While every guy does want to meet a girl that's funny, interesting, and sexual these are general qualities. Love is about something deeper, a feeling that persists long after the first and second sexual encounter.

Do not be surprised to learn that your crushes will fade after the second or third fling with the same woman. However, someone who is truly compatible with you will not be so easy to forget. Something will draw you to her. We used to call that "something" an IT quality, or a soul mate, something chemically unexplainable.

Well, We Know Better Than That Now, Don't We?

The question is what decides the qualities that you find lovable? Your views on real love are shaped by what you experienced as a child, your genetics inherited from your parents, and your environment.

It is a well documented fact that children learn aspects of love from their parents; boys learn how to act in a relationship by watching the behavior of their fathers, and their mothers for the opposite sex role. So it is not unusual to see men falling for women who possess the positive qualities (or indeed sometimes the negative qualities) of their mothers.

This does not mean you are doomed to marry someone just like your mother, which would be creepy, but simply that you do have a type. Since most mothers are nurturing, supportive, independent, intelligent, and charitable it's no surprise these are the "types" that powerful men go for. They want a helper, someone who understands them beyond mind games, player strategy, and peripheral attractions.

On the other hand, if you find that you don't really see any positive qualities that impress you, but remain under a sexual spell, it's very likely not the love of a lifetime.

First, identify the features of love. What does real love feel like?

- You do not want to stop seeing the person.

- Despite all your new instincts to "play" you find yourself wanting to please her.

- You want to give to her and share with her.

- You want to protect her.

- You would not mind meeting her parents.

- You find the idea of having a family with her interesting.

And so on and so on. No, we are not saying you should follow your instincts on this one. As we have been saying the entire book, women do not respond to nice behavior—even if you are soul mates, you need to play this one very carefully.

You can end this experiment by creating a list of qualities that you want and then compare your desired qualities to your current girlfriend.

For example:

Desired Qualities:

1. **Supportive of my career**

2. **Cares about other people**

3. **Really smart about people**

4. **Strong faith in the good of humanity**

5. **Funny**

My Girlfriend's Qualities

1. **Doesn't really care about my job**

2. **Mostly wants sex, doesn't talk about her family**

3. **Book smart, but too trusting of people**

4. **Very cynical**

5. **Very wild**

In the end, you have to decide if these qualities are worth keeping or should simply be passed on. The advantage you have now as an alpha male is that you DON'T have to worry about being alone. You do not have to settle for someone that does not match you, just so you can have someone to keep you company. You will always have the ability to attract a mate and find someone to date, or even live with. The days of settling are over.

If you remain confused about what you want in a relationship then it is best to do some reflecting on your past relationships. For instance, do you find that a lot of your ex-girlfriends (or at least women you have a crush on) tended to be of the same type? Or all had some characteristic that was immediately identifiable? Did you meet them all under similar circumstances?

Now stop thinking about them and put the camera back on yourself for a moment. What do these patterns in your old relationships say about you? What types of relationships make you comfortable? What recurring themes are in these relationships and is this related to self-confidence?

You may even find that with your new knowledge of dating and seduction, you might start looking for entirely different women than in years past.

Love: The Biological View

A less idealistic view of life would be a biological view of love, sex and relationships. In theory, this would be based on evolutionary thought; the Darwinian concept of survival and replication. In theory, the human animal is programmed to survive, adapt to the environment and then replicate through the old-fashioned creative process. These strategies tend to reappear in all of our decision-making. We make "impulsive" decisions based on our perception of surviving from threats (providing for our hunger, defending ourselves against predators) as well as our desire to reproduce with an attractive mate, as well as a mate we subconsciously see as a capable mother to our seed.

There is also the theory that we are overpopulated as a species on earth and thus we are "outdated" models for our environment. This motivates us on an instinctive level to stay away from people with low social value. By wanting to be around people who match us in survival and replication value, we improve our own chances for survival

So it's not at all surprising men are attracted to women who are good homemakers, or who have a stable job, or even women who have large breasts, as this indicates maternal capabilities on a subconscious level.

We are hardwired to seek out popular people, or people who have something of value to share with us. Thus you could view all relationships as simply the trading and negotiation of mutual value. A woman gives you something in exchange for what you can give her.

Even the fear of rejection that you instinctively feel could be traced to evolutionary theory, such as the idea that if a woman rejected your advances, you could anger an entire tribe of her male relatives.

Maslow's Hierarchy of Needs: Abraham Maslow wrote that human beings are primarily motivated by primal needs.   In his reckoning, more simplistic minor needs had to become before major or broad needs.

Physiological needs include: Food, water, warmth, sleep, and sex.

Safety: Shelter, consistency, and comfort.

Love: The need to belong and be accepted for your talents.

Esteem: The respect you get for achieving something yourself and being praised for it.

Self Actualization: Reaching a peak of everything, desiring everything you are capable of becoming, and realizing all latent potential.

Focusing more attention on developing health, wealth, and love, and accomplishing your goals would fill you with a feeling of happiness. Ideally, you focus on keeping all needs balanced. If you do not, eventually your entire quality of life descends and you may even spiral into a depression or habits of self-sabotage.

Furthermore, neglecting one of these major needs will eventually start to weigh down your success in other needs. Without health, you will not maintain wealth. Lacking wealth (or at least a career in something you enjoy doing) will affect your ability to make contacts, network, and "sell" your value to others.

So if you discover that something is off about your dating plan it may be time to focus on your personal development. Are you maximizing your health? Are you working in a career that rewards you? Are you making an effort to love yourself, and create a family and a network of friends?

Love: The Player's View

There is a more cynical view of love in the player lifestyle that cannot be ignored. This one takes a more antagonistic approach to love, suggesting that embracing "love" and acting like a man in love is a mistake. It considers the feeling of love as a desperate fixation, and the ultimate theory is that women do not want a man to be in love with them—but to make them work for his approval.

Of course, you have the power to stay in a monogamous relationship if you so desire, but you will continue taking an alpha male's view of relationships. You avoid qualities associated with traditional "love stories"; neediness, clinginess, jealousy and lovesickness. Your new attitude is counterproductive to these traits. A master seducer doesn't display weakness, nor does he have time.

Of course, monogamy is contrary to the true player's philosophy, even though some guys will go against the school of thought and marry or settle down. In theory, you date multiple women at once since being in love with one woman only will limit your potential and expose you to the risk of fixation and obsession.

There is no question that when you are in love, you are afraid to lose what you have. The player strategy is that you are never afraid to walk away. Rejection, and your partner not feeling the same way as you, fuel a man's low self-image of himself. The player strategy revolts against this natural inclination and instead enhances the role of the dominant man.

Having the attention of many women at once keeps you thinking confidently and logically, and this is what attracts the attention of women. Furthermore, exclusivity is believed by the player to devolve into routine, and then eventually into boredom and resentment. On the other hand, non-exclusivity keeps relationships exciting.

Comfort and tradition, the characterization of traditional love, are contrary to an exciting and sexually fulfilling life, so says the player. Now this section is not to warn you against falling in love. Rather, you have to take this section, and compare it to the two previous sections, and make an educated decision on what **love means to you.**

Even if you do want to love just one woman at some point (which a lot of people do, because eventually their bodies grow older and it becomes more stressful in their 60s to attract a mate as energetically as they once did in their 20s) the player's strategy can be helpful.

The reason being, is that so many men settle into a long-term relationship that they don't really want. They assume that this is a pattern of life, and that routines are normal. They figure they might as well marry because this woman seems to be the best they can do, and she is better than being alone, or better than most other women they meet.

Still, that is not the FULL capacity a man has. A man has unlimited potential to date beautiful women, successful women, and to literally customize the type of woman he goes after, by paying close attention to her qualities and then using seduction strategy to intrigue her interest.

This is a far more exciting view of life; the idea that you do not have to settle for what seems normal. You always have the option of finding a woman who completes you better than your last ex-girlfriend.

Sometimes, it is a learning experience for you. You may think you have paradise in bedding a blonde that is rich, fun to be around, and sensual. However, after a few dates and affairs, you may discover that your ideal of her was not really that satisfying in person. It may be time to do some reflecting and figure out what's more important to you than games, sex, and momentary bliss.

Now the tricky part. Let's say you've had sex with someone, thinking it was just a fling, but then you discovered you really like her and she really likes you.

Now what happens? Do you go back to being Mr. Nice Guy? Or do you continue playing the part of the player until you're a 90-year-old grandpa?

Relax…we have the answers in the next chapter.

The 9 Affairs Every Player Should Have Before He Gets Married

Are you really ready to take the plunge? Are you sure you've had all the wild sex you imagined you could have, now that you "get" women? Maybe it is time you create a checklist of depravity before you head on to the next chapter. You only get to sow oats in life once.

1. No strings attached anonymous sex partner.

Why not try grandmaster style, or at least hit a few clubs and experience quickie sex with someone you are never going to see again?

2. Long-term mistress.

Before you get married, have a "starter mistress." Date someone off and on, creating a friends with benefits scenario and have sex over a period of months or years. The casual feel of a purely sexual fling with a long-time acquaintance will be erotic and therapeutic.

3. Sex with your friend.

Why not enjoy, and get the last laugh by targeting one of your old "friends" who unceremoniously friend-zoned you? Bedding someone who once coldly rejected you is always a wonderful comeuppance.

162

4. May December relationship.

Sex with an older woman is a delicacy that must be experienced, and the younger you are the better. Older women tend to be more confident, less "attached", and very experienced in bed. Maybe she will show you a thing or two.

5. A younger woman.

At the same time, there is no better ego boost than bedding someone who is several years younger than you are and thoroughly fascinating her impressionable mind with your wit, wisdom, and confident older man behavior. Younger women do like older guys; they admire their confidence and their charm, sometimes even more so than men their own age. So even if you do remain single into your 40s and 50s there's always hope.

7. Someone you dislike.

Why not just for the fun of it try seducing a woman you can't stand? Whether it's a work colleague, old acquaintance, someone's ex, or even your old nemesis from high school, seducing someone you have absolutely nothing in common with is always an intellectually fascinating experience—and hot!

8. A single mom.

Many single moms out there are willing to have casual fun, provided you respect their family pecking order and are generous to their child. This is a learning experience, a preview for a future family (if that appeals to you). It is also a chance to make out with a mom, a truly scandalous fantasy that tickles your subconscious longing for bad boy thrills.

9. A wild child.

Moms are usually not the most radical or dangerous of lovers, so make sure to include a Wild Woman on your sexual bucket list. This is the type of girl you will love all of her sexual adventures. She makes you have sex in public. She dares you to do something that scares you. She is bisexual and up for a threesome. You'll remember the affair fondly for the rest of your life.

163

Chapter 14

Putting It All Together And Living Happily Ever After

Wow, you just had sex! Now what? Now comes the complicated part where you figure out what to say, what to do, and what this means for your hypothetical relationship? Are you going to dump her and reveal to the whole community that you are a player? What is the etiquette anyway?

After Sex

The good news is that expectations are low after sex IF you make an effort to be kind, supportive and confident during sex. This means that when you have sex with her, it is okay to tell her she is beautiful. To adore her, and fawn over her just a little bit, showing her that you have a sensitive side. If you create a COMFORTABLE experience for her, she will be grateful.

Yes, she might feel vulnerable and see you in a brand new light (usually a bit starry-eyed, the same way you viewed her when you first met). She herself is being extra careful to not appear needy or overly cuddly. She wants you to think she is cool with a casual encounter, and she really might be.

Your job is to avoid coming across as a jerk or doing anything that resembles gloating, pouting or freaking out. You need to show her you are in complete control and have no regrets about what happened. Your inner calm should rub off on her, allowing her to feel comfortable in your presence. There is no need to eject yourself from the bed as soon as you are finished. Basking in the afterglow is acceptable, and may be the ideal time to engage in flirty, getting to know you better dialog.

Be kind but not too kind. Do not over-sentimentalize and avoid coming across as "grateful" or clingy. At some point, yes, you can leave or she will leave if it's your place. After this happens, it is time to decide your future.

Should You See Her Again?

Contrary to what your guilt might tell you, you are NOT obligated to see her or call her ever again. If you knew, you just wanted a one-night stand, or if you discovered something about her, it is perfectly fine to just lose all contact with her, and let her get the hint. A woman should not feel as if you are breaking up with her after one night. If she does, this means you were making or implying empty promises, or maybe that she was just mentally unbalanced. In either case, avoid this. Casual sex should be casual, fun, and with no expectations on either side.

Now if you do want to see her again, the best course of action is to call her the next day. This may seem contrary to other advice that suggests you wait for phone calls, but this is no ordinary phone call. After a woman has given you the honor of her body, you have an obligation to express interest in continuing the affair. If you forget or postpone this action, she will take offense and will figure the affair was a one-time thing or maybe even a mistake. If you forget to call the next day, expect the whole thing to be over in a hurry. Rest assured she is waiting for that call as she wants to know if this experiment is ongoing.

How Do I Turn A One Night Stand Into A Real Relationship?

The next step is to CONTINUE being an alpha male. This means you are not going to show up with roses at her doorstep. You are going to keep playing it cool. A woman does not want to think that you are rearranging your life for her at this early stage. Neither does she want to imagine that you are sitting at home just obsessing over this one call, as if this is your life's mission.

Ideally, you want to appear busy, even on the phone. So after making initial contact, say something positive and yet not too mushy, and then make it a point to dismiss the call citing that you're busy at work or running errands or with a hobby.

By making her chase you, and trying to find you not so busy, she will actually be impressed by your level of confidence and will feel further motivated to invest in you—a high value guy that meets her list of requirements. You are in control of the situation.

It is generally believed that until you actually get married and have children that you should NOT make a woman the priority in your life. When you do make the mistake of caring too much (and again, we add without any reason to do so except that you want to prove you are some sort of perfect gentleman) you tell the woman you're VERY interested in a commitment.

The pressure is suddenly on. She feels smothered by all of your affection. This doesn't seem like instinct, right? Aren't you supposed to be nice after you have sex with a woman and she feels vulnerable? Yes, you are and you will. However, you are keeping a respectful distance and letting her realize that she does in fact like you, and that she is willing to meet you halfway.

It cannot all be you. When you show her that you are busy and that your life does not revolve around her (and sex!) then you will remind her that you are popular and worth her time and attention.

Remember your goal is to appear busy always. This means:

- You don't tell her you're bored or did "nothing"

- Share your experiences, proving that you are in fact busy and not just making it up. Hopefully, you're not lying…you really ARE busy! (Remember health, wealth, and love balance!)

- Do not call her every day the week after. Do not talk to her for hours on the phone.

- Remember be nice but be busy. Do not bend over backwards for her and ruin your chances when you're so close to the finish line.

Continue With Positive Associations

Let's review the reason for your sudden level of business. It is not to be a brat or to punish your woman for any particular reason. Rather, it is because if you really do want to talk to her non-stop, you will EXHAUST all creative and interesting subjects, and at a time that is way too early for her comfort.

165

Staying busy and limiting your time actually makes it much easier on you to keep her thoroughly entertained when you do have time to talk to her. Your new goal is to have her associate you with positive feelings, in fact, the absolute best interactions with you. She has to learn to love your periodic appearances and then miss you when you are gone.

Soon, she is going to be eating candy out of your hand so to speak. She will love the attention you give her when you see her, and will remember you as the "perfect guy" with no time to spare, and one who always seems to leave her wanting more.

How To Avoid Hurt Feelings

Now you do have to play this next move VERY carefully. Even if you have mutually agreed upon casual sex with a new friend, you must be discreet in how you handle the subject of exclusivity.

The woman is certainly not committed to you, right? And if you snap out a wedding ring, yeah, she's going to freak out and run away.

Now that said, women tend to be insanely jealous of one another. So if you decide to keep dating other women without having "the discussion" you will more than likely hurt your date's feelings and may turn her into a major F-5 player hater. Women hate the idea of you dating other women, even if you are not exclusive. How fair is that?

However, there is a way to smooth things over. After sex, or even before, talk to her and be upfront about what you want in the relationship. No, you do not have to tell her you are a player after sex. What you will tell her is that you are just having fun, just meeting new people, and following wherever your heart takes you. No promises made. No commitment hinted at.

The woman has no reason to think the two of you are exclusive unless she ups the ante and says that's what she wants. Have the conversation at a reasonable time. Give her the option of walking away, because if she wants someone exclusively that's her right—and your right as well. **Do not feel obligated to keep seeing her if you are not enjoying yourself.** You do not owe a woman any set number of days or weeks after sex, just to be a "good boyfriend." You are not a boyfriend at all. As long as you have been honest, there should be no problem in communication.

It is essential that you start this experimental and open relationship on your own terms. You have not agreed to be exclusive and she should know that you are still dating other people, so that there are no misunderstandings.

Now she knows that you are seeing other people, and that they also know of your unattached state. Your goal should be to EXPLORE compatibility, not commit to someone you hardly know and who hasn't even said anything about being exclusive with you. You owe her nothing except a good time, as you have already been showing her.

Continue to be busy but to put on a great show for her. If you really want to reach her and ignite a spark of jealousy, you should drop subtle hints that you are still single. This will probably provoke her. But once again, she sees your value and sees that you are indirectly asking how serious she wants this to be. She will see that you are not one to be taken for granted. You are not a doormat. If she wants to get serious with you she has to meet you halfway and invest herself.

If there is no commitment and the woman is fine with your arrangement, then it is a good idea to start looking for other women "on the side", meaning that at any given time you are dating 3-5 different girls.

The advantages are:

- Easier to get laid every night.

- You can quickly get rid of women who don't work out and replace them.

- She can see that you have high value and are not like other guys.

- You do not risk everything on one endeavor. If one relationship does not work out you have not wasted anytime, you just keep moving down and adding more friends to your "network."

Just be sure to keep things unpredictable. You can't bore her if your intent is to maintain escalated positive associations. Be spontaneous, be into her…, and then make yourself scarce.

Why Women Want To Pay

This does not necessarily apply to women picking up the check, though some men will ask her to pay for herself. Why does a woman want, a NEED to pay in a relationship? Because in line with survive-replicate theory, something that has little to no value is not in demand. A woman must feel that she has paid for something that is valuable. This validates the worth of the item.

Not many people appreciate the value of free gifts but a cash giveaway, something with high value, is always highly contested. Likewise, women must feel that they are invested in the relationship. They want to "pay" in order to justify their feelings for you. If they were not interested, everything you did would be free. Because you have induced her to pay and make an effort in dating you, she thinks you are the real deal.

It's just a part of human psychology; something that is free or cheap is seen as having low value. Therefore, men who give their affection away for free are not inducing the woman to invest anything. She does not feel attracted because she has not taken any steps at all.

Therefore, what is the price you have assigned to yourself? If you do not know, and if the woman does not get the sense that, you have a price, then you are not worth anything in her eyes.

Now the question is, how do you make her "pay?"

Some men take this literally and ask her to pay her own way, or even go so far as to ask her to pick him up, or run errands for him. However, it really goes deeper than that. She has to overcome obstacles to be with you. That is the payment. That is how she is going to look back very soon and realize, "I'm giving too much to this relationship to turn away now." Some of the most powerful ways to show your "high price" include:

- Being willing to be away from her, as you become scarce and thus more rare. Most guys volunteer to an infinite amount of time with her, decreasing their own value and time worth.

- Being unavailable some of the time. This includes not returning her first call (but the second one) and canceling dates occasionally.

- Getting angry and showing your anger over incidents that merit it. Too many guys stifle their anger, putting on a façade of genteelness. They never stand up for themselves, and thus they lose her respect. NOTE: This does not mean you lose your temper or become violent; rather, you are assertive about what behavior you find unacceptable.

Handling Disrespect

If you pay attention (and so few guys actually do) you would be surprised to learn how many women show extreme disrespect for guys they date. Maybe they are oblivious, or maybe they intentionally do it to exert control. One thing is for sure: doing something rude, thoughtless or flippant is not acceptable and you should not let a woman get away with it.

You can either call her on her offensive behavior or simply walk away, letting your actions speak for themselves. Some women do literally test you in this way and they want to know:

- If you are going to lose your temper.

- If you are a whiner.

- If you are a pushover.

- If you are too afraid to speak up.

This is not only player strategy but also basic human psychology. If you do not designate your boundaries at the beginning of a relationship, the other partner will continually test you, and will keep pushing the limits on what you can tolerate. It can eventually reach codependent levels, and is not healthy.

Setting boundaries of acceptable behavior is very important, and even in dating. If you have no boundaries, a woman has no fear of offending you, and is free to exploit you in whatever way she wants. Instant drop in value.

You may even find that when you assert yourself and break it off, she may come back to you even more desperate to get together with you and try again. If this happens, do not be so quick to take her back. Make it conditional. In fact, make her work for it just a little bit, so that she sees the value in the relationship. (Do not make it sexual, as this could affect your long-term future, as she might think you are just a sex-obsessed guy and not an alpha)

To Walk Or Not To Walk

Here is one of the most important lessons in regards "payment" and value. When you tell a woman that you are not going to tolerate insulting behavior then you must MEAN it. That means you must be willing to walk away and not shrink back or negotiate. There are varieties of scenarios that a woman might try to test your reaction. For example:

- Arriving late to a date

- Canceling a date with a vague or silly excuse

- Not returning your phone calls

- Keeping you waiting

And so on. This behavior merits a negative reaction from you. You should be blunt about this and 100% serious—no neg hitting, no comedy. You are assertive and frustrated at her behavior and you're letting her know you're not putting up with it. You can give her the chance to explain herself if you prefer, but the power of the moment comes in your walking away—your willingness to leave the facility or hang up the phone.

This will probably shock her, but it will be so unusual that she will most likely call back or chase you down to talk with you. Some guys actually take advantage of this shock value and make a romantic move right then and there. It is up to you, but your assertiveness must be felt. This demonstrates that your time is valuable and you are indeed worth the trouble, worth overcoming obstacles for.

Relationship Currency

Little things mean a lot in relationships. Your reactions to these common situations will be scrutinized. Play your cards right and keep projecting the right image.

- Give compliments like $100 bills. Do not over-use them but use them strategically. If she compliments you, you can compliment her back. Some girls like plenty of compliments while others are too vain to accept them, at least early on in the relationship. Learn what she likes and give it to her. It always helps to pay sincere compliments, observations that not a lot of people notice. On the other hand, stating painfully obvious compliments (that everyone else does) is a bore. Once you progress to an intimate relationship with her, body compliments are expected. Otherwise, she may get the impression you are literally not attracted to her. So work your way up to the good stuff.

- Treat secrets as currency. A lot of guys reveal themselves quickly, hoping to "call" all of their cards right away to figure out what they feel. However, women like men of mystery. So keep your secrets hidden until the right time comes to reveal them through a fascinating story. You can also exchange some of your secrets, which she is dying to know by now. You treat them as an exchange, something valuable; she will have to bargain to get that information.

- Always make friends with her friends, flirt, and be friendly with them. This will make her only slightly jealous, but in a benign way. Most women love it when their man shows off in front of their friends. Furthermore, if she suspects you like one of her friends, if she still sees value in you, she will work hard to keep you.

169

What About Romantic Gestures?

As you might have noticed over the course of this book we have revealed a progression of attitude. You start out strong and confident, usually neg-hitting a beautiful woman so that you can grab her attention. However, being flirty and funny (even antagonistic) is not the same thing as being mean-spirited or pointlessly vindictive. A lot of guys get this wrong. They may even shun romance, figuring that it's not in character with their tough guy mode.

However, as we said, it is a progression. After you earn some trust and she invests in you, you are free to give sincere compliments and even a romantic gesture. "You mean I can be a nice guy again?" Sort of. You always want to project confidence of course, but yes, you CAN be an old romantic once you earn the trust of this woman. You do not have to always have your guard up. Some grandly romantic and timeless gestures include:

- Writing her a poem

- Sending her a sweet gift card or e-card

- Buying her a gift (Just make sure not to "buy her love", substituting your entertaining and attractive qualities for money; ideally she wants your personality not "things")

- Sometimes the best gift is a surprise. So try to surprise her with a gift by hiding it somewhere and letting her discover it.

- Play games and pleasantly surprise her, by telling her you might be late…and then whisking her away to a romantic dinner, which you pay for. Sometimes the unexpected is the most romantic thing you can do.

- Cook for her

- Read something romantic or erotic (depending on what she likes) together

- Take her on a romantic weekend getaway; do not make plans just go!

- Lastly, share your feelings. Some players are against being romantic, but at some point in the relationship—especially if you make her work for it—it will be a wonderful gift to share with a woman who has earned your respect.

Long-Term Relationships And Aging

When you reach the point where you have had sex and you both feel a connection, it is time to think relationship. Is a relationship different from courtship?

Oh yeah.

This book is not about how to save a relationship or how to stay married for a lifetime—that is an entirely different subject. However, we can elaborate on the dynamic of a long-term relationship and how it differs from courtship.

As we have said, establishing your alpha male confidence is essential in dating. However, as you grow more intimate you must become flexible with your power. Some of the worst "relationships" are the ones where the men are demanding, inflexible and constantly maintaining "power" in the relationship through argument, violence, and aggression.

Living together is not a power play between man vs. woman. It can't be or it will self-destruct, sometimes in a big hurry. (Ever heard of the 30 day divorce? It happens more often than you think) Living together is a negotiation in progress, and it is constantly being updated because circumstances (and sometimes even people) DO change.

A relationship requires four qualities to stay strong and united.

- Honesty and the willingness to express yourself. Not only do you owe it to your partner to be honest, and not keep things hidden, but you also have to be **willing to talk.** This sometimes means expressing your feelings, even your negative feelings. This will protect the two of you from bottling up your anger and exploding into rage, against infidelity (which often happens because you feel you can't talk to your mate) and passive aggressive bullying.

- The ability to compromise. There is no way one partner can dominate the relationship without resentment building up. What we see in courtship, with the man taking charge and keeping control, is not the same thing as a married man controlling his wife and demanding she comply with his orders. It's a different dynamic altogether; it's confidence vs. insecurity. A man who is insecure will try to dominate a woman's behavior. A confident man will only challenge her.

- Patience, tolerance and mildness. You cannot win an argument by shouting, by quick wit, or by using cheap power plays. Emotion runs wild in these situations and the only solution is to REMOVE emotion and hurt feelings and focus on the logic of the situation. This is not the time to be competitive. Your goal is to negotiate logically so you can build a foundation of reason and see the same evidence, come to the same conclusions, and work on a feasible compromise.

- Respect for your partner. So much of this book has been about respect. You must respect your partner by giving her what she wants in the courtship phase and then continue to respect her as the relationship deepens and intensifies. At the same time, being an alpha male is about **having respect for yourself** and not letting a woman take advantage of your kindness. By establishing boundaries early in courtship you can make them stick for the duration of the relationship.

Now here is where it gets tricky. A lot of "nice guys" will eventually find (or shall we say "settle" on a woman they like) and then apply the same nice guy techniques to their marriage as they did in dating. Yes, believe it or not some nice guys do make it all the way to the altar. Guess they are that good looking, huh?

Here is the problem. The patterns they set during courtship, usually pushover behavior where they throw away their own value by fawning over the woman they like regardless of her behavior, will FOLLOW them into marriage.

These are the poor fellows that end up being married to wives who:

- Cheat on them

171

- Stay married out of guilt

- Hardly ever have sex with them

- Are verbally abusive or take their kindness for granted

- Are very insecure, perhaps even codependent

And these guys are only reasonably happy…they're not really as happy as they should be. They are not "in love" with their wife as much as they could be and the wife is certainly not as attracted as she could be. It's a relationship built on settling, not on passion.

So speaking in these terms, YES, you should apply much of what you have learned in courtship behavior to long-term relationships. Well, what does this involve? Does this mean that you should constantly "seduce" your partner even years after you move in together?

On occasion, yes. But no, of course you're not expected to "act" a certain way for years on end. For this entire book what we've been doing is getting you in touch with your REAL instincts, your alpha male instincts, and moving you away from subordinate anti-manly behavior.

Think about some of the lessons you have learned thus far:

- I do not apologize for my opinions.

- I'm not afraid to tease a woman and make her laugh

- I'm not afraid to speak my mind and tell a woman what I find unacceptable

These are concepts that are **within your natural id/ego. In other words, they are not an "act."** They are the same things you would say to a friend, a little sister, a relative, and so on. When you are not sweating over sexual tension, you are simply having a fun conversation, speaking your mind, and using your creativity to arouse interest.

So yes, there is a place for mystery and for unpredictability in a long-term relationship. Just because you get married or live together does not mean you have earned the right to be lazy, take your partner for granted, and generally start reverting to old patterns.

The fact of the matter is that women do NOT feel attraction to men who:

- Try to buy their sympathy

- Yell or berate them

- Have no spine and submit to a woman's authority on everything

- Refuse to say what they're thinking

- Smile and try to be nice rather than engage in an intelligent conversation

172

- Don't know how to flirt and just make the evening unbearably stiff and awkward

As you get over your fear of sexual tension and rejection, you will find it much easier to "BE YOURSELF." Yes, this is what mom always told you about picking up women. "Just be yourself, honey."

It did not make sense then but now it does. Rather than put on some nice guy act or lose your self-respect in your quest to find romance, follow your manly, alpha instincts and do what FEELS right, rather than what seems logical.

Women are not always logical, not always rational. They are emotional creatures and respect a man who can control his emotions, and can give her the emotions she desires to feel.

This will not stop when you get married. This will always be part of your life, learning to be yourself around other people, learning to make people comfortable in your presence, and maintaining a LEADERSHIP role in a world of "followers."

We have reached the end of our educational discourse. However, there is one more point I want to impress upon you. If we could boil down this entire philosophy to one simple sentence, what would I give to you?

It is in these magical words:

Do not be afraid to leave.

Conclusion: Meet The New You

So much of this book's philosophy is summarized with the simple lesson that an alpha male must have the strength to "walk away." We have been discussing the importance of building self-respect and having the courage to speak your mind and "entertain", whereas most guys just put on a Mr. Nice Guy Act.

And therein lies a major revelation about male psyche. Being willing "to leave" is not a bad thing. We tend to think of "men who leave" as scoundrels or deadbeats that abandon responsibility. However, when a man has no responsibility yet, and when he leaves an unhappy relationship, he is maintaining power. He is taking control of himself and analyzing the relationship, realizing that he doesn't have to stay. He can "leave" at any time.

This enables him to:

- Face rejection and laugh it off

- Crack a joke and have fun

- Walk away from women who are shallow

- Walk away from women who are bratty or who take advantage of him

- Value himself, realizing he has great potential to entertain, to arouse, and to play

And this is precisely what many men out there misinterpret. Being a player is NOT about being mean to women or acting like a jerk or being "dominant" in the sense that you dominate, overpower and scare women. It is about making peace with your own emotions, adjusting your reactions and instincts, and playing the game that they want to play.

So often, we see men who misconstrue the player's philosophy and say offensive things, or abuse women, thinking that this is what they want. Wrong. They want emotional fulfillment. It is up to you to be a responsible and smart man and give them JUST ENOUGH "game time" to make them happy, curious and attracted…and then bring things back down to reality.

As you enter these new relationships, now that you are empowered with knowledge, remember that you are now the *experienced lover,* the one who is going to appeal to women on an intellectual and emotional level. Your strengths will be your ability to manipulate her emotions in just the way she wants. She is the inexperienced one looking to you for guidance, for confidence, and for a complete experience.

Part of becoming an alpha male is being able to play this role and NOT ask her for her guidance, and not to expect her to seduce you or to engage sexually with you without any emotional foreplay. You produce the response in her and she follows your lead. It is not a mind game so much as it is a dance between teacher (you) and student.

You could say that a woman never really feels strong passion for you until she realizes she could lose you. This is just a fact of nature. If you crave something so badly and need it in your life, you become dependent on it.

Think about alcohol or drugs. No brainer, right?

Well, can't the same be said for women? When you decide you NEED them, that you require their approval constantly, you become addicted to negativity—you become dependent and actually feed your own insecurity. What if she leaves? What if you fail?

How do you think that shows itself in your behavior? Your posture? Your words?

In contrast, a confident man understands that a woman has the CHOICE to leave him at any time, and accepts this. He chooses to accept this and to not place his value on a woman's opinion. He has made peace with the fact that he doesn't need a woman to stay. He is willing to walk away if the relationship gets boring, if he is disrespected, or if the woman is a beautiful bore.

This simple attitude adjustment explains the male-female attraction phenomenon. "Bad guys" in life (the kind that you dislike, and the type that intelligent women dislike) do share some similarities with players and pickup artists, but there is also a point of deviation.

1. Bad guys challenge women.

2. Bad guys have high self-esteem and aren't afraid to leave.

3. Bad guys prey upon a woman's weakness. (Taking their power way too far to the point of cruelty)

4. He disrespects her and breaks his own word.

5. He lets his weaknesses guide him rather than an actual strategy.

6. He creates a dysfunctional family dynamic, causing drama, which is exhausting, but never boring.

The thing is, all you have to do to attract a woman is to give her the first two points of that list. Challenge and high confidence. The bad boy is guided by weakness and so falls into 3-6, eventually driving the woman away from him, once she comes to her senses and realizes he's a narcissistic jerk.

If you focus on the techniques I have taught you in this book, the emotional and hypnotic techniques that demand a woman's attraction and attention you will be BETTER than the bad boy. You will be her intellectual and emotional match, her soul mate, her sexy teacher who trumps all the other "boys", and her Mr. Right who knows all the right moves.

You will be the "master" of female seduction. While she will not be able to explain why she adores you, her loyalty and desire to you will never waiver. That is the kind of magnetism you can have, if you embrace the philosophy of this book.

Thank you for reading and I hope that you apply these techniques in your own life, customizing the points to your own unique relationship and set of circumstances.

Innovate. Grow. Learn from your mistakes.

Bonus: A Checklist

Before you make a move in your new relationship make sure, you pass the Tao of Seduction test and mark off each item on this checklist!

- I am willing to walk away from any relationship or person that does not meet my high standards.
- I do have standards and have identified them.
- I am going to base my conversation on what she tells me. I do not need to rehearse.
- I am not going to manipulate any woman I meet with "nice" behavior, buying gifts, or any other manipulative tactic.. My personality alone is what will attract her.
- I am confident in my own abilities to attract a partner. I know that I can seduce anyone under the right circumstances because all it takes is a commitment to LEARNING the person.
- I want to make her invest in me and overcome obstacles for me, as this helps her remember that she likes me.
- I have my first "date" planned because I am a take-charge kind of guy.
- I will make it a point to tease her, and give her a hard time just to see her reaction.
- I have a seven-hour game plan strategy and have selected some good bounce locations.
- I want her to send me loud signals, or to kiss me first. I don't need to beg her, or ask her for sex. I will focus on increasing her desire for me.
- I have done my research on her likes and dislikes, as well as her lifestyle and what this indicates about her.
- I have some questions in mind on how to elicit her values.
- I am already recalling past experiences that were emotionally heavy for me, and will use them to "tell a story" and stimulate her emotions.
- I have a wingman for group situations.
- I have plans to talk to several women every week, progressing from friendly conversation to real flirting.
- I will try grandmaster style at least one or two times because I am NOT afraid of rejection. I really do not care.
- I do not have to be a bad boy or a nice guy. I simply have to be a man in control of myself, and a wise lover who knows how women think.
- I love eye contact, I love smiling, and I am a positive person.
- I have set my boundaries for what is acceptable and what is not.
- I will not allow a woman to bore me or put up a shield towards me without calling her on it.
- I am ready to make dating about having FUN again, not all this awkward energy.
- Whenever she peaks sexually, I am going for it because I understand a woman's sexual desire is a passing thing. She needs the emotion of the moment. I cannot be afraid or doubtful about what I want.
- I have decided to take relationships slowly, figuring out what I want as it happens. I am not obligated to stay with a woman I do not like, even after sex.
- I will never be lonely again. I can hook up with any woman, casual or serious, at any time. I no longer live in fear, nor do I need any woman in my life.
- I have read this book and I am ready to practice what I learned. This is the beginning of my new life as an alpha male, Casa Nova type! I look forward to the challenge.